Britain, Europe and EMU

Also by Walter Eltis

ECONOMIC GROWTH: Analysis and Policy

GROWTH AND DISTRIBUTION

BRITAIN'S ECONOMIC PROBLEM: Too Few Producers (*with Robert Bacon*)

THE CLASSICAL THEORY OF ECONOMIC GROWTH

CLASSICAL ECONOMICS, PUBLIC EXPENDITURE AND GROWTH

CONDILLAC: Commerce and Government (*with Shelagh M. Eltis*)

Britain, Europe and EMU

Walter Eltis
Emeritus Fellow
Exeter College
Oxford, and
Visiting Professor
University of Reading

First published in Great Britain 2000 by
MACMILLAN PRESS LTD
Houndmills, Basingstoke, Hampshire RG21 6XS and London
Companies and representatives throughout the world

A catalogue record for this book is available from the British Library.

ISBN 0–333–77337–3 hardcover
ISBN 0–333–77338–1 paperback

First published in the United States of America 2000 by
ST. MARTIN'S PRESS, INC.,
Scholarly and Reference Division,
175 Fifth Avenue, New York, N.Y. 10010

ISBN 0–312–22986–0

Library of Congress Cataloging-in-Publication Data
Eltis, Walter, 1933–
Britain, Europe, and EMU / Walter Eltis.
p. cm.
Includes bibliographical references and index.
ISBN 0–312–22986–0 (cloth)
1. Great Britain—Economic conditions—1997– 2. European Union countries—Economic conditions. 3. European Monetary Union. I. Title.

HC256.7 .E45 1999
330.94—dc21

99–046786

This book is printed on paper suitable for recycling and made from fully managed and sustained forest sources.

10 9 8 7 6 5 4 3 2 1
09 08 07 06 05 04 03 02 01 00

Printed and bound in Great Britain by
Antony Rowe Ltd, Chippenham, Wiltshire

Contents

List of Figures

List of Tables

Introduction

Britain's decision whether to join EMU will be of profound importance. The political issues matter far more than the economic, and they will weigh especially with those who take the decision and with every citizen with a vote in a referendum.

This book is concerned with the economics, which profoundly colours the politics of EMU membership. During most of the post-war period, France and Germany outcompeted Britain. It has sunk deep into the consciousness of many who governed in those decades that Britain has done many things worse than France and Germany. These great nations struck a new balance between the exercise of state power and production through capitalist market economies. They substantially outperformed the British economy: even in 1998, the government's competitiveness White Paper showed that output per worker was 20 per cent higher in France and Germany than in Britain, which (on universally accepted OECD data) had the sixteenth lowest output per head of population in Europe.[1] As a liberal opponent of dirigism who believes in free markets, I have said to my French friends: 'You have followed the wrong policies for two hundred years, and you have emerged 20 per cent ahead of us.'

So what has now changed? How can it be said against this evidence that Britain's prospects are superior to continental Europe's. Are their leading economies now in such serious difficulty that they may embark on desperate policies from which Britain would do well to keep its distance?

Britain's continuing prosperity no longer requires the merging of its currency with an economic super-power. Switzerland prospers with a net of tax income per worker which exceeds that in the United States and Luxembourg,[2] and the Swiss franc is independent of all other currencies. Currency interdependence can produce great prosperity, but so can a currency's complete independence. So one comes to the detailed questions which are the subject of this book.

Part I concerns Britain. Has the economy turned, despite its mediocre past, and does it truly have prospects for growing prosperity if it retains an independent monetary policy?

Part II is concerned with Europe. Are the difficulties of the leading European economies minor and correctible through the intelligence of its political leaders, and cooperation between its workers and managements which served Europe well during most post-war decades? Or are there difficulties they will fail to resolve?

Part III is concerned with EMU. Are there weaknesses in its constitution, and how will it influence Britain if we join? Since I retired from government service in July 1995 I have published a number of papers concerned with these themes, and I have taken this opportunity to bring them together, to re-write most of them, and to integrate their argument.

Part I of this book is concerned with Britain where the key question is: what has truly changed? In Chapter, 1 'Public Expenditure and the British Economy', I am joined by Robert Bacon, co-author of our 'Declining Britain' articles of 1975 and of *Britain's Economic Problem: Too Few Producers* in an account of the new public expenditure policies which were first adopted in 1976 (not 1979) and of the opportunites they created for renewed growth in Britain's private sector. Britain's public expenditure was not slashed, but our new chapter shows that its ratio in GDP remained approximately stable so that private sector wages and profits could expand in line with the growth of the economy. The simultaneous growth of wages and profits contributed to the healing of industrial relations so that, by the 1980s, a very senior trade unionist could say, to be echoed by Tony Blair in 1999, that there were no longer two sides of industry: workers and managements were beginning to cooperate.

What has come of their cooperation? In Chapter 2, 'The Key to higher British Living Standards', I show how wages and profits grew together from 1979 to 1996. It can be shown from OECD evidence that in that period the real net of tax pay of British 'production workers' grew 28 per cent, when German wages rose just $2\frac{1}{2}$ per cent and French wages fell. British living standards therefore rose remarkably compared to those in continental Europe. Profits rose faster still. The British economy was on its way.

But Chapter 3 on 'Closing the British Competitiveness Gap' provides an objective assessment of how much remains to be done. I wrote it with Dr David Higham, a Senior Economic Adviser in the Department of Trade and Industry while I was Chief Economic Adviser to the President of the Board of Trade. The chapter summarises the assessments of comparative British economic performance presented in the 1994 and 1995 Competitiveness White Papers,[3] and like the 1998 White Paper it concludes that a large performance gap remains, but that perhaps two-thirds of Britain's manufacturing underperformance in comparison with France and Germany had been corrected by 1995. I (but not Dr Higham) have added some brief reflections on the reconciliation of our 1995 data with the new 1998 White Paper. In particular Britain's shortfall in GDP per head (4 per cent in comparison with France and 8 per cent in comparison with Germany) is far less than our underperformance per hour, which exceeds 20 per cent. 10 per cent more of the population works in Britain than in France and Germany, and they work for longer hours. The discrepancy in living standards is therefore a good deal less than the discrepancy in hourly economic performance. But the gap needs to be closed.

In Chapter 4, 'The Political Economy of British Foreign Direct Investment' I set out the particular way in which Britain's high profits, comparatively low taxation and improving industrial relations has led to a wave of inward investment from leading international companies which has transformed the performance of some of the weakest areas of manufacturing industry. The new multinational producers have established quality and design standards which have created balance of payments surpluses in computers and colour televisions, and have gone on to transform the performance of British-owned companies: the standards they set have sent a message of 'match-it or die' to British-owned industry.

The first chapter in Part II (Chapter 5) is concerned with 'Europe's Unemployment Crisis'. This shows how relentlessly European unemployment has risen, and how Europe's private sectors have failed to create any jobs on balance since the 1970s. It contrasts the difficulties Europe faces with the analysis the European Commission presented in its White Paper, *Competitiveness and Employment* in 1993 and in 1995. This chapter shows in detail how the European Commission wills the means, but lacks the will, to propose the reforms which can truly begin to create new private sector employment without which unemployment will continue to rise in each European recession.

Chapter 6 on 'The IT Revolution and European Employment' sets out the remarkable impact IT is having in the United States where 43 per cent of all business investment is now concerned with information processing. According to the IFO Institute in Munich, this could create 6 million additional jobs in Europe, but real European investment in IT has so far been at only one-third of the US level. Until 1998 Europe imposed tariffs on IT imports to asssist its own companies, together with anti-dumping duties of up to 60 per cent, in a vain attempt to keep out Asian imports of semi-conductors, but these none the less secured 85 per cent of the European market. Europe was slowing its utilisation of the new technologies to protect producers which scarcely existed. Now that the tariffs and duties imposed through misguided trade policies have been removed, Europe should at last begin to make full use of the remarkable new technologies. These have helped to prolong the US economy's non-inflationary growth which has reduced its unemployment to $4^1/_2$ per cent in comparison with $10^1/_2$ per cent in the eleven-country Euroland.

Chapter 7, 'The lessons for Britain and for Europe from the success of German Counter-inflation Policy', is about the Bundesbank and what Britain and Europe should learn from its success. It shows how Herbert Giersch the first chairman of Germany's economic experts, 'the wise men' whom Ludwig Ehrhardt appointed to advise on economic policy, explained how German inflation could be detached from Keynesian inspired US inflation only if the D-Mark was freed from the dollar. When the dollar link was severed in the 1960s, the dollar was worth 4 D-Marks and one pound sterling was actually worth 11 D-Marks. By following an independent monetary policy, Germany avoided the US inflation it would have had to import if it had continued to maintain its fixed exchange rate with the dollar. That would have nullified any possibility of an independent German monetary policy. The Bundesbank went on to show the world that holding inflation down was the key to low interest rates, and that it did not damage industry and commerce in the long term. Europe has decided to follow Germany by creating its own Bundesbank, but whether it will allow the same independence to the new bankers in Frankfurt as Germany granted to their predecessors is an open question. Leading European politicians are seeking to place their own men at the head of the bank, and some apparently insist that monetary policy is a political question where elected politicians should have the last word.

The first Chapter in Part III, 'The Creation and Destruction of EMU' is re-published here, virtually unaltered, as Chapter 8. I believed in July 1997, when I first published it, that if the international financial community lost confidence in EMU, it could destroy the Euro by speculating against the still nationally described currencies (until 2002) of its weakest members. In July 1997, precisely when I published the article, the European Commission declared that the currencies linked in EMU would legally become units of the same currency, the Euro, so that anyone who speculated in currency markets would be selling Euros to buy Euros, and come out with precisely the euros they began with. Hence the Euro cannot be destroyed in currency markets. But I also referred in my 1997 paper to speculation against the currency in bill and bond markets, where huge gains and losses will arise if there is ever an EMU break-up.

I fully up-date the EMU story in Chapter 9, 'Further Considerations on EMU: It will create Instability and Destroy Employment' which I published in an earlier version in June 1998. This chapter is especially concerned with British entry. It shows how, in our very different financial sector with enormously competitive banks, finance is allocated through the rate of interest. In much of continental Europe, it is largely alloted to borrowers through the administrative decisions of bankers. Because spending is more interest-sensitive in Britain, changes in interest rates have four times as much impact here as in continental Europe considered as a whole. Hence getting the interest rate right matters far more in Britain. We should have learned that lesson when Nigel Lawson set the interest rate too low in his attempt to shadow the D-Mark in 1987–9, and bank lending consequently exploded to raise inflation from $4^1/_2$ to $9^1/_2$ per cent. In 1992, after John Major took Britain into the ERM, Norman Lamont as Chancellor had to shadow German interest rates which were far too high for British conditions. Bank lending collapsed and the economy went into deep recession. If we entered EMU, such episodes would recur because the interest rate which was right for France and Germany would sometimes be wholly wrong for Britain.

This is partly because the structure of the British economy, the only oil producer in the European Union, is very different. The foreign exchange market recognises this by linking sterling far more closely to the dollar than to the leading European currencies. Sterling's fluctuation margins against the dollar have varied little in recent years. If we were obliged to move with the continental currencies instead of the dollar, much of British industry and commerce would be handicapped. A falling dollar, for instance, would undermine our high-tech industries which are more extensive than continental Europe's.

Some believe that Britain should enter EMU to assist the City of London. Switzerland's financial sector prospers despite – indeed, because of – the independence of the Swiss franc. London has narrower dealing margins than Frankfurt and Paris because it is more efficient. That is why the 1998 Bank of England survey of the foreign exchange market showed that London had far more business than Frankfurt and Paris combined, and it will keep it so long as it retains its superior efficiency which is based above all on the intensity of competition in the City of London.

Multinational companies are said to wish for British membership of EMU, but when they were surveyed, only 11 per cent said that a failure to join would adversely influence their investments in Britain. Most regard other considerations which favour Britain as far more significant.

The final question is whether the leading European economies are now in serious difficulty. Their labour markets have become so rigid that their unemployment only falls at growth rates of 3 per cent or more. Those are only attainable for at most two or three years at a time, and during the other seven years out of ten when growth is far less than 3 per cent, unemployment rises.

With the next step rise in unemployment, continental Europe's new generation of political leaders will become desperate. They may seek to subvert the new European Central Bank (ECB). They will inescapably face rising taxation because of vast unfunded pensions liabilities. If Britain is drawn in, it may be asked in one way or another to pay for their mistakes, as it is still paying for the Common Agricultural Policy (CAP), which was part of the package which Edward Heath signed up to in 1972, with two thirds cross-party support in the subsequent referendum in 1975. At the very least a degree of tax harmonisation will be required of Britain on this occasion, and this could undo much of the achievement that the earlier chapters of this book describe.

It may be mainly a political question, but there will be significant economic implications if Britain decides to enter in order to enjoy the supposed political benefits of a place at Europe's 'top table'. It will not be quite the top table, because France and Germany agreed in their treaty of 1963 to meet regularly so that they could arrive at an 'analogous' position on all European questions – and on the principal international issues which concern the two countries.

The book concludes in Part IV with three chapters where the experience of earlier historical periods offers lessons from which we can still learn. Chapter 10, 'John Locke and the Establishment of a Sound Currency', shows how John Locke and Isaac Newton established a secure currency for sterling in 1695 and in 1711. In the 220 years after 1711, when the pound sterling was fixed at £3.17*s*.9*d* to an ounce of gold until 1931 when Britain finally left that standard, British prices rose in total by no more than 29 per cent. John Locke and Isaac Newton served the British people well.

Chapter 11, 'Debt, Deficits and Default', is concerned with debt and default in the history of economics. Britain concluded the Napoleonic wars with their twentieth-century legacy of Waterloo Station and

Trafalgar Square, with a national debt of 275 per cent of GDP, more than four times the level nowadays permitted to those who signed Maastricht. Debt interest was 11 per cent of GDP after the war, and Britain's response was a century of balanced budgets (which initially involved a primary budget surplus of 11 per cent of GDP, more than twice what any country nowadays achieves) which reduced the debt to 38 per cent of GDP before the First World War. Many countries with far less debt have defaulted. The economics of debt and default is a pervasive issue in every century, not least the twentieth, and it will doubtless remain one in the twenty-first.

Finally, Chapter 12, 'Europe's Free Markets Reforms in 1774–6 and Russia's in the 1990s ...', is concerned with the parallel difficulties of Louis XVI's greatest finance minister who sought to create free markets in the French economy, and those which Russia's would-be reformers now face. The frustrations Turgot faced in 1774–6 and those which Russia confronts today have far too much in common, so the events which undermined France's finances fifteen years before the Revolution are relevant to an understanding of our world.

Some of these chapters have benefited greatly from seminars and lectures in many countries and universities. I hope that those who presented pertinent comments and counter-arguments will find in my response in this book that I have listened and learned from what they said.

WALTER ELTIS

Oxford University
September 1999

Notes

1. DTI (1998), charts 3.10 and 3.11, p. 13.
2. According to the most recent OECD estimates, in 1996 the real net of tax income of a single employee with average Swiss earnings exceeded that of a US employee by 10 per cent (at purchasing power parity exchange rates) and a Luxembourg employee by 12 per cent (OECD 1998, p. 39).
3. HMSO (1994, 1995).

Acknowledgements

I am grateful to the Centre for Policy Studies for permission to publish revised versions of the papers, *The Key to Higher Living Standards* and *Further Considerations on EMU: it will Create Instability and Destroy Employment*, and to republish *The Creation and destruction of EMU* as Chapters 2, 8 and 9.

I am grateful to the National Institute of Economic and Social Research, and to my co-author, David Higham, for permission to publish a revised version of the article, 'Closing the UK Competitiveness Gap', from the November 1995 issue of the *National Institute Economic Review* (Number 154, November, pp. 71–94) as Chapter 3.

I am grateful to the Foundation for Manufacturing, which is now associated with the University of Cambridge Institute of Manufacturing, for permission to publish revised versions of the papers, *The Political Economy of United Kingdom Foreign Direct Investment* and *The IT Revolution and European Employment* as Chapters 4 and 6.

I am grateful to the European Policy Forum for permission to publish a revised version of the paper *European Competitiveness and Employment Generation* as Chapter 5.

I am grateful to the Economic Research Council for permission to publish a revised version of the paper, *The Lessons for Britain from the Success of German Counter-Inflation Policy*, as Chapter 7.

I am grateful to Edward Elgar for permission to reprint the article, 'John Locke, the Quantity Theory of Money and the Establishment of a Sound Currency', which was originally published in 1995 in *The Quantity Theory of Money from Locke to Keynes and Friedman*, edited by Mark Blaug, as Chapter 10; and a revised version of the article 'Debt, Deficits and Default', originally published in 1998 in *Debt and Deficits: An Historical Perspective*, edited by John Maloney, as Chapter 11.

I am grateful to the *European Journal for the History of Economic Thought*, for permission to publish a revised version of the article, 'France's Free Market Reforms in 1774–6 and Russia's in 1991–3: The Immediate Relevance of l'Abbé de Condillac's Analysis' (1(1), Autumn 1993, pp. 5–19) as Chapter 12.

Finally, I am grateful to my co-author, Robert Bacon, for permission to make use of and to up-date our article, 'Bacon and Eltis after Twenty Years', which we published in *Britain's Economic Problem Revisited*

(Macmillan, 1996, pp. xxvii-lxvi), the third edition of *Britain's Economic Problem: Too Few Producers*, as the foundation for Chapter 1 of the present book.

Walter Eltis

Part I

Britain

1
Public Expenditure and the British Economy 1996*

Robert Bacon and Walter Eltis

In 1975, inflation in Britain reached 25 per cent, public sector borrowing was 10 per cent of GDP and public expenditure was 48 per cent of GDP. Robert Bacon and I summarised our apprehension of what we then regarded as the very real danger of complete economic destabilisation, in perhaps the most significant paragraph in the 'Declining Britain' articles which we published in *The Sunday Times* in November 1975 and in our subsequent book, *Britain's Economic Problem: Too Few Producers*:

> As the unemployment figures rise, extra jobs can only be provided outside industry and only the government can provide jobs where there is no prospect of profits. Hence, governments are tempted to create still more jobs in the public services, and as they raise taxation to pay for them, in due course company profits and workers' living standards are further squeezed with the result that there is still more pressure against company profits in industry. In consequence industry invests still less, more industrial workers become redundant and still more workers need to be fitted into the public sector. This ever-accelerating spiral leads nowhere except to total economic collapse and it is so deep-rooted in structural maladjustment that it is in no way amenable to tinkering. (1976, p. 24)

* This is a revised and updated version of the article 'Bacon and Eltis after Twenty Years' in *Britain's Economic Problem Revisited* (London: Macmillan, 1996), pp. xxvii–lxvi.

This embodies the three central propositions on which our theory of the potentially economically destabilising influence of growing public expenditure was based:

1. An increase in public sector employment as a ratio of total employment, or indeed in any kind of extra public expenditure as a ratio of total output in the economy, can result in an increase in the real cost of labour or capital or both to the private sector.
2. Any increase in the cost of labour or capital in the private sector will reduce the equilibrium level of private sector output and employment below the level that would otherwise be achieved.
3. Any reduction in the equilibrium level of private sector employment will increase the amount of employment the government will need to provide in the public sector if it has an employment target which it seeks to sustain.

These central propositions were based on a distinction between the sector of the economy which is tax-dependent and the sector from which all taxes ultimately derive. As nationalised industries are in the public sector but are also potentially capable of paying taxes and financing non-taxpaying social services, the actual distinction had to be slightly different from the conventional public/private sector dichotomy. The sector of the economy which does not market its output is the tax-dependent one. None of it is financed by selling its output so it must be entirely financed from taxation or borrowing. The sector which markets its output (which includes all private sector industry and commerce plus the nationalised industries insofar as they cover their costs) is the one from which the government must ultimately derive all its tax revenues.

Our propositions therefore became (1) that any increase in the relative size of the non-market sector would require extra taxation, (2) that this would raise costs and so reduce output and employment in the market sector and (3) that the containment of unemployment would then require still more employment in the non-market sector, where governments could create jobs without regard to their financial viability.

When our argument was first published in 1975 and in 1976 there was ready agreement that the three strands in our theory corresponded to recent developments in the British economy. Employment in the non-market public sector had risen more than 50 per cent in the previous thirteen years and because this was tax-dependent, taxation had had to rise massively. We encapsulated this in our remark that blue-collared workers were having to pay a level of taxation which used to be paid by bank managers and university professors. It was also well understood that market sector employment, and especially that in manufacturing industry, had been declining, and that industry had been insufficiently profitable to finance a significant level of new capacity-extending investment. It was a matter of elementary logic that the creation of still more non-market sector employment would further increase the burden of taxation on the market sector.

The core of our argument was that the market sector, private industry and commerce, was becoming too weak to generate the investment and employment the economy required. Denis Healey, the Chancellor of the Exchequer in Harold Wilson's Labour government responded to our articles in *The Sunday Times* on 14 December 1975 that 'The "Declining Britain" articles have provided the most stimulating and comprehensive analysis of our economic predicament' and that he strongly supported the basic proposition that, 'a faster growth in our manufacturing output will require more investment in industry; this will not be possible unless we limit the increase in the claims on the nation's resources which are made by public and private consumption'.

The publication of our articles in November 1975 and the first edition of our book in March 1976 preceded the economic crisis of 1976, the IMF visit and the massive public expenditure cuts which followed. Real public expenditure was cut more than 8 per cent between the fiscal years of 1975–6 and 1977–8, the largest reduction made by any British government over a two-year period. The IMF visit is clearly the principal explanation of the extent of these cuts, but our (then) novel line of argument and the extensive political discussion it attracted may have contributed to the creation of a climate of ideas where it became increasingly understandable that a Labour government could depart from previous Keynesian orthodoxies.

We now provide an account of how the control of public expenditure evolved after 1975, of how this enabled Britain to achieve a faster rate of growth in workers' living standards than continental Europe with corresponding improvements in industrial relations, and of some of the principal issues which have arisen.

The economic impact of tighter control of UK public expenditure

The containment of the growth of public expenditure was central to the policies of the Conservative governments which succeeded Labour in 1979. None of these cut real public expenditure in the manner that Harold Wilson, Denis Healey and James Callaghan had achieved between 1975–6 and 1977–8, but by restricting its rate of increase they reduced the ratio of general government expenditure in GDP by 4 percentage points from 44 per cent in the cyclical peak of 1978–9 to 40 per cent in the cyclical peak of 1989–90. The policies adopted sought to control the growth of public expenditure in a variety of ways, including the application of tight cash limits to contain pay and employment in central and local government.

Figure 1.1 shows that there was a very clear upward trend in the ratio of government expenditure to GDP until 1975. Since then there have been large fluctuations, with peaks in the recessions of 1980–1 and 1992–3 and troughs in the cyclical peaks of 1978–9 and 1989–90.

Since 1975 the trend has been downwards with the share in 1995–6 close to that experienced in the early 1970s. Within this overall pattern, there have been important sectoral changes. The fall during the 1980s was achieved, despite large increases in social security and health programmes, by reductions in defence, in subsidies to industry, in capital spending and in debt interest.

In *Britain's Economic Problem*, we placed particular emphasis on the growth of employment in the market and the non-market sectors.

Figure 1.1 Ratio of UK general government expenditure to gross domestic product, 1963/4 to 1995/6

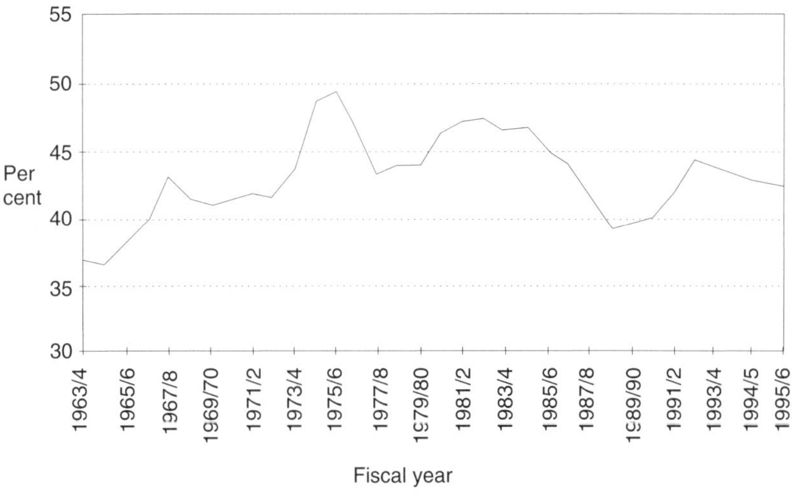

Source: *UK Financial Statement and Budget Report, 1995–96*

Those in the public sector who produce no marketed output depend on tax revenues from those who produce marketed output (mainly in the private sector) to finance their employment, or on government borrowing which will increase taxation in the future. We argued that there would be a strain on resources and an escalation of public expenditure as a ratio of GDP if the numbers producing marketed output declined while the numbers in the non-market sector increased.

Table 1.1 shows what happened to market and non-market employment in the years after the publication of the articles on which our original argument was based. The table shows market and non-market employment in the cyclical peak years of 1961, 1969, 1973, 1979 and 1989. In 1975, 1976 and 1979 we argued that at cyclical peaks employment in the non-market sector can be increased without causing an acceleration of inflation only if it is correspondingly reduced in the market sector – i.e. that at cyclical peaks the economy is at or above its sustainable employment level.

Table 1.1 shows some fall in the ratio of non-market to market sector employment from 1979 to 1989. Non-market employment declined 7 per cent because there was a fall of 2 per cent (129 000) in those who worked for central and local government, and a decline of 82 per cent (282 000) in those employed in the non-market element of the public

Table 1.1 Non-market and market sector employment in the United Kingdom, 1961–89 (000)

	1961	1969	1973	1979	1989
Non-market sector					
General government	3 558	4 198	4 878	5 384	5 255
Public corporations	605	408	378	344	62
Total non-market	4 163	4 606	5 256	5 728	5 317
Market sector					
Private sector	19 303	19 010	18 279	17 944	20 379
Public corporations	1 591	1 662	1 512	1 721	770
Total Market Sector	**20 894**	**20 672**	**19 791**	**19 665**	**21 149**
Non-market/Market (per cent)	**20.0**	**22.3**	**26.6**	**29.2**	**25.1**

Note: Employment in the public corporations is included in the non-market sector to the extent that they receive subsidies and incur *financial* deficits.
Source: CSO.

corporations, mainly as a consequence of the extensive privatisations in the Thatcher decade. In all, non-market employment fell 7 per cent. In the same period, market sector employment grew 7 per cent (by 1 483 000). Private sector employment rose 12 per cent (by 2 435 000), and employment in the market element of the public corporations fell 55 per cent (by 951 000).

The large swing between 1979 and 1989 in the intersectoral head-count had a relatively modest effect on public expenditure totals. Between 1979 and 1989, total employment incomes in central and local government grew 125.3 per cent, while total employment incomes in the whole economy increased 124.2 per cent, so the share of central and local government in aggregate wages and salaries actually increased: the 2 per cent net reduction in general government employment may have disproportionately involved lower-paid staff. In addition, a good deal of the employment swing Table 1.1 shows reflects the direct and indirect effects of privatisations, which had a more significant impact on the government's capital account than on its current account, and therefore the extent to which it could reduce taxation.

Inflation was accelerating in both 1979 and 1989 so at both these cyclical peaks unemployment was below its non-accelerating inflation or 'natural' rate (NAIRU). The OECD estimates that in 1979 the UK 'natural' rate of unemployment was 6.6 per cent and its actual rate 5.0 per cent, while in 1989 its 'natural' rate was 8.8 per cent and its actual rate 7.2 per cent. Hence in both these cyclical peak years market sector employment could not be increased without quite considerable reductions in non-market employment. Over the cycle from 1979 to 1989 considered as a whole the OECD estimates that the natural rate of unemployment averaged 9.3 per cent while the actual rate averaged 10.0 per cent, so the economy was run with perhaps 0.7 percentage points more unemployment than its equilibrium rate because of the priority the government attached to bringing inflation down.

In the seven further complete years of Conservative government from 1989 to 1996 (which was not yet a cyclical peak where full comparisons could be made) a good deal of central government, including especially much of the administration of social security, was reclassified as being discharged by newly created public corporations, such as the Benefits Agency. Total public sector employment, which includes such agencies and new public corporations, fell by 919 000 from 6 080 000 in 1989 to 5 161 000 in 1996, while total private sector employment increased by 129 000 from 20 409 000 to 20 538 000. Employment, mainly in the private sector, increased by a further

1 400 000 from 1996 to 1998, which may be some way from the next cyclical peak after 1989. When the cycle which began in 1989 is completed, total employment will have risen by far more than 600,000.

The 4-percentage point reduction in the ratio of public expenditure to GDP in the complete cycle from 1979 to 1989 was most strongly influenced by reductions in public sector investment, in defence expenditure, in debt interest, through the virtual elimination of subsidies and the elimination of the borrowing needs of the newly privatized public corporations. Walter Eltis showed (Eltis, 1982) how the most powerful net effects of public expenditure cuts on the remainder of the economy are produced by cuts in capital spending and in actual purchases of goods and materials, and it was the slashing of these which had the greatest impact between 1979 and 1989. The opportunity to cut taxation or borrowing which the 4-percentage point reduction in the public expenditure ratio opened up was entirely used to reduce borrowing, so the proportion of current resources which the non-market sector purchased scarcely altered.

In 1979 we developed a table in the *Economic Journal* which showed how marketed output was divided between purchasers in the non-market and the market sectors from 1961 to 1973. We now extend this series to include the cyclical peaks of 1979 and 1989.

Table 1.2 shows that the principal shift from 1979 to 1989 was from the balance of payments to market sector consumption. Those who produced marketed output consumed a higher fraction, and the personal savings ratio actually fell from 9.6 to 5.8 per cent of disposable incomes. In *Britain's Economic Problem* we provided an account of the 'Barber Boom' where bank credit exploded and public and private consumption soared, investment rushed into the housing and property markets and the balance of payments was destroyed. In the 'Lawson

Table 1.2 Where marketed output (net of capital consumption) was purchased 1961–89 (per cent)

	1961	1969	1973	1979	1989
Non-market sector	33.7	36.8	39.8	42.2	41.2
Market-consumption	56.1	51.5	51.8	48.2	53.3
Business investment	7.8	7.4	7.1	4.9	9.4
Investment in dwellings	2.3	3.5	3.5	3.2	3.5
Inventories	1.5	+1.3	+2.3	+1.6	+0.7
Exports *less* imports	–1.4	–0.5	–4.5	–0.1	–8.1

Boom' which concluded the 1979–89 cycle, there was the same over-rapid growth of bank lending because of low real interest rates and further deregulation of banks and building societies. This again encouraged personal borrowing and investment in the housing and property markets. As the personal savings ratio is made up of saving (mainly contractual) for retirement *less* the dissaving of personal borrowers who seek to anticipate future incomes, a large burst of dissaving due to over-optimism by borrowers and eagerness of banks to lend explains the 4-percentage point fall in the aggregate personal savings ratio.

But in the 'Lawson Boom', because there were not competing pressures on resources from the non-market sector, business investment in industry and commerce was extremely strong which helps to explain why the private sector was able to create almost $2^1/_2$ million additional jobs in the decade.

Public expenditure in the United Kingdom and in Europe

It is important to examine how the development of UK public expenditure compares with other countries in the European Union. The information the OECD provides does not permit a sufficient breakdown of the data to provide a series comparable to our Table 1.2, but there is internationally comparable information on public expenditure and taxation as ratios of GDP. Table 1.3 compares general government outlays and current receipts in 1979, 1989 and 1996. The series for outlays omits some capital account public expenditure items, so it shows UK public expenditure falling from 40.9 per cent of GDP in 1979 to 39.8 per cent in 1989, in place of the fall from 44 to $39^3/_4$ per cent of GDP which CSO statistics indicate.

It will be evident that of these fourteen European economies where all but Norway are in the European Union, the UK's public expenditure ratio was the second lowest in both its cyclical peak of 1989 and in 1996, the final year of Conservative government. In 1989 general government outlays were 9.4 percentage points below the average of the thirteen Continental European economies. The United Kingdom cut its general government outlays ratio by 1.1 percentage points between 1979 and 1989 while the thirteen other European economies increased theirs by 3.3 per cent of GDP. From 1989 to 1996, the UK' public spending ratio rose by 3.2 percentage points while the ratio of the thirteen Continental European economies increased by only 0.7 percentage points but the UK's public expenditure was still 6.9 percentage points below the European average in 1996.

Table 1.3 Total outlays and receipts by general government as a ratio of GDP, 1979–96

	Outlays			Receipts		
	1979	1989	1996	1979	1989	1996
Austria	48.2	49.1	51.6	45.8	46.0	47.9
Belgium	57.7	53.6	52.9	50.2	47.4	49.8
Denmark	53.2	56.7	58.2	51.5	57.0	57.4
France	45.0	49.1	55.0	44.1	47.9	50.3
Germany	47.2	44.8	49.1	44.6	44.9	45.6
Greece	30.7	43.6	45.5	28.0	29.2	38.0
Ireland	43.8	48.7	36.3	34.3	36.9	36.1
Italy	41.6	51.4	52.7	31.5	41.6	46.0
Netherlands	53.3	53.9	49.3	49.7	49.1	47.3
Norway	49.5	49.1	45.3	50.8	51.0	51.7
Portugal	36.2	37.6	44.0	30.0	35.2	40.7
Spain	30.1	41.8	43.7	28.3	38.1	39.0
Sweden	60.0	58.3	65.6	57.1	63.7	62.1
Average	**45.9**	**49.2**	**49.9**	**41.9**	**44.9**	**47.1**
United Kingdom	**40.9**	**39.8**	**43.0**	**37.7**	**40.8**	**38.6**

Source: OECD.

The UK's ratio of general government receipts to GDP was the fifth lowest in 1989 and the third lowest in 1996 when it was 8.5 percentage points below the average of the other thirteen. In 1996, not yet a cyclical peak, UK government receipts – that is, taxes and social security contributions, – were 7.0 percentage points below Germany's and 11.7 percentage points below France's.

The immediate effect has been that in the 1990s, the United Kingdom has been able to have lower rates of income tax, corporation tax and above all payroll taxation on the employment of labour than either France or Germany. Overall UK tax rates did not fall between 1979 and 1989 (in Table 1.3 they rise by 3.1 per cent of GDP) but in successive UK budgets special emphasis was placed on reducing marginal rates of taxation, so that by 1989 it had almost the lowest rate of corporation tax in the European Community (33 per cent against the 52 per cent of 1979) and a marginal rate of income tax of 40 per cent when this had been 83 per cent (on earned incomes) in 1979. Average tax levels were also far lower in the United Kingdom in 1996, as Table 1.3 underlines. This is discussed in detail with its full implications for growth and living standards in Chapter 2.

Just how lower UK tax rates have influenced comparative economic performance is a complex question. Lower taxation is one of several considerations which have attracted to the United Kingdom 40 per cent of the US and Japanese investment which has come to Europe since the Second World War. The full implications are discussed in Chapter 4. By 1991, foreign-owned companies employed 17 per cent of the labour, produced 21 per cent of the output and were responsible for 33 per cent of investment in UK manufacturing industry. The average productivity gap between UK and French and German manufacturing industry was halved during the 1980s, when productivity rose more than 40 per cent in the United Kingdom and about 20 per cent in France and Germany.

With rapid productivity growth and virtually no overall increase in taxation as a ratio of GDP, the average net-of-tax earnings of employees in UK manufacturing industry grew 3.1 per cent per annum from 1979 to 1989, while the profits of non-North Sea industrial and commercial companies increased 4.3 per cent per annum faster than the GDP deflator. There were significant industrial relations benefits from this rapid increase in both wages and profits which created what game-theorists refer to as 'positive-sum game' conditions. Betting on horses is a negative-sum game where there are winners and losers, and losses in general to punters and bookmakers together because of the tax on betting. British industry managed to play a positive-sum-game in the 1980s and employees, managers and shareholders were each able to take more money out of the economy because of the large growth in net-of-tax incomes which they were able to generate.

Not surprisingly, game-theorists have discovered that the solution to positive-sum-games is generally cooperation between the players, while in negative or zero-sum-games, where some can win only if others lose, conflict is inevitable. We showed in *Britain's Economic Problem* that in the 1960s and the early 1970s the share of GDP which government took grew so rapidly that what remained for the private sector net-of-tax scarcely increased. It was no wonder that in those decades workers struggled with employers and with other groups of workers to achieve a rising standard of living in an environment where all could not enjoy this. The result was endemic conflict in which wages grew faster than profits, some gained, others lost, and strikes were frequent. In the 1980s employees were able to raise their net-of-tax private consumption by 3 per cent per annum without cutting into profits. As a consequence cooperation to achieve successful production offered more than industrial action could possibly deliver, and at the same time the cost of industrial action to individual unions was raised and the support they would receive from secondary action by other unions was greatly weakened by new industrial relations legislation. The private sector trade unions soon became aware of the significance of these developments. A further favourable result from the creation of an environment where net-of-tax incomes grew significantly year after year was that unions increasingly cooperated with managements to eliminate the over-manning and restrictive practices which had been tolerated in the 1960s and the 1970s. It is now universally understood that all can gain from more efficient production. Walter Eltis was Director General of the National Economic Development Office (NEDO) from 1988 to 1992. In that time he never heard any trade union leader remark that increases in productivity would destroy jobs. He heard many complaints that much of British industry was investing too little, training too little and spending too little on research and development (R & D), which was holding back living standards and competitiveness. The language of the unions had become entirely one of the need to improve productivity and to cooperate to achieve this to the greatest degree managements would allow.

In France and Germany, in contrast to Britain, the average annual growth in real net-of-tax earnings was less than half a per cent per annum in the decade from 1979 to 1989. In both these countries personal taxation and other deductions grew as a ratio of personal incomes, so take home-pay increased far less rapidly than the incomes employees received from their companies. An additional squeeze on the wages workers actually received was due to the continual rise in employers' social security contributions, together with a tendency for real wages to rise more slowly than productivity. In Germany after 1989 there were the added costs of reunification. In the seventeen years from 1979 to 1996 the net-of-tax real wages of German production workers actually fell according to the relevant OECD series while the real incomes of French production workers rose by no more than 3.5 per cent in these seventeen years, or by about 0.2 per cent per annum. In the same period the net-of-tax incomes of British production workers rose 28 per cent, or by about 1.5 per cent per annum (see Table 2.3, p. 41) The net effect has been that while most French and German workers are well paid, their average living standards have risen extremely little in the last two decades. French and German trade unions have therefore begun to develop the attitudes the British unions used to have in the 1960s and the 1970s when employees gradually realised that they could gain significantly higher living standards only by getting larger pay increases than others, which was most readily achievable through the threat of industrial action. In France and Germany in the 1990s, the new frustrations are beginning to show with more frequent and extensive strikes.

While these have all but disappeared in the UK private or market sector, there are areas of the public sector where the 'cash limits' used to control public expenditure have been set so low that negligible real income growth has resulted. This has produced precisely the zero-sum conditions which used to prevail in the private sector and it has naturally led to a continuation of union militancy.

If the private market sector is achieving rapid productivity growth, it should be possible to increase levels of pay in the non-market public sector at parallel rates. There is no statement in *Britain's Economic Problem* where we suggest that individual levels of pay for those who produce unmarketed public services should be held back in comparison with pay in industry and commerce. If real output is growing fast enough in private industry and commerce to permit positive-sum wage bargaining, the same should be attainable in the public sector through the restoration of pay arbitration based on fair comparisons. By 1999 it has been learned throughout Europe that responsibility for the control of inflation rests on effective monetary and fiscal policies, and if the aggregate of pay increases is successfully contained by these, it will not be inflationary to allow the 20 per cent of employees in central and local government to enjoy the same average rise in living standards as the 80 per cent in the private sector.

The UK's combination of positive-sum conditions in the private sector and zero or negative-sum conditions in some of the public sector can be seen as a fundamental tension between two broad principles which influence the relative size of the public sector. The first is that the private sector will function effectively only if net-of-tax real incomes advance sufficiently rapidly to permit the establishment of positive-sum conditions for those who work in industry and commerce. This requires an adequate rate of productivity growth, while a sufficient fraction of the fruits of growth must be retained by those who produce in the market sector. But there is a second principle which is also important.

Evidence from a variety of countries, as surveyed by Norman Gemmell in 1993, shows that as families become richer they spend growing fractions of their incomes on health, education and personal security. These are actually describable as 'superior' goods and services, because the rich spend a higher fraction of their incomes on them than the less well off. The expenditure elasticity of demand for health, education and personal security – i.e. *the proportional increase in demand for these divided by the proportional increase in aggregate expenditure* exceeds 1. If a society determines that these will mostly be provided by the state, then its government will need to increase their provision more rapidly than the national income if it is to follow the preferences of its population. The fundamental implications are the subject of the next part of the argument.

Populations need to spend more on health and education as real incomes grow

The international tendency for public expenditure ratios in GDP to grow is sometimes referred to as 'Wagner's Law'. Adolph Wagner, a late nineteenth-century German economist believed that redistributive social welfare was itself a 'superior' good and that for this and a number of further reasons (set out in Gemmell, 1993) public expenditure would increase as a share of the national income as an economy's incomes per head grew. In the late twentieth century this 'law' has fitted Europe well, but not the United States and Japan. But it is evident that if taxation and public expenditure ratios show an ever-rising trend, because a wealthier economy redistributes more, a point will come where that development will produce economic destabilisation. Even if there is sustained majority political support for continuing redistribution, those whose economic actions are also guided by personal motivations will be aware that the rates of return from tax evasion and tax avoidance all the time increase as average tax rates rise, while the net-of-tax returns from productive investment and employment will decline as the adverse impact of taxation on industry and commerce increases. To continually increase the rate of return from tax evasion and avoidance and reduce the return from productive investment and employment must eventually undermine an economy's growth potential. This is an error which the United States, the Pacific Rim economies, and (since 1976) the United Kingdom have been careful to avoid. The 'law' of ever rising *redistributive* taxation should be resisted, but not the wishes of a population for a greater supply of 'superior' goods such as education, health and personal security which families would themselves buy more of as their incomes grow if they were not predominantly provided by the state.

In theory, a good deal of expenditure on health and education could be arranged through the private sector, but in practice all OECD governments take responsibility for the establishment of minimum standards out of national and local budgets. Increasing provision of health and education is therefore likely to impose a rising trend on these items of public expenditure. The cost of other public expenditure categories such as national defence and industrial and agricultural subsidies may fall, as they did in Britain from 1979 to 1989, so a rising overall trend in public expenditure is potentially avoidable, but a population's desire for improving health, education and personal security (which is independent of whether it also wishes to redistribute more: it may or it may not) is likely to exert some upward pressure on public expenditure.

There are therefore tensions between the need to create positive-sum conditions in the private sector and the need to provide the rising standards of health, education and personal security which families' revealed preferences indicate. With the high rate of productivity growth which much of Europe achieved in the 1950s and the 1960s it was possible to achieve both. Thus, from 1965 to 1977 West German non-market expenditures rose one-and-a-quarter times as fast as marketed output, but private consumption and investment were still able to grow at annual rates of almost 4 per cent and 2 per cent, respectively. That combination of some growth in the public expenditure ratio and a quite rapid rate of increase of real personal consumption may have come close to tracking the preferences between private consumption and government provision of health, education and other public goods which German electorates desired at that time. In contrast, in Britain over this period, public consumption and investment grew twice as fast as marketed output per head and almost four times as fast as private consumption and investment. That almost certainly represented a faster shift in favour of the government provision of health, education and other public goods than implicit preferences called for, and this over-rapid shift in favour of the public services reduced the private sector to near zero-sum conditions with the consequences we set out in *Britain's Economic Problem*.

From 1979 to 1989 the relative rates of growth of public provision and private rewards for UK market sector producers were reversed. With a slight fall in the ratio of public expenditure to GDP, the provision of public goods and services grew less than private consumption and investment. This slower growth in public expenditure may have compensated for its over-rapid expansion in the previous 20 years, so the relative growth of the two sectors may have come close to following the underlying preferences of the population, if the period from 1961 to 1989 is considered as a whole. After 1979 it was central to

Conservative Party strategy to reduce the growth of public expenditure in relation to the national income, and it won four successive general elections with a clear intention to break away from former trends.

Despite the fall in the ratio of total public expenditure to GDP from 1979 to 1989, spending on health and 'public order and safety' – mainly police and prisons – actually increased as ratios of GDP. Public expenditure on health grew one-and-a-half times while real expenditures on 'public order and safety' increased more than twice as fast as GDP. These estimates of real rates of increase do not allow for the 'relative price effect' that expenditures on public services are usually subject to more inflation than the majority of private sector purchases. Private and public sector purchases are both deflated by the economy's general rate of inflation, but nominal expenditures on health and law and order both grew faster than GDP, and the evidence from family expenditure surveys that families spend more on these as their real incomes grow refers only to their nominal expenditures. There is no evidence that families correct for the 'relative price effect'. Hence the growth of public expenditure on health and personal security from 1979 to 1989 may well have corresponded to family preferences as revealed by personal expenditure patterns.

But in the continual pressure to reduce public expenditure from 1979 to 1989 education grew two-thirds as fast as GDP, although it is universally regarded as a 'superior' good. That has been largely made good since 1989, for in the seventeen years from 1979 to 1996 considered as a whole, the share of public expenditure on education in GDP rose, and it increased almost one-and-a-half times as fast as GDP to conform to the private perception that this should grow faster than expenditures in general. In the longer seventeen-year period from 1979 to 1996, expenditure on public order and safety grew three times and expenditure on health almost twice as fast as GDP.

Since 1990 total public expenditure has grown substantially relative to GDP but its level is still well below the EU average. Social provision for the unemployed and for those on low incomes automatically rises when the economy is in recession so the increase in total public expenditure since 1990 has had a significant cyclical element. From the cyclical peak of 1989–90 to 1992–3, general government expenditure rose from 39.6 to 44.2 per cent of GDP. In 1997–8, perhaps some way below the next cyclical peak, it came back to 39.6 per cent of GDP, precisely the 1989–90 level.

The evidence indicates that the Thatcher and Major governments increased the share of total public spending in what many would regard as the areas where there is most justification for a growing share, and this development is likely to continue. There is none the less a widespread belief that public health, education and law and order have been under-provided for. This is despite the evidence from the national accounts that public expenditure on these has grown sufficiently faster than GDP to reflect the preferences of the population. It is unlikely that families would have increased their relative expenditures faster than the government if the decisions had been theirs.

The widely voiced dissatisfaction with some of these services most plausibly reflects the way in which the police, the prisons, the national health service and state education are organised and managed, which Conservative governments finally came to recognise as the key issue which deserved attention. The Major government introduced the 'Citizen's Charter' in 1993 which set out the quality of service which individuals were entitled to receive, and the increasing freedom to manage internal budgets within health and education were directly concerned with the quality of the public services and the priority the government attached to this. Tony Blair's Labour government appears to be reversing some of the freedom to manage internal budgets which the Conservatives introduced in their final years, but it may be strengthening the influence of inspectors of schools.

We reiterated in *Britain's Economic Problem* that extra resources had been poured into health and education, that a high fraction of these had been channelled into administration and that consumers had not perceived commensurate improvements at the sharp end. We in *Britain's Economic Problem*, quoted from a study by Max Gammon which showed from official National Health Service (NHS) statistics that from 1965 to 1973 the number of occupied beds in NHS hospitals in Great Britain had fallen from 451 000 to 400 000 while the number of administrators and clerical staff in the Hospital Service had increased from 48 000 to 72 000. These series cannot be extended on a precisely comparable basis, but current official series show that the available beds in English NHS hospitals were 435 000 in 1966, 391 000 in 1976 and 231 000 in 1992–3. The number of administrators managers and clerical staff in the NHS in England almost doubled from 83 000 in 1974 to 152 000 in 1992. The trend which Max Gammon originally diagnosed has therefore continued relentlessly through Labour and Conservative governments and many Secretaries of State for Health. The manifest difficulties experienced by many of those who require hospital treatment throws considerable doubt on whether the apparent imbalance between the substantial reduction in the number of beds in the last thirty years, and the continuing increases in managerial administrative and clerical staff, have been well judged.

The questions which are most widely debated on health and education in the 1990s underline how the most significant public expenditure issues now centre on how the public services are administered and organised and not on the rates of growth of financial expenditures. It is becoming increasingly recognised that we must learn to measure the *outputs* of public services – the levels of literacy and mathematical attainment in our schools (where there are comparative international studies), the proportion of crimes 'solved' by the police, the extent of hospital waiting lists and whether these are growing or declining. If *inputs* into these services advance – that is, if there are more teachers, more policemen and more employees of the NHS, but numeracy and literacy fail to advance, as many crimes remain unsolved and hospital waiting lists remain as long – the public will not accept that the *output* of these services is improving. These have become the issues that matter.

Successive UK governments have sought to reconcile constraint over financial *inputs* into public expenditure with improvements in the quality of *outputs* by adopting management techniques which increase value for money. By 1997, the underlying perception of successive Conservative governments had become that the financial inputs the UK public services received were becoming appropriate in relation to the national income, and that the higher standards of provision the public desired would be best delivered through improvements in the management of these resources.

Their policy of maintaining a near-stable share of public expenditure in GDP (apart from fluctuations inherent in the cycle) reflected the difficulties the United Kingdom had experienced in the past from over-rapid change. Too fast an increase in public expenditure from 1961 to 1976 had left workers facing slow or zero growth in what their real wages would buy, which had led to frustration and zero-sum behaviour. At the other extreme, some over-rapid reductions in the 1980s and the 1990s had led to zero- and even negative-sum conditions among those who provided certain public services which created frustrations and resistance of a different kind. The adverse pressures from too little private or too little public consumption are most easily containable in a rapidly growing economy where both can be increased at rates which command general assent.

In the particularly damaging scenario with which *Britain's Economic Problem* was concerned, increases in the public expenditure ratio first produced worker frustration, and then went on to damage investment and therefore the productive base and the economy's underlying rate of growth. That gradually made it more difficult for a society to satisfy its combined aspirations for private and public consumption, and if pushed relentlessly, it went on to create a situation where the frustrations from inadequate growth of private consumption and the necessity for cuts in public consumption were encountered at the same time.

Can Britain's economic problem recur?

Our analysis suggests that a return to the destabilisation sequence from which Britain suffered in the 1960s and the 1970s would need a recurrence of two significant developments.

First, extra public expenditure would again have to be allowed to cream off most of the fruits of growth. In 1997 Britain's public expenditure ratio was $8^1/_2$ percentage points below the EU average, so there are many items of expenditure, and especially on the infrastructure, state pensions and social benefits, where Europe spends considerably more than the United Kingdom. Those who believe that the other countries in the European Union have achieved a superior economic and social balance between public and private provision could seek future public expenditure growth at rates considerably faster than the output of the economy. This would also occur if Britain succumbed to political pressures from the leading European governments and, through them, the EU's Council of Ministers, to conform to a wider range of European levels of economic and social provision and, of course, minimum European levels of taxation. If for this and other reasons, UK public expenditure and tax ratios returned to the sustained expansion which occurred from 1961 to 1976, the ratio of taxation in GDP and in all paypackets and salary cheques would rise continuously. Powerful adverse effects similar to those of the 1960s and the 1970s would return if the United Kingdom private sector was again allowed to return to near zero-sum conditions, where the real net-of-tax pay of the average worker scarcely grew. The need to limit the relative growth of the public sector so that there is room for private sector net-of-tax incomes to grow at adequate rates must continue to be understood. Otherwise trade union militancy and endemic strikes will return in both the private and the public sectors.

A second serious danger would arise if future governments returned to the former practice of acting as employer of last resort in an effort to bring unemployment back to the far lower levels of the 1950s and the

1960s. Tax and public expenditure ratios would then escalate without limit, as in Sweden in the 1960s and the 1970s and the early 1980s (the details are set out in Chapter 5). There have been voices which have begun to suggest that a situation has been reached in Britain where only the state can provide adequate employment for the uneducated and the unskilled. There are vast areas of under-provision to which the state could contribute by harnessing the energies of those who cannot find employment in private industry and commerce. If pay for new public sector jobs is raised well above present benefit levels to encourage more of the unemployed to move into work, and if central government and local authorities created many more jobs which the unskilled could perform, unemployment could appear to fall, though not for long, as the Swedish example illustrates.

But to restore the role of the government as employer of last resort, and to allow a disproportionately rapid rate of growth of public expenditure, would involve a return to past policies, and this would resurrect the economic conditions from which Britain suffered in the later 1960s and the 1970s. Some believe that these would not recur if, in the next decades, renewed growth in the public sector is accompanied by sustained control over inflation through the independent control over monetary conditions that was granted to the Bank of England in 1997 (the subject of Chapter 7 below).

Many in economics and politics forget previous disasters and the political and intellectual battles which had to be won to re-establish the foundations of a viable economy. Another crisis like those the United Kingdom survived in 1976 and 1979 could recur if the combination of policies which destabilised the economy in the 1970s is allowed to re-emerge. Precisely how a return to these policies could re-establish the conditions for economic destabilization is set out in the technical Appendix which follows.

Appendix: a technical presentation of our underlying argument that excessive non-market sector growth destabilises economies

Our underlying theoretical argument was based on three propositions: that a fraction of tax increases will be passed on, that the consequently higher cost of labour will reduce market sector employment and that a reduction in market employment will force taxation up further because workers no longer employed in the market sector will be an added burden on the finances of the state. If these effects are sufficiently powerful they can produce the complete destabilisation which threatened the United Kingdom in the 1970s, but which was averted by the re-establishment of control over the growth of public expenditure in 1976 and in 1979. Our academic argument rests on the power of these propositions. We begin with whether higher taxation will actually raise the real cost of labour.

There is now much econometric evidence which indicates that a fraction of tax increases is passed on. This was summarised by Robert Bacon in 'The Effects of Public Employment and Other Government Spending on the Rate of Wage Inflation' (1980), and in a further survey, 'Real Wages and Taxation in Ten OECD Countries', which Anthonie Knoester and Nico van der Windt published in 1987. A 1990 OECD study found that on average, for sixteen OECD countries, a 1 per cent increase in the 'tax wedge' (the excess of the total amount companies pay to employ a worker over what the tax system allows the worker to receive) induced an immediate increase in labour costs of $^1/_2$ per cent. Virtually all well-based wage equations show that changes in the direct taxation of wages influence the pace of wage increases, while changes in indirect taxes and employers' social security contributions influence these through their effect on prices, which will be wholly or partly passed on into higher wages. There are three significant transmission mechanisms.

First and most simply and directly, the supply curve of labour is universally seen as depending upon expected real earnings net of tax. An increase in the taxation of wages will reduce what workers receive at the previously established real wage. Workers will supply less labour at that wage if there is any sensitivity of the supply of labour to the rewards of the worker. The new equilibrium between the supply of labour and the wage will be at a level where companies pay more but workers receive less than in the previous equilibrium where there was no taxation of wages. Empirical evidence does not suggest that there is much sensitivity of the supply of labour to the real wage, but there is some, so higher payroll or income taxation is associated with a lower supply of labour and a higher cost of labour to companies.

Robert Bacon shows how the argument can be generalised so that workers are influenced both by the part of the real wage which is available to buy marketed output, and also by the social wage, the public services they benefit from, and also the availability of leisure. In this broader and more general approach, there is still some tendency for higher taxation to reduce the supply of labour and increase its cost to industry and commerce, unless the increase in the social wage is seen as a greater priority than increases in the market wage.

A second consideration which leads to the passing on of some taxation of wages is based on the influence of workers' expectations. Their supply of labour will depend on the real net-of-tax incomes they expect to receive in the 'year' for which they are bargaining. In order to continue to enjoy the same real standard of living, they bargain for pay increases which cover the price increases they anticipate (the current rate of inflation if their expectations 'adapt' to immediate experience), *plus* whatever further pay increases they would require to cover additional deductions from their paypackets or salary cheques. Employees will therefore enter wage negotiations with a larger target increase if tax deductions are growing. Employers will face strong resistance to increases which fail to compensate for higher taxation, and the bargain that results will be influenced by this. The argument is often extended to suggest that workers' wage demands are based not merely on what they believe will produce a specific net-of-tax real wage, but in addition they will expect a real wage which grows in line with what they have received in the immediate past. Again, rising taxation will add to the wage increases they require to achieve any target net-of-tax real wage path.

A third line of argument, much present in *Britain's Economic Problem*, suggests that in addition to what has been said so far the pace of wage increases is influenced by whether wages are above or below the level at which the labour market is in equilibrium. If the wages which workers seek run ahead of the real wages the economy can deliver because aggregate demand is limited through monetary and fiscal policy, growing unemployment will result. This will pull back the pace of wage increases, so employees' efforts to pass taxation on will raise unemployment rather than wages. Any developments (through government action or equilibrating market forces) which re-establish the former 'natural' level of unemployment will at the same time have to establish the higher real wages workers required at the original unemployment level.

These theoretical lines of argument, and others like them, have led to a plethora of wage equations which have been widely tested and are compatible with the view that employees pass a fraction of tax increases on through higher wages.

We can now examine the first of the three fundamental relationships which have the potential in combination to produce economic destabilisation: the connection between an increase in taxation and a consequent increase in the real cost of labour.

For this presentation of the argument, it will be assumed that an economy has a uniform proportional rate of tax of T which is levied on all incomes. A uniform rate of tax of T levied on all outputs (value-added) would have quite similar general effects. If employers could not pass an increase in T on in higher prices, workers would pay none of the higher taxation unless money wages *fell*, while if employers could raise their prices in response to higher indirect taxation, workers would recover part of tax increases if they could raise money wages. In the example which follows, T is raised by 1 percentage point because there is an initial increase in public expenditure by 1 per cent of GDP, and the budget is balanced. If the wage (and therefore the cost of labour) is W before tax, it will be $W(1–T)$ after tax, and if taxation rises by 1 percentage point, the proportional fall in the wage after tax is the increase in tax, $0.01W$, divided by the original pre-tax wage of $(1–T)W$. Hence the proportional fall in net-of-tax wages is $0.01W$ divided by $(1–T)W$, or $0.01/(1–T)$. Net-of-tax wages therefore fall by the 1 per cent increase in taxation times a multiplier of $1/(1–T)$. The size of this multiplier will be 1.18 if T is 15 per cent, 1.67 if it is 40 per cent, 2 if it is 50 per cent and 3 if it is 67 per cent. We therefore have the important proposition that a tax increase will reduce net-of-tax wages by a multiple of the increase in taxation. This multiplier of $1/(1–T)$ means that in a highly taxed economy like Sweden where taxation takes almost two-thirds of the national income, $1/(1–T)$ will approach 3. With a multiplier of 3, an increase in taxation of 1 per cent of the national income would reduce net-of-tax earnings by 3 per cent. A Swedish worker earning a money income of 300 Kronor, would have only 100 after tax if incomes were taxed at a rate of 67 per cent, and a tax increase of 1 per cent on his total income of 300 would remove a further 3 Kronor from his paypacket, and leave him with a net-of-tax income of 97 instead of 100, a reduction of 3 per cent.

The equivalent multiplier will be about 2 in most of Europe where taxation averages 50 per cent of GDP, perhaps 1.67 in the United Kingdom where it averages 40 per cent, and little more than 1 in an economy like Hong Kong where average taxation is only 15 per cent.

If a fraction, $Ç$, of tax increases is passed on in higher wages, then an increase in taxation by 1 per cent of all incomes will raise the cost of labour $Ç/(1–T)$ per cent. If $Ç$ is 1 so that tax increases on wages are fully passed on, then a 1-percentage point tax increase would raise the cost of labour 3 per cent in an economy with 67 per cent taxation, 2 per cent in a typical European economy and 1.2 per cent in an economy like Hong Kong. If $Ç$ is $^1/_2$, so that workers are able to pass on half of tax increases, a 1-percentage point tax increase would produce an increase of up to $1^1/_2$ per cent in the cost of labour in an economy like Sweden, a 1 per cent increase in Western Europe and a 0.60 per cent increase in Hong Kong. In general we can write:

$$\text{Elasticity of cost of labour with respect to taxation } (E_{W/T}) = Ç/(1-T) \quad (1.1)$$

The second link in the potential destabilisation chain is that an increase in the cost of labour will reduce market sector employment. Here we can use the concept of the elasticity of substitution between labour and capital, *the decrease in the quantity of labour which is employed (relative to capital), divided by the relative increase in the cost of labour*. If the elasticity of substitution between labour and capital is $-^1/_2$, a 1 per cent increase in the relative cost of labour would produce a $^1/_2$ per cent fall in the amount of labour employed. Estimates of the elasticity of substitution between labour and capital have virtually always found a figure of less than 1 (Sato, 1970; Arrow, Chenery, Minhas and Solow, 1961), so a 1 per cent increase in the relative cost of labour is almost invariably associated with a fall of less than 1 per cent in employment. If we write $\tilde{o}$ for the elasticity of substitution between labour and capital, and $E_{N/W}$ for the elasticity of market sector employment with respect to the cost of labour, then in general:

$$\text{Elasticity of market sector employment with respect to the cost of labour } (E_{N/W}) \text{ equals } \tilde{o} \quad (1.2)$$

Equation 1.2 under-states the full adverse impact of a higher cost of labour on the employment the market sector provides. The impact of the elasticity of substitution between labour and capital shows what the fall in employment will be when the market sector's capital stock is at a particular level. In *Britain's Economic Problem* we also emphasised the way in which tax increases which workers pass on reduce net of tax profits and market sector investment. This will have an adverse *dynamic* impact on the market sector's capital stock and the employment it can provide, which will therefore fall more sharply than is indicated by expression (1.2) which describes a *static* movement along a given production function.

The third link in the potential destabilization chain is between a fall in market sector employment and the consequent need to increase taxation, either to provide alternative public sector employment for newly redundant workers, or else to finance their unemployment. If the marginal product of labour in the market sector is β times its average product and 1 per cent of market sector employment is lost, then β per cent of the tax-paying part of the economy will cease to function. Taxation would need to be raised by β percentage points if a worker made redundant in the market sector is employed in the public non-market sector (in existing office accommodation) at a similar wage. If those made redundant in the market sector are merely allowed to become unemployed, they might cost the state as little as one-third of their former marginal products. If the state takes the view, which used to prevail in Sweden, that the government normally acts as employer of last resort, such workers will be found employment in the public non-market sector at a cost to government finances which would correspond at least to their previous marginal product in the market sector. If the state had to provide new capital installations in addition it would have to provide total funds which exceeded workers' previous marginal products. If the alternative public sector provision is μ times as expensive as the private sector provision that is eliminated by increased taxation, and the elasticity of the rate of taxation the economy requires to balance its budget with respect to the level of market sector employment is $E_{T/N}$, then in general:

Elasticity of the tax rate with respect to market sector employment
$(E_{T/N}) = -\beta\ \mu$ (1.3)

The full destabilisation sequence has the three elements that (1) tax increases raise the cost of labour, (2) increases in the cost of labour reduce market sector employment, and (3) reductions in market sector employment cause an increase in taxation. This will start the whole sequence off again and produce a second round of the same developments, and after that a third. A significant question is whether the second round of tax increase which come at the end of (1), (2) and (3) will be larger or smaller than the initial increases, and whether the tax increases which subsequently set off a third round are larger or smaller than those which set off the second. If the tax increases that set off each round become progressively larger the economy will explode into destabilization. Alternatively if the tax increases in the second round are significantly smaller than those in the first, the sequence will in due course diminish to insignificance. The dynamic sequence could be *explosive*, with tax increases becoming larger in each successive round, or *damped*, with tax increases continually diminishing.

Whether the tax increases which set off the second round are larger than those which initiate the process will depend on the size of the three links in the dynamic chain. Thus the initial tax increase raises the cost of labour by a multiple $E_{W/T}$, the elasticity of the cost of labour with respect to taxation. This extra cost of labour then reduces market sector employment by a multiple $E_{N/W}$, the elasticity of market sector employment relative to the cost of labour. This reduction in market sector employment then goes on to increase taxation by the further multiple $\boldsymbol{E}_{T/N}$, the elasticity of taxation with respect to market sector employment.

The extent of the increase in taxation that initiates the second round will be the initial increase in taxation times the combined effect of the three elasticities. Hence:

> Increase in taxation that initiates the second round equals the increase that initiates the first times
> $E_{W/T} \times E_{N/W} \times E_{T/N}$ (1.4)

We can use the statements we derived for the three elasticities, $E_{W/T}$, $E_{N/W}$, and $E_{T/N}$ in expressions (1.1), (1.2) and (1.3) to derive a numerical value for (1.4) which tells us whether the potential destabilization sequence will be explosive or damped:

> Increase in taxation in the second round equals the increase that initiates the first round times
> $-[Ç/(1-T)]\ \tilde{o}\ \beta\ \mu$ (1.5)

So the sequence will be explosive if $[Ç/(1-T)]\ \tilde{o}\ \beta\ \mu$ exceeds unity. Let us begin by considering what values these might have in a British sequence with the economy as it is developing in the 1990s. It could be suggested that the trade unions have become quite weak so that Ç, the proportion of what workers lose from tax increases that they are able to pass on, could be as low as 0.3. Taxation itself is close to 40 per cent of GDP, so $1/(1-T)$ may be about 1.67. The elasticity of substitution between labour and capital, $\tilde{o}$, is perhaps about –0.6, it appears close to this in many studies, while μ (the budgetary cost of supporting those who lose their jobs in the market sector as a ratio of their former wage) might be quite low, perhaps as little as 0.4, because such workers are not found alternative government employment and unemployment benefits have become a low fraction of earnings. The marginal product of the workers who lose market sector employment might be about 0.7 times the average product of labour in the market sector, so β might be about 0.7. In all, with these assumptions, $-[Ç/(1-T)]\ \tilde{o}\ \beta\ \mu$ would come to $0.3 \times 1.67 \times 0.6 \times 0.4 \times 0.7$ which equals 0.084. With an economy that follows that description, an initial increase in taxation would set off an echo sequence which was perhaps one-twelth as great. That would indicate that there is no present risk of a destabilisation sequence.

We can contrast this with the situation which prevailed in the United Kingdom in 1976 when we published the first edition of *Britain's Economic Problem*. At that time, the trade unions were far more able to pass taxation on than in 1999 so *Ç*, the proportion of a tax increase which is passed on, may have been as high as 0.6 as against the 0.3 we are supposing in 1999. *T*, the proportion of taxation in GDP, was similar to the 40 per cent of 1998. At that time workers made redundant in the market sector were found equally well paid work in the non-market sector and the cost to the state was not merely the provision of a public sector income equivalent to their former wage. Paying newly employed public sector workers the same wage would have made μ equal to 1.0, but capital costs also had to be incurred to provide office blocks and other appropriate accommodation in the public sector. This will have raised μ to perhaps 1.3. Thus the total cost of employing an extra worker in the public sector was perhaps 1.3 times the level of income the marginal worker received in the market sector. $\tilde{\sigma}$, the elasticity of substitution between labour and capital, and β, the ratio of the marginal product of labour to the average product will have been similar to their assumed values in 1999, – 0.6 and 0.7. With these assumptions, $-[Ç/(1-T)]\ \tilde{\sigma}\ \beta\ \mu$ would come to 0.546, so in the economic conditions which prevailed in 1976, a tax increase would have opened up a dynamic sequence which produced further tax increases and consequent declines in the market sector, at repeated intervals. These subsequent tax increases would have gradually diminished in extent, by perhaps about one-half in each round.

That is where Britain might have headed in the absence of the significant policy change in 1976 that the government would cease to act as employer of last resort, and the further policy change in 1979 that the ratio of taxation in GDP would be contained. These significant decisions virtually eliminated the potential destabilisation sequence. If they were reversed, the possibility of destabilisation could recur.

2
The Key to Higher British Living Standards*

Prologue: a small trade dispute in 1979

In May 1979 when Margaret Thatcher won her first general election the print unions were in dispute with *The Times* and *The Sunday Times*. The printers' world was transformed a few years later but in 1979 they still had the power to prevent the publication of any newspaper for up to a year. During the election campaign Harold Evans, editor of *The Sunday Times*, expected that the dispute would be resolved before the election and invited me to write an article on the economic implications of the election, but he was unable to publish it because Times Newspapers failed to appear during the campaign.

Now, twenty years later, the article I wrote in 1979 which is reproduced on pp. 29–33 below provides an account of what some of us then hoped for. After that, I go on to contrast my optimism in 1979 with what Margaret Thatcher's and John Major's governments actually delivered.

It emerges that a good deal that I expected in 1979 was actually achieved, including a large rise in the living standards of British workers in comparison with those in France and Germany. Perhaps the most vivid contrast between 1979 and 1999 is that it has become unthinkable that anyone should have the power to silence *The Times* and *The Sunday Times* during an election campaign.

* This is a revised and up-dated version of the paper *The Key to Higher Living Standards* (London: Centre for Policy Studies, 1996).

The hopes of 1979: if the Conservatives win, will Britain catch-up with Europe?[1]

For a gambler, Britain has the best prospects for growth in living standards of any EEC economy. According to recent North American research the growth of the world's developed economies is explained by the theory that they are catching-up with the level of efficiency that the United States has already achieved. Those like Japan and Italy which have had the most ground to make up since the Second World War have had the most sensational growth. One country has stood out from the statistics of catch-up – Britain. While every other country has seized the opportunity to take American technical efficiency on board and move ever nearer to North American living standards, Britain has remained doggedly 40 to 50 per cent behind the United States. We have failed to take the easy road of merely copying what the efficient already do.

But Britain has the same opportunity to catch-up as everyone else, and like the rest we shall in the end. Will we start to do so in the next five years? If we do, we shall for the first time enjoy West European growth rates in output and living standards, and because we are now significantly behind the French and the Germans, we shall actually be able to grow faster. Will we?

Elections are times of hope and they present opportunities for new departures. We hoped for much in 1964 and 1970, but in practice the Wilson and Heath governments offered repeated incomes policies, devaluations, monetary expansion, and an ever-growing public sector. Each year we fell still further behind. Do the Conservatives now offer a genuine chance of catch-up?

Their tax-cutting and expenditure-reducing policies are the main departure from the past, and it is a marginal tax rate of 60 per cent or less which could bring Californian efficiency and enterprise to Britain. It is in California that the Laffer curve was invented. Professor Art Laffer made the profoundly simple observation that a tax rate of 100 per cent yields no revenue. Treasuries are a little apt to assume that a tax rate of 90 per cent will yield more revenue than a tax rate of 80 per cent, while a tax rate of 100 per cent will yield the most revenue of all – everything that everyone earns. In fact by the time tax rates reach 100 per cent taxpayers will have arranged to be in another country, given up work, or joined the unofficial economy which, according to the Head of the Inland Revenue is now producing $7^1/_2$ per cent of Britain's National Product. If 100 per cent taxation yields no revenue and 0 per cent taxation yields no revenue, the government gets more money by taxing at some rate in between. In Figure 2.1 the revenue-maximising tax rate has been set at 65 per cent. If that is about right, any tax cuts from the present 83 per cent (and 98 per cent for investment incomes) down to 65 per cent would actually bring extra money to the government and allow other taxes to be cut. The taxes of over 65 per cent have driven taxpayers out of the country and caused distortions and irregularities which have cost the country revenue. If that is right, cutting marginal tax rates to 60 per cent or so to bring taxes into line with those in the remainder of the EEC would cost virtually nothing, and that is widely recognised today. But would it have a significant effect on the country's underperformance?

Hard evidence on the damage done by high marginal taxation is notoriously difficult to establish since underperformance has many possible causes. But there is a strong *a priori* case that high marginal taxation could explain a good deal, and it should be remembered that

Figure 2.1 The rate of taxation and total tax revenue

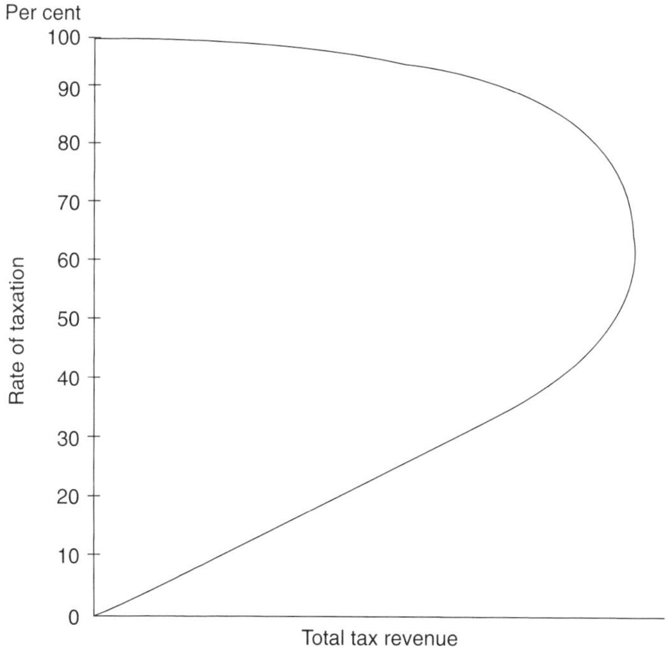

it never fell below 75 per cent, a far higher rate than is now contemplated, in the time of Mr Macmillan and Mr Heath. Many think of wealth and job creation as coming mainly from the large well known companies. The self-employed and those who work in the private services where many firms are small increased by 1 085 000 from 1966 to 1977 while industry lost nearly 2 million jobs in this period. There is general agreement that the solution to Britain's employment problem must now come from faster expansion of the country's small businesses. With luck the large companies may hold their jobs, but expansion will have to come from below, from new firms with ideas, and from men and women who see gaps in the markets around them. At present the Inland Revenue assumes that partnerships and close companies distribute a considerable fraction of their profits, and then taxes these profits at up to 98 per cent, so these rates of taxation are levied on many of those who have most to offer.

In the larger corporations, executives will value money and what it can buy, security, and a quiet and comfortable life – the on-the-job leisure which many Town Halls now offer. If the tax system denies managers extra money, they will rationally take extra security or leisure instead. There will be many dedicated men and women who will do the right thing without financial reward, but what of the others, perhaps the majority. If a major reorganisation of the company and its operations will involve extra work and no extra money, why bother? If difficult negotiations with the trades unions to raise productivity would involve no extra money and sleepless nights and long days, why trouble? If the effect of the risks involved in introducing an important new product which might sell on world markets is no extra money after tax if it succeeds and a lost reputation if it fails, why take the risk? If a promotion involves little extra money but a change of house and schools, why disrupt the family? A believer in the power of market incentives would expect that those who actually want more money and what it can buy are now abroad, while it is the risk avoiders and the seekers of on-the-job leisure – and the dedicated – who have remained in Britain.

The Conservative proposals to cut the top rate of tax to 60 per cent or below might transform the business world. It could release the energies that everyone knows are there. It is the main Conservative trump. However, until it is played, no one will know if it is the ace or the three of trumps. But there are no other proposals on offer which stand the slightest chance of leading to catch-up. According to recent leaked documents, the industrial strategy of the 1974 Labour government has involved investing the entire growth of the economy in loss-making projects. The Government may have found one or two winners, but the cost of the losers is astronomical. Indications are that the Conservatives would leave detailed decisions on where money should be invested to those whose professional responsibility it is to take these decisions, and that they will seek to cut overall taxation to a level where businesses, both large and small, have the financial incentives and the resources to follow through their judgements.

In 1974–5 many of the cleverest Oxford and Cambridge graduates went into government services. In 1978–9 with astronomical taxation their most profitable employment opportunities have been as accountants. If taxes come down in the 1980s and civil service expansion ceases, they might actually help to finance social welfare by taking part in the revival of the economy, like their opposite numbers in Germany, France and the United States.

The extra energies and the extra talents that far lower taxation might draw into industry and commerce would produce a significantly faster rate of growth of *supply*. It used to be believed and it still is in the Fenland swamps where a few Keynesians cluster together for comfort that extra demand will raise the level of output and employment. The bottleneck now is in fact getting people to produce. If there is a greater willingness to raise the supply of internationally competitive goods and services produced in Britain, a world market for manufactures where Britain supplies only 9 per cent, and a home market where foreigners now supply 35 per cent will provide ample scope for the enterprising.

The hope must be at the most fundamental level that workers will welcome increased living standards once output starts to grow as fast as in Western Europe. Faster growth once it gets under way will also be able to offer them improved social services, even though these will take *a lower share* of the National Income. At a stagnant National Income there is no scope for real improvements to social services, and this lesson should certainly have been learned in the recent years of stagnation. If workers are offered more, it will be rational for all but the wreckers to accept it, and cooperate to achieve the productivity growth which alone can bring it about. Legislation will apparently seek to ensure that the aspirations of workers for higher living standards will not be blocked by union leaderships through strikes which a minority starts and the majority cannot end, and through closed shops which ensure that strikes remain solid even if many wish to continue to work. If new legislation makes unions less trigger happy, there will be less industrial action and the critical unemployment rate where wages explode upwards could fall. Strikes will of course be inescapable if the leadership of a union and the rank and file are both convinced that industrial action is needed, but the Conservatives must hope that what they have to offer – renewed growth and catch-up – will win over enough of the rank and file.

An additional policy influence on the labour market is that lower taxes on wages will raise the net-of-tax incomes of those at work relative to those of strikers and the unemployed. The Conservatives will therefore need a lower public expenditure ratio, not only to restore workers' incentives, but also to help restore the balance of the labour market on which so much depends.

If the industrial relations policies fail, there will be obvious difficulties. A combination of tight money and militant trades unionism can only produce higher unemployment while inflationary expectations are painfully choked out of the economy. That could postpone any enterprise-led recovery. An early success for the new policies will therefore require both quick, large and tangible incentive effects from lower taxation and the victory of moderate trades unionism over militancy. The true outcome may be harder and slower.

The reality: which hopes were realised in 1979–97?

I was right to fear that squeezing inflationary expections out of the economy would be painful and 'postpone any enterprise-led recovery'. Before the 1979 election Margaret Thatcher asked a group of Conservative-minded economists whether if she did what everyone was advising and controlled the money supply output would still be at the 1979 level five years later. That is almost exactly what happened: real GDP rose by no more than $^{1}/_{2}$ per cent between 1979 and 1984. In 1979, when her government took over, the British economy was simultaneously suffering from several fundamental weaknesses. Taxation, and especially marginal taxation, was far too high to provide adequate incentives for workers and managements. Trade unions were obstructing the efficient management of many companies. The consequently weakened companies were producing with inadequate productivity and they had too few well designed and reliably manufactured world-class products to sustain adequate profitability in world markets which were becoming increasingly competitive. In addition, deep-rooted inflationary expectations were high, with the consequence that British interest rates were far above those in the United States, Germany and Japan.

These weaknesses could not all be corrected at the same time, and the key decision for the new government was which to address first. Dealing with some would necessarily stand in the way of the creation of an appropriate environment for the correction of others. The critical and immensely controversial decision (364 economists objected including virtually all former Chief Economic Advisers) was to begin by sharply bringing down inflationary expectations which required far higher interest rates and increasing taxation to halve the budget deficit. The rise in real interest rates and consequently in the exchange rate, and the increases in taxation (apart from marginal rates which were slashed at once) greatly exacerbated the difficulties of managements and led to an initial fall of 15 per cent in manufacturing output which was made good only eight years later in 1987. Unemployment rose from 1.1 million in 1979 to $2^1/_2$ million in 1982 and more than 3 million in 1986, after which it began to fall. But the decision to start by bringing inflation down proved vital. Would companies have actually achieved significant structural reforms if, as so often in the past, the Government had allowed inflation and the exchange rate to track whatever prices businesses needed to charge to cover unreformed costs? After the painful start, fundamental structural reforms in the quality of managements and companies started to come through and some of the favourable 1979 predictions began to be fulfilled.

The increase in productivity

The central prediction in my 1979 article was that lower taxation and other favourable supply-side reforms could lead to a catch-up of UK productivity towards the far higher levels that other leading economies were achieving.

This has clearly occurred in manufacturing industry. In 1979, manufacturing productivity was 51 per cent higher in Germany, 34 per cent higher in France and 86 per cent higher in the United States than in the United Kingdom. By 1994, manufacturing productivity was only 14 per cent higher in France and Germany while the productivity advantage of the United States over the United Kingdom had fallen from 86 to 58 per cent (Figure 2.2). Hence by 1994, manufacturers had made good more than two-thirds of the productivity shortfall with France and Germany and almost one-third of the productivity gap with the United States. Japan's productivity advantage of more than 30 per cent changed very little between 1979 and 1994. There was little further change in 1994–6.

Figure 2.2 Comparison of manufacturing productivity between the UK and other leading economies, 1979–94

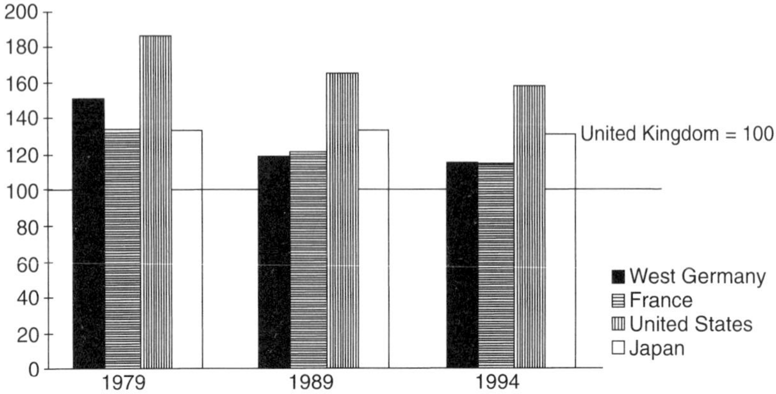

Note: Productivity is measured by output per hour worked.
Source: *Competitiveness: Creating the Enterprise Centre of Europe* (London: HMSO, June 1996), p. 19.

My 1979 analysis went on to predict that British productivity catch-up would go on to produce faster growth in both output and living standards. Figure 2.3 shows that from 1979 to 1989 the UK's GDP per head grew slightly faster than that in France, Germany and the United States, but the advantage was no more than $^1/_4$ to $^1/_2$ per cent per annum, so in the first Conservative decade overall UK output per head grew by only 3 to 5 per cent more than in France, Germany and the United States. The decade from 1979 to 1989 represents a complete economic cycle in which comparisons may safely be made. After 1989 there was a deep recession followed by an incomplete recovery and Figure 2.3 shows that from 1989 to 1995 the UK's GDP per head grew a little less than in France, Germany and the United States. This means that when the period from 1979 to 1995 is considered as a whole, GDP per head increased at much the same rates in Britain, France, Germany and the United States. That suggests that while there was considerable catch-up in manufacturing, where Britain used to be especially weak, there was virtually none when the economy is considered as a whole. In 1980 UK GDP per head ranked 12th among Europe's seventeen economies which were then members of OECD (the fifteen members of

Figure 2.3 Growth of GDP per head in the world's leading economies, 1968–95

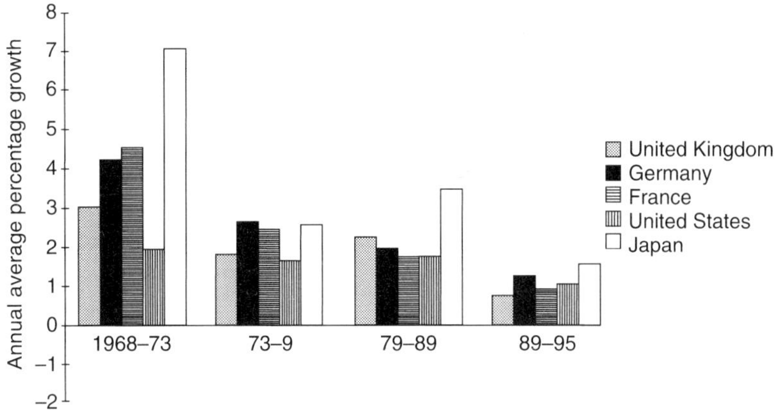

Note: The last period (1989–95) is not a complete economic cycle.
Source: *Competitiveness: Creating the Enterprise Centre of Europe* (London: HMSO, June 1996), p. 18.

the European Union, *plus* Norway and Switzerland) while in 1997, eighteen years later, it still ranked 12th.

Manufacturing industry where such productivity catch-up as occurred was achieved was 26 per cent of the economy in 1979 and only 21 per cent in 1996, so its influence on overall productivity growth has diminished throughout the seventeen years. This has been dominated by the far larger service sector where it appears that British, French and German productivity may have grown at very similar rates.

Public expenditure and taxation

Another contrast between my hopes of 1979 and the achievements of the next seventeen years has been the failure to reduce the ratios of total taxation and public expenditure in the national income. In 1979 '[the Conservatives'] tax-cutting and expenditure-reducing policies' were 'the main departure from the past'. In 1979–80 UK general government outlays totalled 40.9 per cent of GDP, while in 1996 they were 43.0 per cent. General government receipts, mainly taxes and social security contributions took 37.7 per cent of GDP in 1979 and 38.6 per cent in 1996. Therefore, despite great hopes and repeated efforts to contain and reduce spending, public expenditure has not fallen since 1979, while total taxation remains at almost the same ratio of GDP as it was when Margaret Thatcher was first elected.

While British ratios of taxation and public expenditure in GDP have remained all but stable, some European ratios have risen sharply. Table 2.1 shows the ratios of current outlays (most general government expenditure) and current receipts (most taxes and social security contributions) of the larger EU economies and the United States and Japan. From 1979 to 1996 UK government outlays increased by 2.1 per cent of GDP while the average outlays of the countries now in the European Union increased by an average of 6.1 per cent of GDP. UK government expenditure at 43.0 per cent was 6.9 percentage points below the EU average. At the same time UK tax and social security receipts at 38.6 per cent rose by 0.9 percentage points while the average level of the present EU economies increased by 5.5 percentage points. In 1996 UK general government receipts were 6.9 percentage points below the EU average. In contrast, Japanese and US government outlays and receipts have been little more than 30 per cent of GDP and they are far below those of all European economies.

The United Kingdom has therefore failed to achieve the significant reductions in public expenditure and taxation which were widely hoped for and expected in 1979. Some may even have hoped to get these down to US and Japanese levels, but British taxation and public expenditure have increased less than in most of Europe.

Table 2.1 Ratios of public expenditure and taxation in GDP, 1979–96

	General Government					
	Outlays			Receipts		
	1979	1989	1996	1979	1989	1996
EU average	43.8	46.7	49.9	40.0	44.1	45.5
United Kingdom	40.9	39.8	43.0	37.7	40.8	38.6
France	45.0	49.1	55.0	44.1	47.9	50.3
Germany	47.2	44.8	49.1	44.6	44.9	45.6
Japan	31.1	30.6	35.9	26.3	33.1	31.7
United States	29.5	31.9	32.4	29.8	30.2	31.5

Source: OECD, *Economic Outlook*.

Growth in living standards

It might be expected that disappointment that Britain's rate of growth has not exceeded France's and Germany's, and because overall taxation failed to fall, the 1979 prediction that the living standards of British workers would catch-up with those in the leading West European economies will have been disappointed. The evidence provided by estimates of average consumption per head supports that relatively pessimistic conclusion. Table 2.2 shows private consumption per head estimated at purchasing power parities for the total populations of the United Kingdom, France, Germany, the fifteen countries now in the European Union and also the United States and Japan.

Table 2.2 suggests that in the seventeen years from 1979 to 1996, UK private consumption per head increased very slightly $4^1/_2$ per cent above the average level in the European Union to $5^1/_2$ per cent above this, so it rose only very slightly faster than the European average. In these seventeen years French consumption per head fell by 12 percentage points relatively to the European average while Germany's rose by $4^1/_2$ percentage points. The United Kingdom, which moved up 1 percentage point in relation to the European average, therefore gained 13 percentage points relative to France but lost $3^1/_2$ percentage points relative to Germany (where consumption in the former East Germany advanced considerably after 1990). US private consumption per head was about 60 per cent above European levels throughout the period, while Japanese consumption per head grew sharply in relation to all the European countries. Figure 2.2 showed the extent to which Japanese growth in GDP per head exceeded that of the leading European economies from 1979 to 1996 so it is scarcely surprising that Japanese private consumption has also increased far faster.

Table 2.2 Private consumption per head at purchasing power parities, 1979–1996

	1979	1996
EU average	100.0	100.0
United Kingdom	104.5	105.5
France	115.5	103.5
Germany	99.0	103.5
Japan	100.0	120.0
United States	164.5	160.5

Source: OECD, *National Accounts: Main Aggregates 1960–97.*

Figure 2.2 showed that from 1979 to 1995, output per head grew at much the same rate in the United Kingdom, France, Germany and the United States, while overall taxation did not fall significantly in the United Kingdom. It is therefore unsurprising that private consumption per head increased at quite similar rates in Britain, France, Germany and the United States, and that the considerable catch-up in manufacturing productivity which Britain achieved after 1979 failed to raise private consumption in the manner I had hoped for in 1979. But Table 2.2 may exaggerate the real level of UK consumption in 1979 when sterling was greatly overvalued, which made British consumption appear very high in dollars and D-marks. If this is not entirely corrected for in the OECD's purchasing power parity (PPP) estimates, real British consumption will have been lower in 1979 than Table 2.2 indicates, and it will have grown more in relation to consumption in France and Germany than the table shows.

In 1979 I anticipated that the adoption of new policies which favoured tax incentives and the supply-side of the economy would raise private consumption, and I also hoped that this new approach would greatly raise the comparative level of the wages British workers received. My expectation was that productivity catch-up would raise wages and lead workers to appreciate that cooperation with managements would raise their standards of living far more substantially than successful industrial action could possibly achieve, so they would cease to elect militant trade union leaders to represent them and there would be an end to strikes which 'a minority starts and the majority cannot end'.

Quite surprisingly in view of the lack of overall tax reductions and the absence of superior overall growth, the prediction that the achievement of industrial catch-up would greatly raise British wages has been entirely fulfilled. At first sight it will appear startling that comparative wages per worker can have risen exceptionally in Britain when consumption per head rose at much the same rate as in France and Germany but this occurred because British taxation was rearranged so that it fell far less heavily on productive activity.

While the Conservative governments failed to reduce overall taxation as a ratio of GDP, they greatly reduced marginal rates of tax, and especially those that fall on workers and companies that produce. The standard rate of income tax which most workers pay was reduced from 33 per cent in 1979 to 24 per cent in 1996, while a still lower rate of 20 per cent that is marginal to some workers was introduced in 1992. So far as the higher rates are concerned, my 1979 prediction that the top rate of income tax would be reduced from 83 per cent on earned incomes and 98 per cent on investment incomes was fulfilled in Sir Geoffrey Howe's first budget when he reduced the top rates to 60 per cent on earned incomes and 75 per cent on investment incomes, and in 1988 Nigel Lawson reduced the top rate of income tax further to 40 per cent on all incomes. Lawson also cut the rate of corporation tax from 52 to 35 per cent, and he largely financed this by at the same time greatly reducing the value of allowances. Norman Lamont went on to cut corporation tax further to 33 per cent. Gordon Brown, the first Labour Chancellor in 1997 has actually cut it further to 31 per cent. Small companies pay a still lower rate, which has been reduced to 23 per cent.

The strategy of favouring producers over non-producers was reinforced by successive Conservative governments who took the decision to adjust the level of social benefits for pensioners, the unemployed and those receiving family income support to increases of no more than the rise in retail prices. Previous governments had increased benefits in line with the economy-wide increase in wages, so that the increases in the standard of living that workers obtained from the overall growth in productivity were shared with pensioners and the unemployed, whose benefits were raised at the same rate as the pay increases which workers enjoyed. The new policy froze the real value of benefits. This meant that the consumption available to workers from rising real wages increased year by year in relation to the consumption available to non-producers, and because workers have not had to share the fruits of economic growth with pensioners and the unemployed, their taxes have risen less than they otherwise would.

In France and Germany, in contrast, the taxes and social security contributions which workers have had to pay have increased sharply so that their net-of-tax incomes have grown far less than their productivity. In consequence, while overall consumption per head has increased at fairly similar rates in Britain, France and Germany, the proportion of that consumption which has gone to those who produce has increased in Britain while it has fallen in France and Germany. For this reason and others, workers' real take-home pay has increased far faster in Britain.

Each year until 1996 the OECD published a comparative account of the real pay of production workers in each country – that is, of unskilled manual workers (or C2s as social commentators now describe them), and the deductions for tax and compulsory social security contributions from their pay. This information allowed the increase in real take-home pay in each country to be estimated on a comparable basis. The OECD sought to compare the real take-home pay of workers of equal skill in each country, and it allowed for taxes and social security contributions in a uniform manner. The information was tabulated for both single workers and married couples with two children; the information for single workers is presented in Table 2.3 because married couples often enjoy the additional benefit of a second part-time or full-time income and the OECD does not provide the additional information of the impact of these extra incomes on real take-home pay. The real incomes which production workers derive from the pay of a single earner is in contrast entirely comparable between the various countries.

Table 2.3 sets out the remarkable result that in the seventeen years from 1979 to 1996 the real take-home pay of British production workers increased by more than 28 per cent, while the real take-home pay of German workers declined by 1.5 per cent, the real take-home pay of French workers increased by less than 4 per cent and the real take-home pay of US workers fell by 6 per cent. Only Japanese workers achieved an increase in real take-home pay in any way comparable to that achieved in Britain.

The evidence presented in Table 2.3 shows a remarkable advance in the comparative standard of living *of those who work in Britain*. The net-of-tax pay of British workers increased by 25 per cent relative to French workers, by 30 per cent in relation to German workers and by 34 per cent in relation to US workers. Hence so far as workers' living standards are concerned, the hopes of 1979 were entirely realised. The real increase of 28.2 per cent in seventeen years, or of 1.47 per cent per

Table 2.3 Increases in the real take-home pay of production workers (per cent)

	Increase from 1979 to 1996	
	Real wage	Real take-home pay
United Kingdom	21.5	28.2
France	14.0	3.3
Germany	14.7	–1.5
Japan	28.0	26.2
United States	–7.5	–6.2

Source: OECD (1980–96, 1998).

annum, is much in line with the UK's growth in *per capita* GDP set out in Figure 2.2. This showed that GDP per head grew at 2.2 per cent per annum in the complete cycle from 1979 to 1989 and by 0.7 per cent per annum in the recession and partial recovery from 1979 to 1995, so an average increase of 1.47 per cent in the two periods taken together is close to the rate at which production per head advanced. The data indicate that the net-of-tax real incomes of British unskilled workers grew approximately in line with productivity. Because taxes and social security contributions increased far faster than earnings in France (from 20.3 per cent of earnings in 1979 to 27.8 per cent in 1996) and Germany (where they increased from 31.6 per cent in 1979 to 41.3 per cent in 1996) take-home pay increased far less than productivity.[2] Wages themselves also rose less than productivity. In the United States the wages of unskilled workers fell sharply in relation to the wages and salaries of the skilled in the 1980s and the 1990s.

Many British workers will have achieved considerably greater increases in real take-home pay than the OECD data indicates. The Office of National Statistics publishes a 'tax and price index' which shows the pay increases a worker requires to compensate for price increases and changes in taxation. This shows that from 1980 to 1996 pay increases of 5.2 per cent per annum would have been needed to compensate for price increases and tax changes while average earnings actually increased at an average annual rate of 7.7 per cent. Therefore according to the official UK indices, real take-home pay increased by more than 2.4 per cent per annum and by more than 45 per cent in sixteen years against the real increase of 28 per cent or 1.47 per cent per annum that the OECD series shows. The UK average earnings series will include the wage and salary increases of the skilled as well as the unskilled, while the OECD series focuses on the pay of unskilled production workers. Series for the net-of-tax pay of the skilled as well as the unskilled are not available for the other OECD countries, so it is only the pay of unskilled production workers that can be compared on a uniform basis.

The bulk of the British increase in real take-home pay occurred before 1992. According to the OECD data for production workers, 25.6 of the 28.2 per cent increase in real take-home pay in Britain was achieved between 1979 and 1992 and it rose by only a further 2 per cent from 1992 to 1996. The average earnings of all workers outpaced the tax and price index by 39.8 per cent between 1980 and 1992, but employees gained only a further 4.4 per cent between 1992 and 1996. Therefore only a small fraction of the gain in workers' real incomes occured in the 1992–7 parliament which proved so catastrophic for the Conservative party and government. In the three parliaments in the thirteen years from 1979 to 1992, workers' net of tax real incomes increased by an average 8 per cent in each parliament.

The interesting conclusion remains that when the period from 1979 to 1996 is considered as a whole, unskilled workers obtained substantial pay increases in Britain and skilled workers still greater increases, while real take-home pay stagnated in the leading European economies and fell in the United States.

Rising profits and employment and transformed industrial relations

Because of the extent to which taxes on productive activity have fallen in Britain it has also been possible for the share of profits in the national income to increase. In 1979 the gross trading profits of industrial and commercial companies within the United Kingdom were £23.9 billion out of a GDP of £198.2 billion, or 12.1 per cent of GDP. In 1996 gross trading profits were £117.8 billion while GDP totalled £742.3 billion, so profits had risen by 3.8 percentage points to 15.9 per cent of GDP. If North Sea profits are excluded, the increase is still greater, by 4.7 per cent of GDP from 9.3 per cent of GDP in 1979 to 14.0 per cent in 1996. The British economy has therefore been able to increase both real wages and real profits. This has produced a growing realisation that the interests of workers and managements are entirely reconcilable. Shortly before its closure in 1992 a leading trade unionist remarked in the tripartite National Economic Development Council (NEDC) that descriptions of workers and managers as 'the two sides of industry' referred to a world which had passed: in most of British industry workers and managements are now on the same side.

That has been far from the situation in France and Germany. A consequence of the near-zero increase in the net of tax earnings of production workers has been that the trade unions of both countries have become increasingly militant. Because the average production worker has gained virtually nothing in fifteen years, those who have fallen below the average have experienced declining real incomes. French and German workers have come to appreciate that if they fail to get the general level of pay increases, some of their traditional standard of living will disappear, while the principal opportunity to achieve rising real incomes has to come from above-average pay increases. Those with special bargaining power who produce indispensable goods and services have supported union leaders who were prepared to take the lead in recommending strike action because it was this that now offered the best prospect of rising living standards. At the same time the weak have supported militancy in France because a willingness to take to the streets has been needed to protect traditional living standards. As the frequency of strikes grows in France and Germany, labour market conditions begin to resemble those which Britain experienced in the 1970s.

In Britain *private* sector strikes virtually ceased. New legislation has required ballots before union leaders can call strikes, so these have to be supported by a majority. Arthur Scargill's manipulation of two-thirds of his members into a coalminers' strike without a ballot in 1983–4 prevented any general support from outside his union. Secondary strike action by unions not directly involved in a dispute has been made illegal and escalating fines rapidly showed recalcitrant union leaderships that the new laws had to be obeyed. Private sector workers who achieved average increases in real take-home pay of 28 to 45 per cent in seventeen years have come to appreciate that they stand to gain far more from the successful performance of their companies (which strikes would disrupt) than from industrial action, and on several crucial occasions they have declined to vote for this. In the past Ford has often set the lead for pay increases in the car industry, and in 1995 the unions made their customary demands which management declined to grant in full. The Ford unions then recommended industrial action which their members declined to support. The remarkable fall in UK strike activity is illustrated in Figure 2.4.

There have in contrast been continuing strikes in Britain's public sector where unions seek to influence government. In the railways before privatisation, successful industrial action repeatedly prevented the achievement of efficiency gains comparable to those which managements were achieving in the privatised nationalised industries – for instance, in electricity generation where productivity has been raised by 15 to 20 per cent per annum since 1990–1 without a day of strikes.

In the private sector substantial increases in real take-home pay have undermined workers' potential support for industrial action while increased pay flexibility has rewarded those who have cooperated to achieve efficiency gains. At the same time the managements which have achieved the efficiency gains have received net-of-tax financial rewards which have fully justified the energies and managerial skills they have directed to the transformation of their companies.

Many managers have the ability to supervise the progress of a successful company on an established basis. There are in contrast few with

Figure 2.4 Number of labour stoppages in the United Kingdom, 1975–95

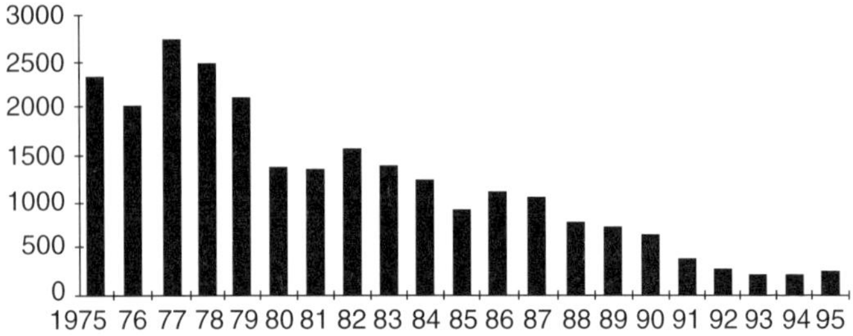

Source: *Labour Market Trends*, Office for National Statistics (June 1995).

the personal and technical skills and energies needed to turn an unsuccessful high-cost company around and search committees seek such talent. Where such managers can be found – Sir Graham Day who turned round Rover which lost £1$^1/_2$ billion in the year before it was sold to British Aerospace and Sir Ian Macgregor who transformed British Steel and led British Coal while the miners'strike was defeated are obvious examples – they will command very high financial rewards because they will be recognised as being among the very few with the particular qualities required to transform companies.

The absence of incentives to devote exceptional energy and skill to the transformation of companies was a feature of the high-tax world of 1979 when manufacturing productivity fell far below European standards but managers stood to gain little personally by re-locating inefficient colleagues and disturbing potentially disruptive trade unions. In that world there was no market in Britain for highly rewarded 'company-surgeons' and those with these particular abilities mostly worked overseas. In Britain there was a general acquiescence in continuing inefficiency and a tolerance of mutual on-the-job leisure. The night shift in British Leyland was even allowed to bring in beds, and my Italian professorial host in a visit to Naples who was driving a Leyland car told me that he did so because 'it is the only one the mafia does not steal'.

The reductions in the top rates of tax which Sir Geoffrey Howe initiated led to an enormous opening up in the highest executive salaries without which those with the power to transform companies would not have been identified or rewarded. Without that, a considerable proportion of the very substantial manufacturing productivity gains of the 1980s and the 1990s would not have been achieved.

The prediction that reductions in the highest marginal rates of tax would also increase total tax revenues so that instead of costing money they would add to the resources government had at its disposal to reduce the taxes of the lower paid has also been fulfilled. In 1978–9 the most highly paid 1 per cent of taxpayers contributed 11 per cent of total income tax revenues while in 1995–6 the most highly paid 1 per cent contributed 15 per cent of total revenues. In 1978–9 the highest-paid hundredth of taxpayers were paying tax rates of 75 per cent and above while in 1995–6 they were paying no more than 40 per cent, but despite being left 60 per cent of their incomes to spend themselves they contributed 15 per cent of total income tax revenues against the 11 per cent the best-paid hundredth had previously contributed. The remaining 99 per cent of income taxpayers are therefore better off because the highest-paid 1 per cent are contributing 4 percentage points more than before. The reductions in the highest rates of tax have led the most highly paid to declare far more income for taxation within the United Kingdom so they pay more at 40 per cent than they had previously been paying at 75 per cent and above. In addition, the highest paying are earning more because they are receiving salary in place of the less efficient rewards of more secure job tenure and an acquiescence in incompetence with which those who ran many British companies were more generally rewarded in the 1960s and the 1970s.

The prediction that these developments would lead an increasing fraction of the most talented university graduates to work in industry and commerce like their opposite numbers in other leading economies has been fulfilled. Leslie Hannah (1994) has documented the increasing extent to which graduates with First Class Honours degrees now work in industry and commerce and Figure 2.5 shows how from 1979 to 1992 the number of Firsts who went into industry and commerce approximately doubled while the numbers who went into the Civil Service or stayed in education has remained approximtely the same. In the 1950s about the same number of Firsts became civil servants, remained in education and went into industry and commerce. By the 1990s, about 100 went into the Civil Service, 100 remained in education while almost 1500 went into industry and commerce. This continuing trend in favour of industry and commerce has been influenced by the signal that they offer immeasurably greater material rewards, and these have resulted from the opening up of the tax system. The growing entry of the most talented into industry and commerce, and the promotion of some to the highest levels, is one influence that is gradually transforming British managements. The time when Keynes

Figure 2.5 Destination of male UK graduates with first class honours degrees, 1950–92

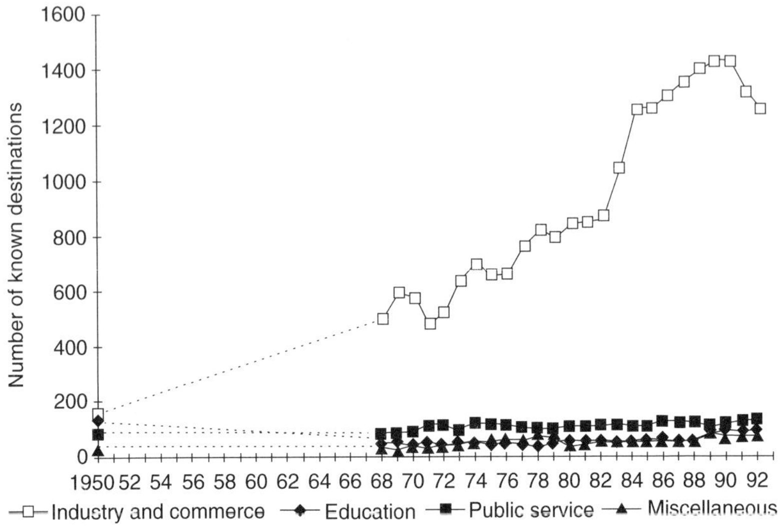

Source: Leslie Hannah. *Education, Employment and Business Leadership* (London: Foundation for Manufacturing and Industry, 1994).

could say that British industry was controlled by the stupidity of fourth-generation men has long gone.

The underlying performance of the economy is also being improved by a substantial growth in small businesses, which is another consequence of far lower marginal taxation. The total number of firms in the United Kingdom rose from 1 890 000 in 1979 to 3 090 000 in the cyclical peak of 1989. There was a fall in the subsequent recession, and in 1993 the number was down to 2 810 000, but this still showed a rise of 920 000 from the 1979 level. The number of the self-employed shows similar growth. These totalled 1 906 000 in 1979 and increased by more than $1^1/_2$ million to 3 526 000 in 1989: in 1996 they totalled 3 283 000, a rise of 1 377 000 from the 1979 level. Income from self-employment rose from 9.2 cent of GDP in 1979 to 11.6 per cent in 1989 after which it fell back to 10.9 per cent in 1996.

The growth in self-employment by more than 1.3 million is a principal reason why UK unemployment rates are now among the lowest in Europe. On a standardised OECD basis average unemployment in the countries now in the European Union rose from 5.7 per cent in 1979 to 10.8 per cent in 1996. In these seventeen years French unemployment rose by 6.4 percentage points from 5.2 to 11.6 per cent, German unemployment by 5.7 percentage points from 3.2 to 8.9 per cent, and UK unemployment by 3.3 percentage points from 5.0 to 8.3 per cent. Without the two-thirds growth in self-employment and the increase of nearly a million in the number of small businesses, unemployment in Britain might have risen as much as in the rest of Europe.

It is now far more widely understood than in 1979 that sustainable growth in employment depends above all on an economy's ability to supply internationally competitive goods and services. The transformation of performance of so many companies, the closing of much of the productivity gap in manufacturing industry, the increase in private service sector activity where small companies excel and the transformation of labour relations in the private sector are important elements in Britain's progress since 1979. But such catch-up as has been achieved is incomplete. Average productivity is still between 10 and 20 per cent above the average British level in France and Germany, and productivity has grown at very similar rates in these three economies since 1979.

But equal performance has been achieved since 1979 when British growth used to be inferior. It is especially hopeful for the future that significant features in Britain's equal overall performance offer much in the next decade. Britain has superior labour relations in 1999 because France and Germany have caught 'the British disease' of endemic strikes. Britain has lower taxation, and this is an important element in the attraction of so many of the world's leading companies to Britain. The extent to which American, Japanese and German companies have been attracted to Britain is the subject of Chapter 4. There are exceptional opportunities for Britain in the next decade provided the underlying achievements of the last twenty years are not thrown away.

The challenge continues

Britain's improved labour relations, the significant catch-up in manufacturing productivity and the attraction of so many of the world's leading companies have depended on the creation of an economic environment where wages and profits can both rise and where labour and capital work closely together to raise economic performance.

This was underpinned by the containment of public expenditure and taxation as ratios of GDP. In 1979 it appeared possible to greatly reduce both taxation and public expenditure as ratios of the national income, but despite sometimes fierce assaults on expenditure, containment is all that was achieved. The ageing of the population has produced substantial requirements to increase expenditure on health and pensions, and while it has been possible to reduce other items, the relentless upward impact of unfavourable demography has prevented an actual reduction in the public expenditure ratio. The United States spends far less than Europe on social welfare, with a consequent public expenditure ratio of little more than 30 per cent, but there is a high and visible social cost. The example of Asia, where there are fast-growing economies with public expenditure ratios of far less than 30 per cent, is sometimes extolled. Much of Asia retains the institution of the extended family where private responsibility for the welfare of quite distant relatives is universally accepted. Those who fall ill and the aged can mostly count on the support of their relatives and this greatly reduces the need for state welfare which absorbs between 10 and 20 per cent of GDP in Europe. Whether a family welfare safety net is preferable to Europe's state safety net is a complex and far-reaching question, but a widespread acceptance of Asian family responsibilities does not exist in Europe, and it cannot be created. Compulsory private insurance could not replace state welfare for at least a generation and the insurance industry would be reluctant to take on many who are most likely to require a safety net. A truly radical reduction in UK public expenditure from the level of 40 to 43 per cent of GDP which has prevailed since 1979 may therefore be unachievable.

But the near constant ratios of public expenditure and taxation which have been achieved since 1979 are entirely compatible with the continuing growth of workers' living standards in line with the productivity of the economy. The considerable rate of increase in real take-home pay, strong incentives and the far higher profits which British industry and commerce can now earn have sufficed to confer considerable competitive advantages on Britain in relation to the leading European economies.

The examples of France and Germany show how easily upward creep in taxation and public expenditure can cause stagnation in workers' living standards and the destruction of the foundations of harmonious industrial relations. Productivity grows by no more than $1^1/_2$ to 2 per cent per annum in the leading Western economies, so stable public expenditure and tax ratios make possible an average rate of growth in workers' living standards of no more than $1^1/_2$ to 2 per cent. Chapter 1 showed how even a slight diversion of this potential gain to the public sector can produce stagnation in private living standards and a return to the zero-sum pay conflicts of the 1970s.

The underlying strategy of preventing increases in the ratios of public expenditure and taxation in GDP is therefore radical in its potential consequences. Its core is concern for the living standards of those who lack the skills to command high pay. This considerable proportion of the labour force can easily be left with a standard of living which scarcely exceeds social benefit levels. Many lower-paid production workers, the C2s whose living standards have risen so considerably since 1979, regard as unjust a lack of material advantage from their willingness to work. In 1806 Thomas Robert Malthus criticised bounties given to those whose earnings were judged insufficient because these 'diminished exactly in the same proportion that command over the necessities of life, which the classes above them, by their superior skill and industry would naturally possess'.[3]

The governments of 1979–92 favoured those who work for wages, and the net-of-tax incomes of lower-paid production workers rose in line with national productivity. By permitting the net-of-tax incomes of all workers to rise at least as fast as national productivity the Conservatives gained considerable electoral support in 1983, 1987 and 1992 from lower-paid working families which had previously been regarded as predominantly Labour supporters. The living standards of many such workers failed to rise equally in the 1992–7 Parliament for a variety of reasons.

It is important that growth in the net-of-tax incomes of lower-paid working families should resume. That is especially important for industrial relations in Britain. The prime need is to sustain a continual advantage in the living standards of the relatively unskilled who work over those who mainly rely on social benefits. That margin of advantage from work can only be maintained if the ratio of public expenditure in GDP continues to be held down. If it is, British labour relations should retain their superiority over those in continental Europe, and there might well be continuing electoral support for governments which, like the Conservative governments of 1979–92, preside over rising living standards for the great majority of those in employment.

Notes

1. This section reproduces an article *The Sunday Times* commissioned to appear on 29 April 1979.
2. OECD (1998), which is used to obtain information on the increase in tax deductions from 1994 to 1996, does not use quite the same wage series as the previous volumes, but it shows the same percentage deductions as the earlier series for 1979 and 1994 so the new figure for deductions in 1996 will be consistent with those in 1994.
3. Malthus ([1806]1989, I, p. 351).

3
Closing the British Competitiveness Gap*

Walter Eltis and David Higham

Introduction

Improving national competitiveness has become a key policy theme of the 1990s. The UK government published White Papers on competitiveness in 1994, 1995, 1996 and 1998. The United States, Germany, Canada, Australia and Spain are some of the other countries that have published similar reports. The European Commission has followed up its 1993 White Paper entitled *Growth, Competitiveness, Employment* with the establishment of a high-level Competitiveness Advisory Group.

Yet the concept of national competitiveness has been attacked by many leading economists. Krugman (1994), for example, has said that 'competitiveness is a meaningless word when applied to national economies. And the obsession with competitiveness is both wrong and dangerous'.

Two main criticisms have been made of competitiveness as a guide to policy. The first is that the competitiveness of a nation (rather than that of a firm) has no agreed meaning in economic theory and can therefore mean different things to different people. Corden (1994)

* This is a revised and slightly up-dated version of the article, 'How Much of the UK Competitiveness Gap has been Closed?', in *National Institute Economic Review*, 154 (November 1995), pp. 71–94. We are grateful for helpful assistance and comments from colleagues in the DTI during 1994–5. The DTI and David Higham are not responsible for any changes to the original text.

identifies three different measures of national competitiveness in common usage: sectoral competitiveness; relative cost competitiveness (the real exchange rate); and productivity.

The UK White Papers, like Porter (1990) and the US Competitiveness Policy Council (1993), use the third of Corden's definitions by viewing competitiveness as the ability to raise living standards. Competitiveness is defined as:

> the degree to which a country can, under free and fair market conditions, produce goods and services which meet the test of international markets, while simultaneously maintaining and expanding the real incomes of its people over the long term. (HMSO, 1994, 1995)

This definition focuses on productivity rather than on the real exchange rate. A country with low productivity levels may still be competitive in relative cost terms provided that its (nominal) exchange rate is low enough, but its living standards will generally be lower than those in countries with higher productivity levels.

The second criticism is that using competitiveness as a synonym for raising productivity in the domestic production of goods and services may encourage protectionism by giving a misplaced emphasis to countries as rivals, and to the role of trade and the balance of payments in economic performance. The UK White Papers recognise this danger and stress that trade is not a zero-sum-game and that living standards are determined by productivity growth and not by trade performance.

In spite of these criticisms, a long-term concept of competitiveness remains of use to policy makers for two reasons. First, because it emphasises international benchmarking. The key issue for policy is whether productivity in the UK is below its own potential, given its national preferences and technological capabilities, rather than the potential of other nations. However, there is much we can learn about economic policy and institutional arrangements from countries with faster (or indeed, slower) productivity growth than ourselves. Second, it implies that the search for improved economic performance is never ending. That is why the White Papers focus on international comparisons of performance over the long term.

The government's competitiveness analysis

Living standards are generally approximated by real output per head measured at purchasing power parities. If output per head grows then the real incomes of the population can increase. If output per head grows faster in one country than in others, the real incomes of its population will increase more rapidly. Raising output per head is therefore a central objective of government policy. In 1997 the UK's output per head was the nineteenth highest in the OECD. However, only Luxembourg, the United States, Norway and Switzerland exceeded UK GDP per head by more than 20 per cent (Figure 3.1).

The 1998 Competitiveness White Paper shows that in 1997 GDP per head (at purchasing power parities) was 4 per cent above the UK level in France and 8 per cent higher in Germany (Figure 3.1). Output per hour worked was more than 20 per cent higher in France and Germany but labour force participation was 10 per cent higher in the United Kingdom than in France and Germany: 75.3 per cent of those of working age were employed in Britain, while only 67.2 per cent worked in France and 68.5 per cent in Germany. Average hours worked were also higher in Britain, so because more worked and for longer hours, the gap in output per head of population was far narrower than in productivity per hour, where Britain was 20 per cent behind.

Productivity is a key determinant of living standards in the long run. International comparisons of productivity levels are difficult to make with precision and are affected by the timing of the economic cycle. In 1994 the United Kingdom appeared to have closed about three-quarters of the West European productivity gap in manufacturing industry that existed in 1979 when French and German manufacturing productivity were (respectively) one-third and one half above that in the United Kingdom (Figure 2.2, p. 36). British attention is most often focused on comparisons with France and Germany, because that is where we are most immediately aware of any differences. The outstanding achievements of Japan and the Pacific rim set a still greater challenge. Figure 2.2 showed that between 1979 and 1994 UK manufacturing companies slightly narrowed the productivity gap with Japan, but that a large gap remained.

Manufacturing is only about one-fifth of the UK economy and much less is known about productivity in the much larger service sector. However, given that private sector services produce about 50 per cent of value-added and that the overall gap in GDP per head between the United Kingdom and France and Germany is roughly the same as the productivity gap in manufacturing, the productivity gap in the service sector is probably quite similar to that in manufacturing.

Figure 3.1 GDP per head, 1997

Note: At purchasing power parities.
Source: DTI calculations, using OECD data.

Comparative productivity in the individual services is difficult to measure, partly for conceptual reasons and partly because adequate data are not available. McKinsey (1992) suggest that in the late 1980s UK services lagged behind the United States in productivity, except in air transport. According to the study, the United Kingdom achieved 80 per cent of US productivity in retailing, 60 per cent in banking and 50 per cent in telecommunications. However, UK productivity in some of these sectors appears to have improved significantly in the 1990s.

The 1994 and 1995 White Papers argued that improving the underlying performance of the UK would involve action in ten key areas: the macroeconomy; education and training; the labour market; management; innovation; fair and open markets; finance for business; communications and the infrastructure; the commercial framework; and the business of government.

This approach is based on theoretical and empirical analyses of economic growth and on detailed study of the sources of productivity differences between nations. Both theoretical and empirical work emphasise that higher investment in physical capital alone is not the route to permanently higher growth. Investment in people and ideas is also important. Both also show that economists have not yet fully explained the process of growth and that much depends on intangible factors such as social attitudes. Crafts and Toniolo (1995) provide a survey of the literature.

An important influence on the White Papers is the literature on 'growth accounting' associated with Denison (1967) and with Maddison (1991). This seeks to decompose the growth in output into that part which is due to growth of the quantities of factors of production (physical capital and labour), their quality (for example, labour skills) and the efficiency with which they are combined. Key results are that the quality of factors is an important influence on growth and that a substantial proportion of economic growth can be attributed only to 'technical change' (sometimes referred to as total factor productivity or TFP). For example, Maddison found that as much as 40 per cent of UK growth between 1973 and 1987 was not explained by changes in the quantity and the quality of factors of production. Considerations influencing technical change might include managerial inefficiencies, restrictive labour practices and the degree of competition in the economy.

More recent work by Romer and others (see Romer, 1994 for a brief survey) uses more refined theoretical tools to provide a fuller explanation of the behaviour of 'technical change'. Typically, this work –

generally known as 'new growth theory' – emphasises the role of broad capital accumulation (that is, investment in people as well as machines), the ability to absorb new ideas (Romer, 1993) via, for example, inward investment, and the scope for 'catchup'.

The 1994 and 1995 White Papers were also influenced by comparisons of productivity differences across countries. An early study by Pratten (1976) found that around half of the observed productivity gap between UK and German industry was related to behavioural factors such as labour relations, manning levels and efficiency. Caves (1980) found that in a comparison of US and UK manufacturing industry British productivity was lower in industries requiring technical and managerial skills, those organised on a large scale and those subject to strikes. Prais (1981) found a key role for vocational training in explaining productivity differences between UK, US and German industry. A series of studies (see, for example, Mason and van Ark, 1993) carried out by the National Institute of Economic and Social Research over a number of years, comparing the performance of similar manufacturing plants in different countries, have emphasised the importance of education and training and the flexibility of the workforce in explaining productivity differentials.

The White Papers examine UK performance in each of the ten areas and propose government initiatives to improve performance. Policy seeks to control public expenditure in a manner which will reduce borrowing and tax rates as the economy recovers. There will therefore be a trade-off between control of the macroeconomy – one of the considerations which influences competitiveness – and the extra financial resources government can deploy to enhance education, training, the infrastructure, and government-funded research and development. The next two sections examine performance in some key areas.

Education, training and investment

As noted above, increased emphasis is being placed on the role of human capital in economic growth. Considerable progress is being made to correct weaknesses in education and training. In 1992, UK graduation rates in higher education were the third highest among the countries listed and almost as high as Japan's (Figure 3.2). The participation rate in higher education has risen from 14 per cent of each generation in the mid-1980s to close to 30 per cent in 1994 (Figure 3.3). The proportion of 17-year-olds in full-time education or training has been rising steadily year by year (Figure 3.4). The proportion of employees of

Figure 3.2 Graduation rates in 1992

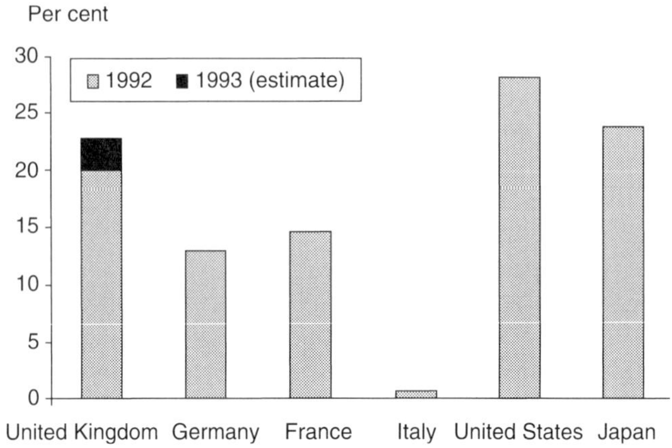

Note: The last period (1989–95) is not a complete economic cycle
Source: OECD.

Figure 3.3 Participation in higher education, 1978–94

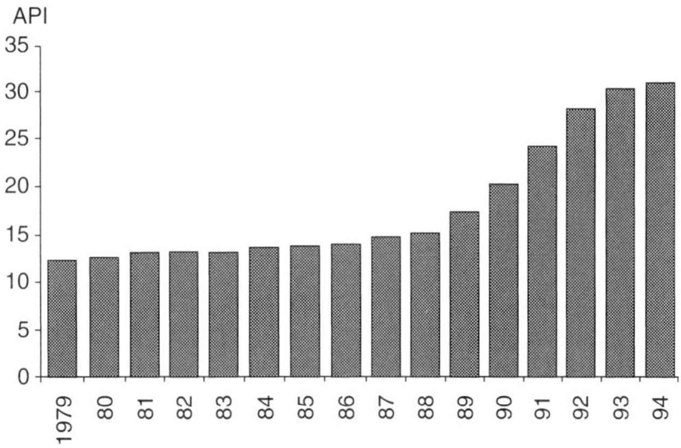

Note: API = initial entrants to full-time HE aged under 21 as a proportion of the average of the number of 18 and 19 year olds in the population
Source: Department of Education

working age receiving job-related training rose from 10 per cent in the mid 1980s to about 15 per cent in 1994 (Figure 3.5). The new national qualifications structure now covers 85 per cent of occupations. However, concerns remain about the breadth of attainment.

Figure 3.4 Proportion of 16- and 17-year-olds in full-time education or training, 1984–94

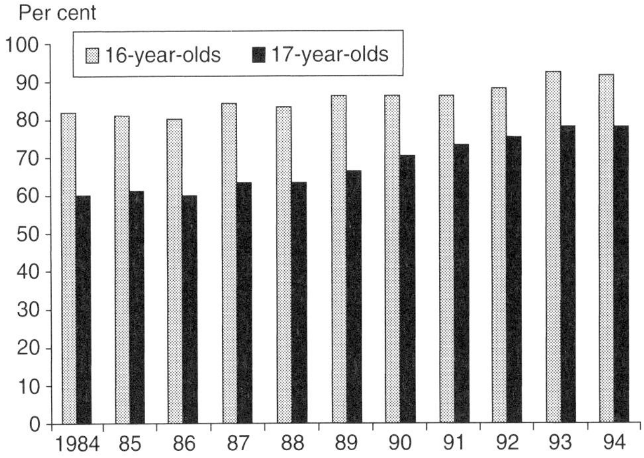

Source: Labour Force Survey.

Figure 3.5 Proportion of employees of working age receiving job-related training, 1984–94

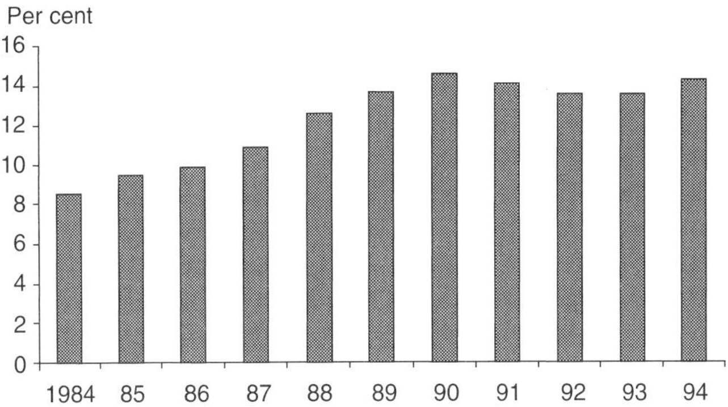

Note: data refer to Spring of each year, Working age is defined as men aged 16–64 and women aged 16–59
Source: Labour Force Survey.

In 1994, only one-third of 15-year-olds obtained GCSEs at Grade C and above in English, maths and a science. Moreover, around one-third of those of working age did not expect to pursue any further training.

Contrary to popular belief, capital investment is an area where UK performance differs little from that of other leading West European economies. Figure 3.6 shows that, from 1980 to 1993, UK business investment was higher, on average, as a share of GDP than that of other G6 economies (with the exception of Japan). Investment in machinery and equipment – which some have seen as especially important for the growth process (DeLong and Summers, 1991) – has also been much the same in the UK as in Germany (Figure 3.7). Manufacturing investment has been almost as high as a share of manufacturing output as in Germany (Figure 3.8). It is interesting that the investment gap between the United Kingdom and France and Germany is now a narrow one. Western Europe as a whole and not merely the United Kingdom invests less and grows less than the Pacific rim.

UK business investment remained at comparable levels from 1993 to 1997 because of the buoyancy of the economy. The 1998 White Paper shows that in the 1990s, France and Germany invested between 10 and 20 per cent more *per worker* in the business sector, but that reflects their 20 per cent advantage in output per worker. The shares of investment in output remained very similar.

One area of relatively low UK investment is in business-financed research and development where the United Kingdom spent 1.1 per cent of GDP, about the same as France, while the expenditures of Germany at 1.4 per cent of GDP and the United States at 1.6 per cent

Figure 3.6 Business investment as a proportion of GDP, 1960–93

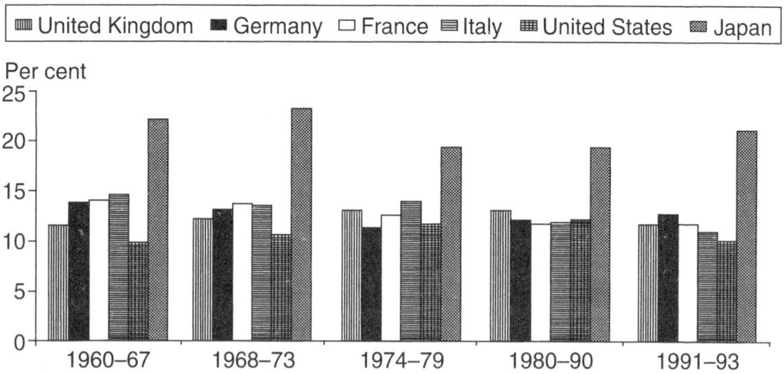

Source: OECD.

Figure 3.7 Investment in machinery and equipment as a proportion of GDP, 1960–93

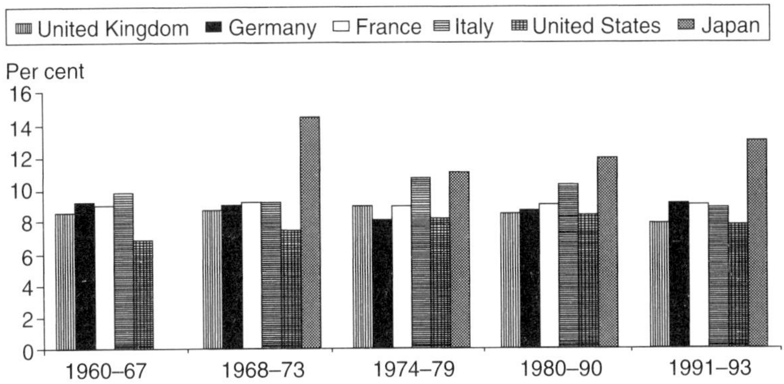

Source: OECD

Figure 3.8 Manufacturing investment as a proportion of manufacturing output, 1968–93

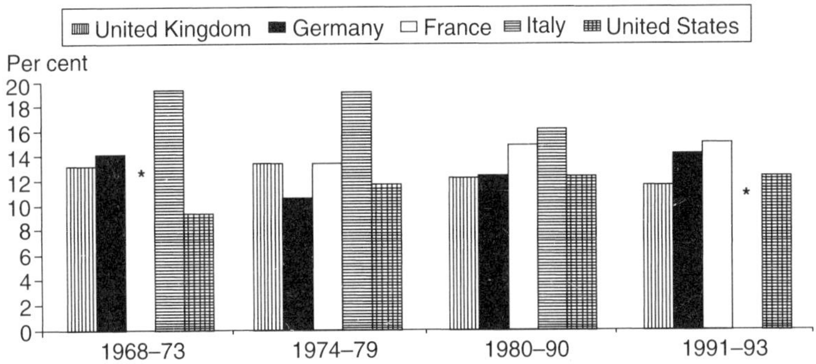

Source: OECD

and Japan at nearly 2 per cent of GDP were considerably higher (Figure 3.9). On the other hand, a higher fraction of UK visible exports are at the high-tech end of production than for France or Germany (HMSO, 1995).

Figure 3.9 Business and enterprise expenditure on R&D, 1993, per cent of GDP

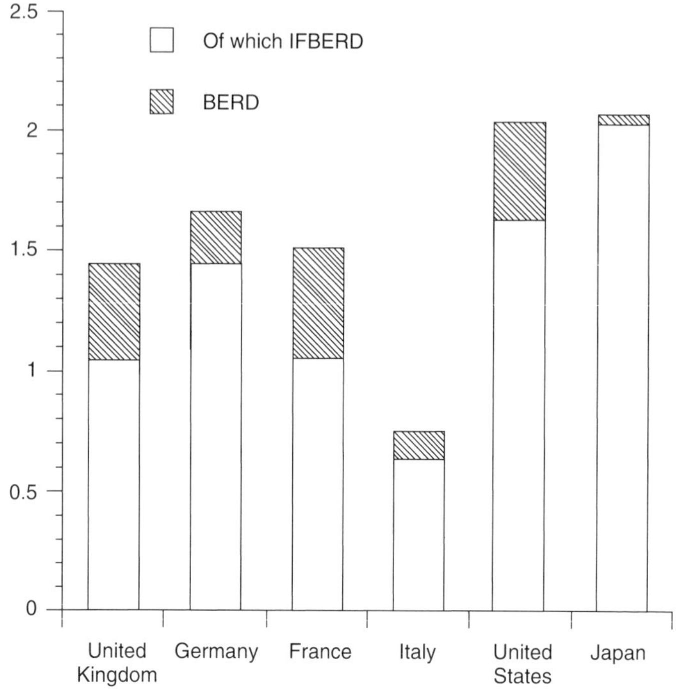

Note: Data for France, United States and Japan refer to 1992.
BERD is Business and Enterprise Expenditure on R&D.
IFBERD is that part of BERD which is industrially financed.
Source: OECD.

Finance for industry

The cost and availability of finance is an important factor for the competitiveness of industry. The cost of capital is notoriously difficult to measure. It is affected by (unobserved) inflationary expectations, the nature of the project chosen and the detailed operation of the systems of both corporate and personal taxes. Although the cost of debt is observable fairly easily, estimates of the cost of equity are heavily dependent on the underlying model of asset pricing used. This explains part of the wide variation in the estimates of the cost of capital in the United Kingdom relative to its major competitors revealed in studies such as McCauley and Zimmer (1989), Fukao (1993) and Coopers and Lybrand (1993).

Increased efficiency within the financial system will, other things being equal, lead to a lower cost of capital. One major aspect of this internal efficiency can be measured by looking at the spread between bank borrowing and lending rates. This spread was as high as 35 per cent in medieval times, and it has come down continuously as competitive banking systems developed and expert knowledge reduced risk to both lenders and borrowers.

Table 3.1 sets out estimates provided by the Bank of England of the spread between prime bank lending rates and deposit rates in the UK and a number of other leading economies. Between 1992 and 1997 this averaged 3.44 percentage points in the UK and 3.54 in Germany, which had narrower spreads than France's 4.10, Italy's 4.71 and Sweden's 5.29 percentage points. United States and Japanese spreads were lower than any in Europe, but it has now emerged that many of the Japanese banks were making vast losses in this period, in part by charging too little to industrial and commercial borrowers to reflect a true assessment of the risks involved. Most companies have to pay more than prime rates, and terms and conditions for refinancing differ, but this Bank of England evidence presents an *a priori* case that those who made use of UK and German banks were more favourably placed than those who made use of the banking systems of France, Italy and Sweden.

It is arguable that much of industry's concern about 'short-termism' is not related to the efficiency of the financial sector or the cost of capital, but to the comparative narrowness of the gap between the interest rates at which companies borrow and the profits they have been able to earn. This has left UK lenders and borrowers vulnerable to small fluctuations in profits which would not have destabilised loans to the same extent in economies where profits were higher, and has obliged many companies to maximise profits over shorter time horizons, increasing the influence of short-term considerations in business decisions. Figure 3.10 indicates that profitability has been consistently lower in UK manufacturing industry than in industrial and commercial companies considered as a whole, so on balance UK profits have been lower in manufacturing than in the service sector. If the rise in profitability in the 1990s is sustained, it will considerably widen the excess of profits over interest costs and we may hear less of 'short-termism' from now onwards.

Table 3.1 International interest rate spreads, 1992–97

	1992	1993	1994	1995	1996	1997	Average
UK							
Prime Lending rate	11.50	7.00	6.50	7.25	7.25	7.00	7.75
Deposit rate	7.46	3.97	3.66	4.11	3.04	3.63	4.31
Spread	4.04	3.03	2.84	3.14	4.21	3.37	3.44
Germany							
Prime lending rate	11.00	11.00	9.00	7.50	6.25	4.60	8.23
Deposit rate	8.01	6.27	4.47	3.85	2.83	2.69	4.69
Spread	2.99	4.73	4.53	3.65	3.42	1.91	3.54
France							
Prime lending rate	10.35	10.00	7.95	8.25	7.00	6.30	8.31
Deposit rate	4.50	4.50	4.56	4.50	3.67	3.50	4.21
Spread	5.85	5.50	3.39	3.75	3.33	2.80	4.10
Italy							
Prime lending rate	13.00	13.63	9.88	9.34	11.50	9.75	11.19
Deposit rate	7.11	7.79	6.20	6.45	6.49	4.83	6.48
Spread	5.89	5.84	3.68	2.89	5.01	4.92	4.71
Sweden							
Prime lending rate	14.50	12.50	9.50	9.50	9.30	5.35	10.11
Deposit rate	7.80	5.10	4.91	6.16	2.47	2.50	4.82
Spread	6.70	7.40	4.59	3.34	6.83	2.85	5.29
United States							
Prime lending rate	6.50	6.00	6.00	8.50	8.50	8.25	7.29
Deposit rate	3.68	3.17	4.63	5.92	5.39	5.62	4.73
Spread	2.82	2.83	1.37	2.58	3.11	2.63	2.56
Japan							
Prime lending rate	5.88	4.50	3.00	3.00	1.63	1.63	3.27
Deposit rate	3.35	2.14	1.70	0.90	0.30	0.30	1.45
Spread	2.53	2.36	1.30	2.10	1.33	1.33	1.82

Source for Prime lending rate: Datastream. Source for Deposit rate: IFS. We are grateful to Andy Haldane of the Bank of England for help in compiling our original 1995 table, and to Jayne Willis of the Bank of England for extending these data sources to 1997.

Some UK policies which have changed business conditions

Four approaches to policy made a particularly favourable contribution between 1979 and 1996: privatisation, inward investment; the growth of small businesses; and labour market policies.

Figure 3.10 Profitability in industrial and commercial companies and in manufacturing, 1970–93

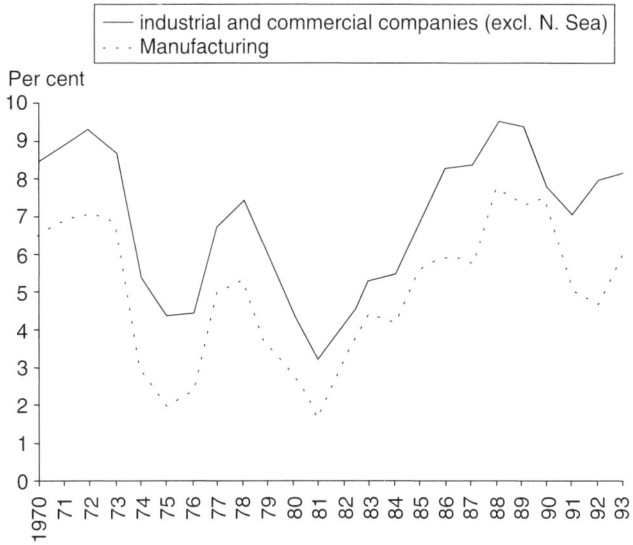

Note: Net rate of return on capital employment.
Source: CSO.

A major influence on UK performance in the 1960s and 1970s was inefficiency in the use of resources (Bean and Crafts, 1995). For example, Vickers and Yarrow (1988) found that in many of the major nationalised industries weak monitoring and control mechanisms led to inadequate control over construction costs and the inefficient use of labour. Many of the privatised utilities have significantly raised productivity, particularly when exposed to competition (Table 3.2).

The United Kingdom has higher ratios of inward and outward direct investment to GDP than any other major economy. Foreign-owned companies employ nearly one-fifth of the labour in UK manufacturing industry, produce nearly one-quarter of the value added, and are responsible for almost one-third of all capital investment.

Foreign-owned companies produce over two-thirds of data processing equipment and office machinery, nearly one-third of motor vehicles and parts, one-third of instrument engineering products and one-fifth of electrical and electronic engineering products. At the same time, foreign-owned companies were responsible for nearly three-

Table 3.2 Productivity growth in the privatised utilities, 1984–91

Privatised utilities	Year in which privatised	Average annual increase in labour productivity[a] since privatisation
British Telecom	1984–5	7.0
British Gas	1986–7	3.7
Water	1989–90	1.7*b*
National Power	1990–1	20.7
PowerGen	1990–1	15.5
Regional Electricity Companies	1990–1	6.0
Public sector utilities	*Reference year*	*Average annual increase in labour productivity since reference year*
British Rail	1984–5	0.7
Royal Mail	1984–5	3.3
Nuclear Electric	1990–1	24.7

Notes:
a Physical units delivered per employee: BT, connections; British Gas, temperature adjusted Gwh; Water, Litres/day supplied; electricity, Twh; British Rail, weighted sum of passenger miles and tonnes; Royal Mail, domestic and international letters.
b This table takes no account of improvements in water quality and service provision, and demand management measures which have reduced the amount of water being put into supply.
Source: Company accounts to 1993–4; for Gas, British Gas accounts to December 1995 and Financial and Operations Statistics 1993; for water, *Waterfacts*, various years.

quarters of investment in motor vehicles and parts, over one-half of investment in electrical and electronic engineering and one-third of investment in instrument engineering. The contribution of foreign-owned companies to the UK economy is set out in detail in Chapter 4.

Inward investment consists of two types of inflow. The first is purchases of new fixed assets by foreign firms financed from abroad, often at greenfield sites (for example, Nissan), but also at established sites (for example, Ford). The other is mergers such as Nestlé-Rowntree where the investor firm pays for existing assets. There is no reason *a priori* to think that greenfield investors will have the most positive impact on productivity. However, firms are more likely to improve performance if they are installing modern equipment and this tends to be more the case at greenfield sites. Furthermore, introducing new working practices has been easier at greenfield sites with no history of poor industrial relations. Table 4.2 (p. 77 below) shows that the value-added per head of foreign owned companies was 40 per cent higher, and their investment to output ratio was 50 per cent higher, than that in the UK-owned sector of manufacturing industry, although it must be remembered that inward investors tend to have larger plants and to be in faster-growing sectors.

Foreign-owned companies may account for about two-fifths of total exports of manufactures. The United Kingdom now has export surpluses in computers and colour televisions, sectors dominated by foreign-owned companies. Evidence from Blake and Pain (1994) suggests that while inward investment has raised the UK export share, outward investment has reduced it. However, a number of other studies – see, for example, Dunning and Walker (1982), Balasubramanyam (1993) and KPMG (1995) – suggest that exports and foreign direct investment tend to complement each other.

The benefits of inward investment go beyond the share of foreign firms in output, investment and jobs (PA Cambridge Economic Consultants, 1995). Some of the most productive companies in the world have been attracted to the United Kingdom, introducing techniques of quality control and a managerial 'style' which have spread very widely to UK-owned companies. In Sunderland, Nissan has been able to select just 10 per cent of those who wished to work for it, to train these workers to very high standards and to achieve quality control and productivity levels which equal those in the Nissan plants in Japan. This may be an important benefit of inward investment since although the UK-owned sector of manufacturing industry includes some of the world's leading companies, it also appears to include a long tail of under-performers struggling to remain competitive (IBM/LBS, 1994). However, it must be recognised that some of the benefits from improving managerial techniques are likely to have been gained by UK companies regardless of whether inward investors had located in the United Kingdom or overseas.

Inward investment has also influenced the UK's comparative strength at the high-tech end of world trade. As noted earlier, business financed R&D in the United Kingdom is between $^1/_2$ and 1 per cent of GDP below that in the United States and Japan. As the spread of technology has become easier, the UK economy benefits if it is producing the products of inward investors, even if much of the R&D is undertaken overseas. The scientific and technical content of UK production may therefore now be considerably in advance of that implied by the actual fraction of R&D which is undertaken in the United Kingdom.

Econometric and survey work both suggest that the main determinants of international investment flows are potential markets and the price and quality of factors of production. Many firms invest and expand in the United Kingdom because of the size of the local market and its proximity to Europe. Pain (1993) finds that growth in EU demand is an important determinant of the level of foreign investment in the United Kingdom and also estimates that a 1 per cent rise in relative UK labour costs will ultimately reduce the inward investment stock by just under 1 per cent. Taxation will affect relative factor costs for firms; either directly through corporation tax and employers' social security payments, or indirectly through other taxes that may bear on firms. For example, personal tax levels may affect companies if higher income taxes oblige firms to pay a higher pre-tax wage to get the staff they require. Cummins and Hubbard (1994) suggest that differentials in corporation tax are a determinant of the location of investment by US firms. Similarly, Young (1994) found that the tax regime on US firms was a significant factor in explaining their investment in the United Kingdom in the period 1970–91.

This bodes well for the United Kingdom since the overall burden of taxation has been lower than the average for other EU countries since 1980 (Table 3.3). The top rate of income tax and national insurance

Table 3.3 Current receipts by government as a percentage of GDP, 1980–96

	1980–89	1990–6	1996
Austria	47.2	47.6	47.9
Belgium	51.6	48.8	49.8
Denmark	55.6	56.6	57.4
France	46.4	49.2	50.3
Finland	45.4	52.7	54.0
Germany	45.1	45.3	45.6
Greece	33.4	35.2	38.0
Ireland	41.5	37.2	36.1
Italy	37.8	45.7	46.0
Netherlands	54.3	49.7	47.3
Norway	53.7	50.8	51.7
Portugal	36.2	39.6	40.7
Spain	33.9	39.3	39.0
Sweden	59.4	59.9	62.1
United Kingdom	41.2	38.9	38.6
Average of EU15	43.5	45.8	46.4

Sources: OECD *Historical Statistics* 1960–93, Table 6.6: *Economic Outlook*, December 1998, Annex Table 29.

contributions in the United Kingdom is 40 per cent. This is the lowest in the European Union, matched only by Greece. The United Kingdom also has the lowest main rate of corporation tax of any major industrialised country and employers' social security contributions are low. As a result, taxes on business have been a smaller proportion of GDP in the United Kingdom than in our major European competitors and Japan (Table 3.4).

Other significant factors influencing inward investment include the unambiguous welcome that the government gives to the entry of foreign firms, the generally good experiences of long established foreign firms in the United Kingdom and the position of English as the first or second language of nearly every country. Deregulation in the City of London in 1986 also encouraged investment in the financial sector.

There has been an economy-wide shift in favour of smaller businesses. Since 1979, the number of firms in the United Kingdom has risen by over 1 million. In part, this reflects the growing importance of the service sector where smaller firms are more viable and economies of scale are less important. But it also reflects improved and more flexible technologies (especially developments in IT) which have allowed a smaller scale of firm to be efficient. As a result, there has also been a shift towards smaller firms within manufacturing: the proportions of manufacturing employment in large and small business units were reversed between 1975 and 1995. Reductions in corporate and income tax rates during the 1980s have encouraged new businesses by providing greater incentives to invest and by increasing the reserves of small firms which often have limited access to capital markets (Bannock and Albach, 1991). Deregulation and simplification have also helped

Table 3.4 Taxes on business[a] as a share of GDP, 1980–93

	1980	1985	1990	1993
United Kingdom	7.8	8.1	7.5	5.9
France	14.9	15.4	15.0	14.5
Germany	9.2	9.5	8.8	9.1
Italy	11.2	11.9	13.2	17.3
United States	7.6	7.0	7.1	7.2
Japan	9.3	10.1	11.5	9.4

Note:
a Taxes on business are defined as the sum of corporation tax, payroll taxes and employers' social security contributions.
Source: Revenue Statistics of OECD member countries 1965–1994.

smaller firms (Small Business Research Centre, 1993). Although most of the growth in small firms is from self-employed and two-employee firms, these provide a seed-bed and training ground for entrepreneurs. Some new businesses go on to become significant new innovative companies and therefore enhance the economy's overall rate of technical advance.

A final notable development in the 1980s was a great improvement in the efficiency of the UK labour market. A range of econometric studies has shown that this was associated with at least a once-for-all improvement in labour productivity – see, for example, Denny and Nickell (1992) and Gregg, Machin and Metcalf (1993). The number of days lost through strikes fell sharply and UK private sector employment increased when it fell in the European Union as a whole. Demarcation disputes and official and unofficial industrial action have virtually disappeared. Industrial relations legislation has strengthened the democratic control of trade unions. It has also made it illegal for strikes to spread into companies not directly involved through secondary action.

New well-paid jobs are being created in the sectors of the economy which are gaining international business. These have often been sited in regions where unemployment used to be comparatively high. Many inward investors have been choosing greenfield sites away from customary industrial areas of the United Kingdom. Evidence suggests that the regional balance of the economy has been improving, although marked differences remain within regions. It can be argued that this should slowly reduce the non-accelerating inflation rate of unemployment (NAIRU) and so allow the economy to achieve macroeconomic equilibrium at a lower unemployment rate than in the past. (OECD, 1995, presents evidence that the UK NAIRU has fallen). Sustained economic growth can in any case gradually reduce the NAIRU as workers adjust their behaviour to take advantage of increased employment opportunities. The hysteresis literature indicates that, provided the economy does not grow too rapidly for adjustments to behaviour to occur, the NAIRU can slowly track actual unemployment downwards. In the 1990s the UK unemployment rate has fallen well below the EU average and it has fallen in comparison with unemployment in a good deal of Europe without a marked acceleration in inflation.

The gap that remains

Figure 3.11 shows that in 1992 the gap between UK and German productivity varied considerably by industry. In chemicals, the United

Kingdom matched German levels, and exceeded them in food and drink. Germany was far ahead of the United Kingdom in machinery and transport equipment, electrical engineering, textiles and clothing. In pharmaceuticals, the fastest growing area of the chemical industry, the United Kingdom has the largest company in the world, Glaxo–Wellcome with research and development of 16 per cent of value added. Sir Geoffrey Owen (1994) has suggested that one of the factors behind the UK's superior comparative performance in pharmaceuticals has been that it is comparatively more effective at research than in the mechanics of production. The United Kingdom used to have no shortage of university graduates but a considerable shortage of skilled labour. With pharmaceuticals the development of new drugs which depends mainly on research is the principal challenge and their manufacture after that is relatively straightforward.

The inferiorities in the mechanics of production during the 1970s and 1980s may now be being corrected. The data in the 1995 White Paper indicate that skill shortages may be diminishing.

How the quality of UK exports has been changing in comparison with those of our principal international competitors was estimated in 1996 by P.A. Brenton and P.J.N. Sinclair of the University of Birmingham in an unpublished paper commissioned by HM Treasury, 'Explaining Recent British Export Performance'. They found that in the 1980s the quality of UK exports rose in comparison with those

Figure 3.11 Productivity in UK and German manufacturing industry, 1980 and 1992

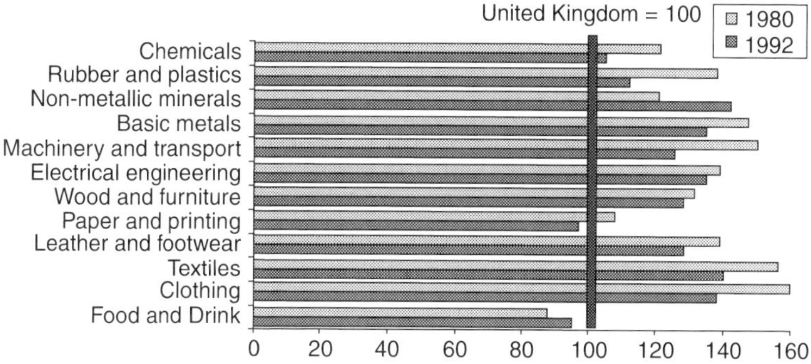

Note: Productivity measured as output per hour worked
Source: O'Mahony.

produced in France and Germany in ten industrial groupings out of eighteen, and that in the other eight, evidence on quality change 'was generally insignificant, and occasionally adverse'.

The sectors where relative quality advanced significantly against both France and Germany include iron and steel, plastics, man-made fibres, chemicals, office computing and accounting machinery and motor vehicles. In radio, television and communications equipment quality advanced in comparison with Germany but not France. Brenton and Sinclair attribute the relative quality improvement in motor vehicles and radio and television equipment 'in large measure to the arrival of superior technology introduced by the foreign firms and the response this induced on the part of indigenous enterprises (match it, or die)'. Some of the considerations which used to be most responsible for weaknesses in competitiveness are being corrected. If that is so, the influence of inward investors with their higher productivity and investment than most UK-owned businesses has been crucial. It could also be argued that British businesses are now better managed than a decade ago and that companies are responding more rapidly to opportunities to sell in world markets. Whatever the reason, there is a possibility that there has been a significant performance change since the mid-1980s which has led to a better trade and inflation performance than anyone anticipated. (For a discussion of the evidence for an improvement in the United Kingdom's underlying export performance see Blake and Pain, 1994.)

Although the underlying performance of the UK economy improved during the 1980s, productivity levels in both manufacturing and services still appear to lag behind those in the leading West European economies. Moreover, manufacturing productivity has grown far faster than manufacturing output for reasons discussed in Eltis (1996). Closing the remaining productivity gap and ensuring a sustained growth in output will require further improvements in performance.

4
The Political Economy of British Foreign Direct Investment*

Introduction

Foreign direct investment (FDI) is transforming the world economy, and the questions it raises are debated in every country. Is it in the interests of a country to receive large inflows of FDI which enhance its productivity and employment, but at the same time increase the extent of foreign control of its industry and commerce? If UK companies invest abroad, are they depriving their countrymen of jobs and incomes and the UK government of tax revenues? Is foreign investment by British companies a vote of no confidence, or an indication that businesses are so well managed that they can produce competitively in a variety of environments?

These are important and controversial questions. This chapter will outline some of the most significant statistical information and present the principal economic arguments in four stages: (1) the detailed extent of UK inward and outward investment, (2) the similar trends in other leading economies, (3) the international competitiveness of Britain as a productive base and (4) the implications of Britain's exceptional levels of inward and outward direct investment.

The chapter shows that Britain has the highest ratios of inward and outward investment to GDP of any leading economy. Foreign-owned companies produce with higher average labour productivity than British-owned manufacturers: they invest more, pay their employees

* This is a revised and up-dated version of *The Political Economy of United Kingdom Foreign Direct Investment* (London: Foundation for Manufacturing and Industry, 1996)

more and the research and development (R&D) they undertake is at a similar level. Evidence from other leading economies shows that there has been a similar world-wide tendency for foreign-owned companies to perform more strongly than domestically owned industry and commerce. The United Kingdom has been exceptionally successful at attracting inward investment in relation to the rest of Europe, in part because of the advantages of the English language, Britain's comparatively low taxation and the highly competitive costs of those with scientific and IT skills.

Economic theory indicates that inward investment offers considerable benefits to employees, and British trades unions have strongly supported it while employer organisations have not been opposed. Companies have gained because inward investors have had a growing impact on the establishment of best-practice in British-owned industry. Economic theory indicates that outward investment raises employment and tax revenues in foreign countries rather than at home, but much of it is complementary to home investment. The establishment of production facilities and distributive outlets throughout the world increases the world market share of leading British companies. The option of insisting that they invest in Britain no longer exists, and the best approach of government is to continue to create an environment where all companies, British and foreign-owned, find the United Kingdom a highly competitive productive base.

Foreign direct investment and the British economy

More than 20 per cent of the output and 30 per cent of the investment of British manufacturing industry is produced by foreign-owned companies. If we add to this the extent to which British manufacturing output is produced by British-owned companies which are multinational and have the continual option to switch their production overseas, it can be concluded that more than half of manufacturing output comes from companies with a presence in several countries. These will only manufacture in Britain while it pays them to do so.

British direct investment in the rest of the world far exceeds FDI in Britain (Table 4.1). In 1997, British companies and individuals owned direct investments outside the United Kingdom of £225.8 billion, while the total assets of foreign-owned companies in the United Kingdom were £170.6 billion. Foreign direct investment into the United Kingdom exceeded outward direct investment only in 1990 at the peak of the 'Lawson Boom'. In the aggregate, from 1987 to 1997,

Table 4.1 Direct investment overseas: by the United Kingdom and within the United Kingdom 1987–97

		UK investment overseas (£ billion)	Foreign investment in the United Kingdom (£ billion)
Assets of all companies	(1997)	225.8	170.6
Income of all companies	(1997)	32.7	18.4
Dividends and interest in	(1997)	16.1	11.0
Investment in:	(1997)	36.3	23.3
	(1996)	22.5	16.6
	(1995)	28.2	12.9
	(1994)	22.2	6.1
	(1993)	17.9	10.3
	(1992)	11.1	9.2
	(1991)	9.1	9.1
	(1990)	10.6	18.6
	(1989)	21.5	18.6
	(1988)	20.9	12.0
	(1987)	19.2	9.5
Total 1987–97		219.5	146.2

Source: NSO: *United Kingdom Balance of Payments*, 1998 edn.

British direct investment overseas totalled £219.5 billion while foreign direct investment into Britain totalled £146.2 billion. British companies and individuals are therefore consistently buying and creating British-owned assets in the rest of the world at a far faster rate than the British economy is becoming foreign-owned.

With a net balance of British capital in the rest of the world, the United Kingdom has a favourable net income from the foreign ownership of companies. Britain receives more income and more interest and dividends from its ownership of companies overseas than it pays out to those who own companies in Britain. In 1997 the United Kindom received a total income of £32.7 billion and paid out £18.4 billion. The interest and dividends Britain received exceeded those paid out by £5.1 billion. In the aggregate, British companies and individuals are net direct investors in the rest of the world, and this makes a substantial contribution to the current account of the balance of payments.

Between 1980 and 1990 Britain's foreign direct investment into the rest of the world, and the inward investment into the United Kingdom were both greater as ratios of GDP than the outward and inward investment of the Netherlands, Switzerland, the United States, France, Sweden, Italy, Germany, Spain or Japan (Figure 4.1). The tendency for Japan and the United States to create and buy up companies in the rest of the world is much discussed, but the tendency for Britain to do this is far greater. Britain is the largest outward investor and it also has the largest inward investment (when these are both expressed as ratios of GDP). It has proved to be both the most open economy for investment from the rest of the world, and also the economy which invests most freely overseas.

The foreign companies which have chosen to produce in Britain are making a very favourable contribution to productivity and investment. Table 4.2 presents striking data which show how much more strongly foreign-owned companies have performed in manufacturing industry than indigenous British-owned companies. In 1992, labour productivity in foreign-owned companies was 1.4 times as great as in the British-owned sector of manufacturing industry. Investment per worker by the foreign-owned companies was more than twice as great. The new foreign-owned companies were on average larger and more capital-intensive than the majority of British manufacturing companies, which explains some of these discrepancies but many were also outperforming the larger British-owned companies. The presence of the

Figure 4.1 International comparison of inward and outward foreign direct investment, 1980–90

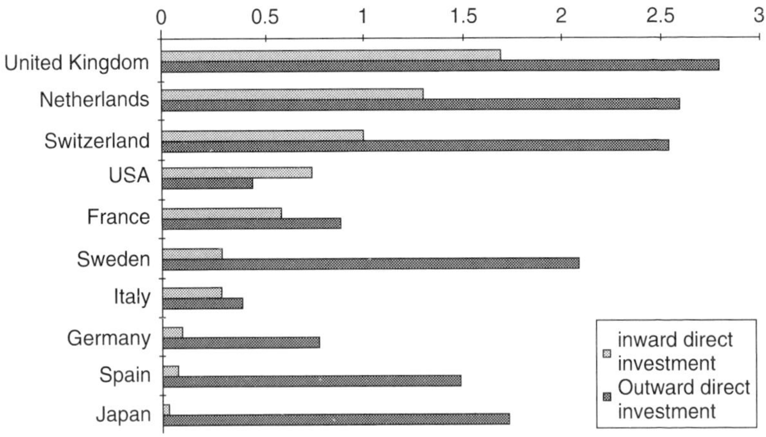

Source: CBI *Making it in Britain, Partnerships for World Class Manufacturing* (London: CBI).

Table 4.2 Foreign- and United Kingdom enterprises in United Kingdom manufacturing industry in 1992

	Foreign-owned	UK-owned	Foreign/ United Kingdom
Proportion of total employment	0.179	0.821	0.218
Proportion of total value-added	0.234	0.766	0.305
Valued-added per worker as a ratio of UK average	1.307	0.933	1.401
Proportion of total investment	0.316	0.684	0.467
Investment per worker as a ratio of UK average	1.765	0.833	2.119
Investment/value-added as a proportion of UK average	1.350	0.893	1.512

Source: CSO Census of Production 1992.

foreign-owned element in British industry therefore substantially increased both its productivity and its investment.

This is not a new phenomenon. Foreign-owned companies produced 23.4 per cent of manufacturing output in 1992 but they were already producing 18.1 per cent in 1981 (Table 4.3), so in the eleven years from 1981 to 1992 which nearly corresponds to the Thatcher decade, the share of the foreign-owned sector of British manufacturing industry grew by just 5 percentage points. Nor is there anything radically new in the comparatively high labour productivity and investment of foreign-owned companies. It can be inferred from Table 4.3 that their labour productivity was 28 per cent higher than that of the UK-owned companies in 1981 and their advantage had become 40 per cent by 1992. Foreign-owned manufacturing companies invested 95 per cent more per worker in 1981 and 112 per cent more in 1992, while their investment as a share of value-added was 1.53 times higher in 1981 and 1.51 times higher in 1992. The impact of foreign-owned companies was therefore already favourable in 1981 and still more favourable in 1992.

Table 4.3 also offers useful sectoral information. The striking changes between 1981 and 1992 include an advance in the foreign-owned element of office machinery and data processing from 28.5 per cent in 1981 to 69.0 per cent in 1992. There are other sectors where the

Table 4.3 Share of foreign-owned enterprises in United Kingdom industry in 1992

	Value-added	Employment	Investment
Total manufacturing	23.4	17.9	31.6
(in 1981)	(18.3)	(14.9)	(25.5)
Office machinery and data processing equipment (in 1981)	69.0 (28.5)	43.1 (38.2)	56.2 (65.5)
Motor vehicles and parts	46.6	43.1	71.2
(in 1981)	(43.3)	(36.1)	(47.2)
Chemical industry (1990)	35.2	33.4	29.1
(in 1981)	(34.0)	(30.8)	(48.1)
Instrument engineering	30.3	23.4	32.0
(in 1981)	(29.9)	(30.1)	(35.8)
Electrical and electronic engineering (in 1981)	29.1 (21.8)	26.5 (21.4)	41.1 (29.4)
Mechanical engineering	23.0	19.0	28.3
(in 1981)	(24.1)	(19.8)	(29.0)
Metal manufacturing	19.1	16.3	19.6
(in 1981)	(13.1)	(11.1)	(20.6)
Food, drink and tobacco	21.5	13.2	19.2
(in 1981)	(15.2)	(11.1)	(15.6)
Textiles, clothing and footwear	7.2	5.4	11.7
(in 1981)	(4.5)	(3.4)	(5.0)

Source: CSO *Census of Production* (1981 and 1992).

foreign-owned element increased, but less strikingly. In motor vehicles and parts (where Ford and Vauxhall have been prominent since the inter-war years), 43.3 per cent was produced by foreign-owned companies in 1981 and 46.6 per cent in 1992: the foreign-owned proportion of investment increased strikingly from 47.2 to 71.2 per cent. In electrical and electronic engineering, the foreign-owned element increased from, 21.8 to 29.1 per cent of output, and from 29.4 to 41.1 per cent of investment. In chemicals, the foreign-owned proportion of output was high but it rose by only 1 percentage point (from 34.0 to 35.2 per cent) while the share of investment actually fell. This is a sector where several of the British-owned companies, including especially Glaxo-Wellcome and ICI, are world class. One area where British-owned manufacturing industry has been notably weak, and where it has lost substantial output, employment and world market share, has been textiles, clothing and footwear. Here the foreign-owned element was only 4.5 per cent of output in 1981 and 7.2 per cent in 1992.

Some have argued that when foreign-owned companies enter the United Kingdom their tendency is to establish 'screwdriver' operations, where British workers are employed to assemble and carry out elementary manufacturing tasks on products which are designed, developed and partly manufactured elsewhere. Figure 4.2 is important because it contradicts this assertion. It shows that in 1989 foreign-owned companies, which were responsible for about 21 per cent of the turnover of British manufacturing industry, performed 19 per cent of its R&D. The proportions of output and of R&D by foreign-owned companies in Britain were therefore almost the same, so their contribution to British R&D is parallel to that of British-owned companies. Table 4.4 actually shows that in 1990 the foreign-owned companies in Britain registered 70 per cent as many European patents as British-owned companies: while in 1978–86 they registered 40 per cent as many US patents.[1] In

Figure 4.2 Share of foreign affiliates' R&D and turnover in total manufacturing R&D and turnover in 1989

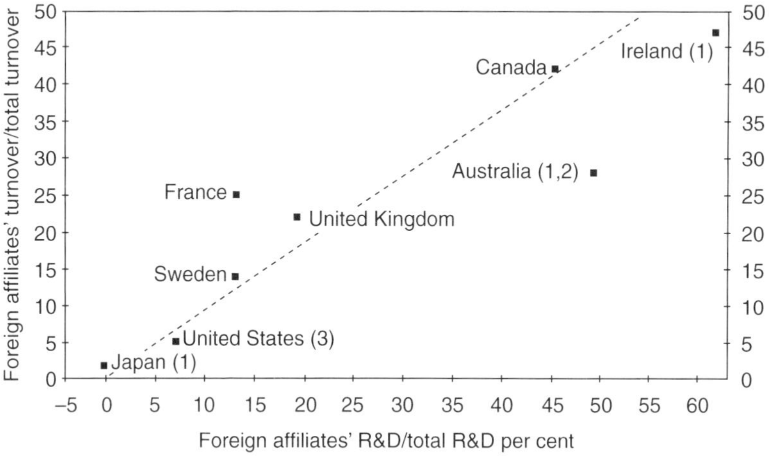

Notes: 1. Production.
2. 1986/87.
3. Value added.
Source: OECD, EAS Division, Industrial Activity of Foreign Affiliates Data Bank.

Table 4.4 Share of domestic and foreign firms in European patent-taking in 1990 (percentage share of all patent-taking in Europe)

		France	Germany	United Kingdom	Netherlands	Switzerland	Italy
Domestic firms		6.4	16.0	2.7	2.1	2.2	1.7
Foreign affiliates		1.4	3.3	1.9	0.5	0.3	0.6
Of which	EU	0.6	1.3	0.6	0.3	0.2	0.3
	EFTA	0.1	0.9	0.1	0.0	0.0	0.1
	US	0.6	1.1	1.0	0.0	0.0	0.0
	Japan	0.0	0.0	0.1	0.0	0.0	0.0
	Other	0.1	0.0	0.1	0.0	0.0	0.0
Geographical share of total (per cent)		7.8	19.3	4.6	2.6	2.5	2.3
Share of foreign affiliates in national total (per cent)		22.0	21.0	70.0	24.0	14.0	35.0

Source: Science of Technologie Indicateurs 1994, Remi Bare (ed.), Economica, Paris.

contrast, in France, Germany, the Netherlands, Switzerland and Italy, the proportion of European patents taken out by foreign-owned companies was far lower than Britain's 70 per cent: 14 per cent in Switzerland and little more than 20 per cent in France and Germany.

There are several reasons why foreign-owned companies find the United Kingdom an attractive base for research and development. These include the 'Scientific Research Allowances' which may allow companies to offset 100 per cent of the cost of their research plant and machinery against tax, while technically skilled staff are far cheaper to employ than in other leading European economies. Table 4.5 shows how, in 1994, the cost of employing a computer programmer was 46 per cent higher in France and 73 per cent higher in Germany than in Britain. The cost of employing a systems analyst was 38 per cent higher in France and 26 per cent higher in Germany. These discrepancies arise because British wages and salaries are lower (when measured in a common currency) and social add-on costs are far lower: non-salary costs are three times as great in France, and one-and-a-half to two-and-a-half times as great in Germany. There is widespread evidence that Britain has fewer skilled craftsmen than France and Germany, but employees with job-specific skills such as those of a

Table 4.5 Selected pay differences in 1994 (US $)

	Germany	France	Britain
Computer Programmer			
Salary per year	40 124	26 311	25 529
Non-salary costs*	13 951	19 210	5718
Total costs	54 075	45 521	31 247
Britain = 100	173	146	100
Systems analyst			
Salary per year	49 286	44 050	41 808
Non-salary costs*	15 821	27 113	9680
Total costs	65 107	71 163	51 488
Britain = 100	126	138	100
Textile worker (hourly)			
Salary per year	13.12	9.73	8.23
Non-salary costs*	7.38	6.76	2.04
Total costs	20.50	16.49	10.27
Britain = 100	200	161	100

Source: The Economist (30 July 1994).

computer programmer or a systems analyst are largely interchangeable between the three economies. Because British computer experts cost between three-fifths and two-thirds as much to employ as those with the same specific skills in France and Germany (and this was also true of chemists, engineers and draftsmen) multinational companies found it more economical to undertake research in Britain than in other leading West European economies. The entry of such companies therefore had no tendency to weaken the level of R&D undertaken in Britain and it may well have strengthened it.

A further consideration is that foreign ownership often leads to the sharing of successful research. ICL and Fujitsu are leading international computer manufacturers and each undertakes substantial research. Fujitsu now owns ICL and each has complete access to the other's research. It has been suggested by senior ICL executives that the pooling of R&D has proved far more important to their creation of new products than the availability of extra financial resources from their wealthier foreign parent. ICL's research is at the same time fully available to Fujitsu. A former Chairman of Sony, Akio Morita, has said that you have to make your own products obsolete before somebody else does it for you. Any well managed international company will wish its subsidiaries to pursue R&D and be part of the knowledge-sharing process which drives the conglomerate forward in international competition.

The new businesses which entered Britain in the 1980s and the 1990s include some of the world's leading companies and many of those especially associated with high-tech production have been Japanese and German-owned. Figures 4.3 and 4.4 show how rapidly the entry of Japanese- and German-owned companies has been advancing. 181 Japanese and 271 German companies were manufacturing in Britain in 1992. Figure 4.5 shows that US-owned participation in British manufacturing industry is still greater. Ford and Vauxhall have been in the British economy for a very long time.

The contribution to the British balance of payments of the entry of Japanese- (and other Pacific Rim)-owned companies has been especially striking. In Chapter 3 (p. 71–2) Brenton and Sinclair's 1996 study, 'Explaining Recent British Export Performance', was referred to, and their conclusion that in the 1980s the quality of UK exports rose in comparison with those produced in France and Germany in ten industrial groupings out of eighteen, and how this was partly the result of, 'the arrival of superior technology introduced by the foreign firms and the response this induced on the part of indigenous enterprises (match it, or die)'.

Figure 4.3 Growth of Japanese-owned manufacturing in the United Kingdom, 1972–92

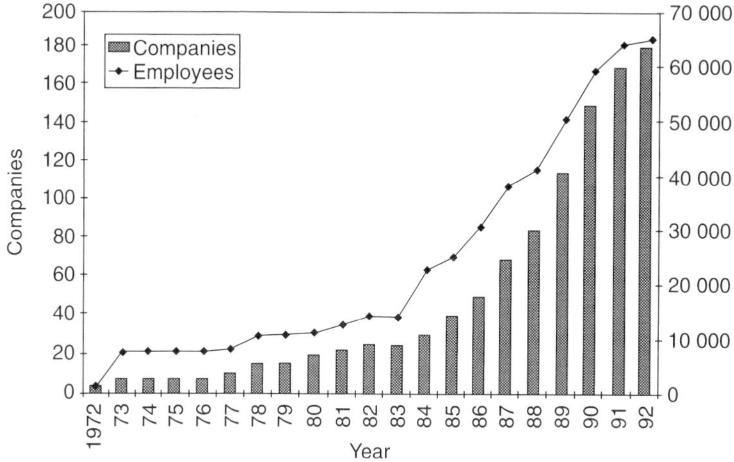

Figure 4.4 Growth of German-owned manufacturing in the United Kingdom, 1970–90

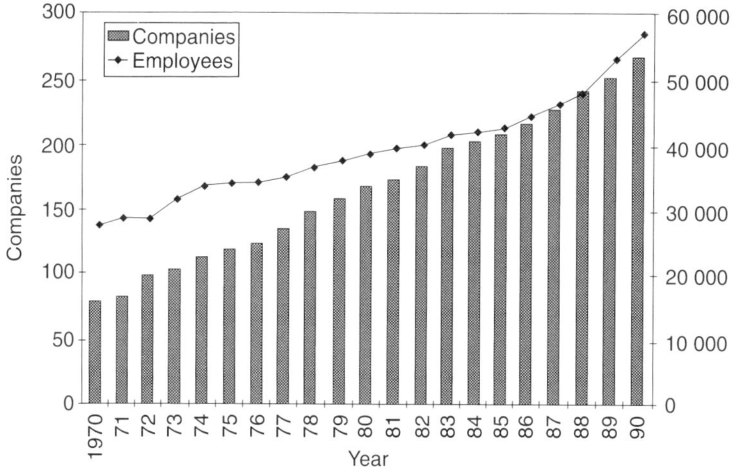

Figure 4.5 Inward direct investment in the United Kingdom attributable to overseas companies, 1981–9

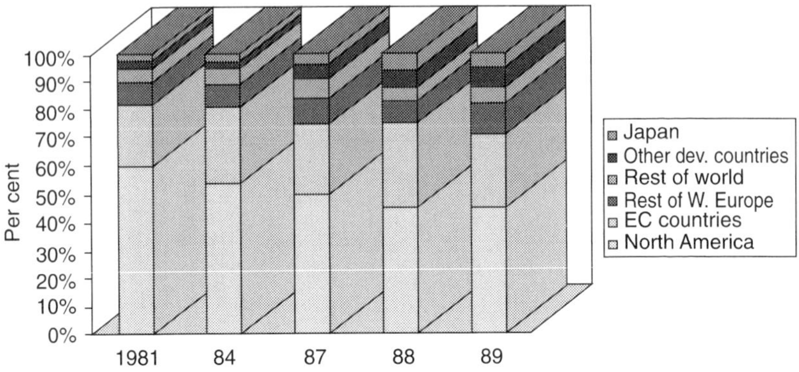

Figure 4.6 sets out the companies which manufactured television sets in the United Kingdom between 1967 and 1991. In the 1960s and the early 1970s these mainly had familiar British names such as Pye, Decca, Ferguson, Philips, Rank and GEC. These had disappeared by the 1990s and been replaced by Sony, Matsushita, Toshiba, Mitsubishi, Hitachi and JVC. The British- and European-owned producers could not match the rising quality and reliability standards of the Japanese and their lower manufacturing costs. The British balance of payments in colour televisions was transformed. A trade deficit in finished television sets in the 1970s and the early 1980s became a surplus, and since 1988 there has been a growing export surplus in colour televisions (Figure 4.7). The same has been true of finished computers where the British-owned producers have been driven out of production or taken over, and a trade deficit has been converted into a substantial surplus. This data is for finished televisions and computers and there may still be a trade deficit in colour television and computer components.

Colour television and computers are sectors where the British-owned producers have been entirely outcompeted. In motor vehicles, no significant British-owned assemblers survive, although there are several British-owned component suppliers some of which operate successfully on an international basis.

The evidence presented indicates that the entry of foreign-owned manufacturing companies has raised productivity and investment in

Figure 4.6 The displacement of British by foreign-owned firms in the manufacture of television sets, 1967–91

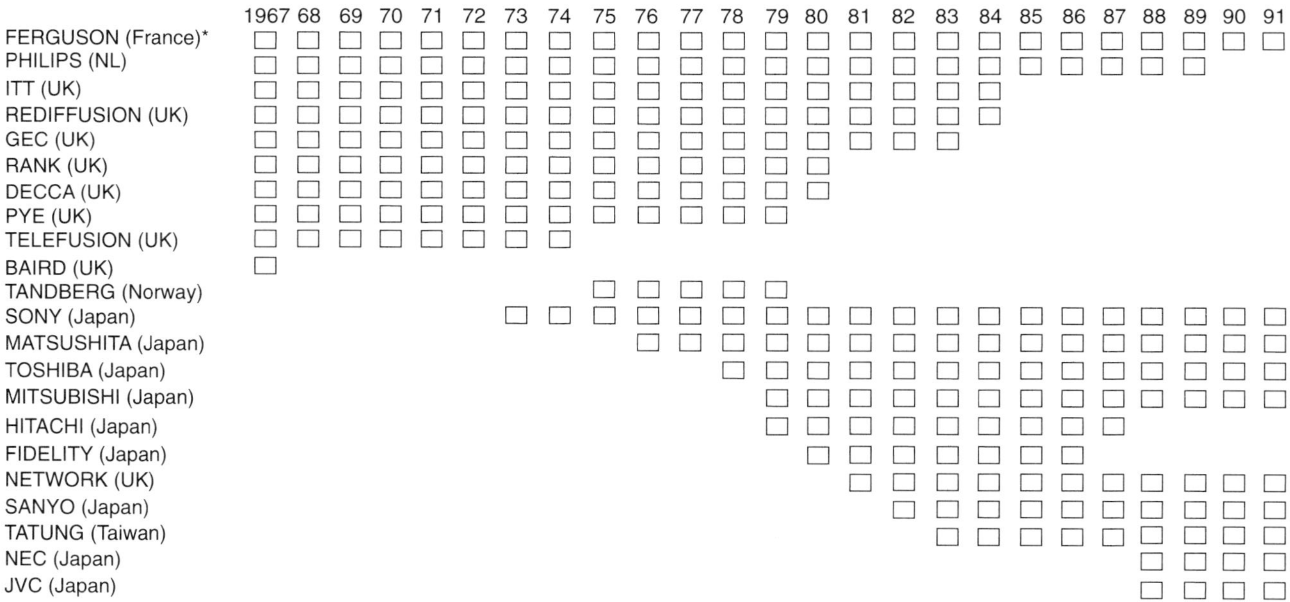

Note:
*Ferguson was acquired by Thomson (France) in 1987.
Source: The Open University.

Figure 4.7 UK trade in colour televisions, 1970–91

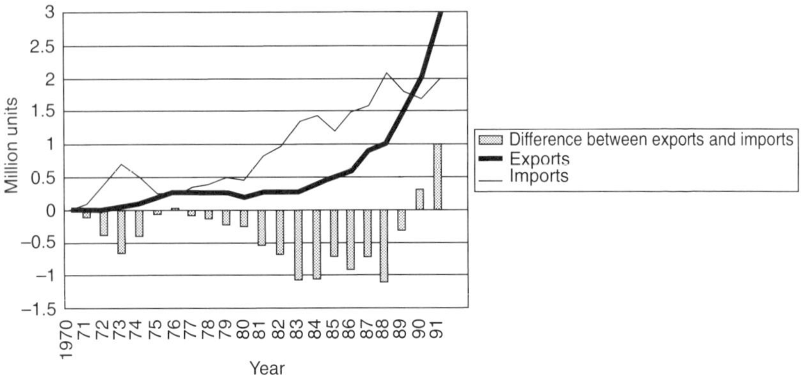

Source: BREMA.

Britain and that it has almost certainly enhanced R&D and improved the balance of payments.

The similar impact of foreign direct investment in other leading economies

The impact of foreign-owned companies has been very favourable in the United Kingdom. The OECD evidence presented in Figures 4.8 and 4.9 and in Table 4.6 suggests that it has been similarly favourable in several other countries. Employment fell substantially in British-owned manufacturing industry from 1980 to 1990. Figure 4.8 shows that it also fell in domestically-owned manufacturing industry in Sweden, the United States, Portugal, Finland, Ireland, Norway, Austria, Australia, France and Canada. Only Germany, Japan and Turkey have experienced growing employment from their domestically-owned manufacturing companies. But for the United Kingdom, foreign-owned manufacturers increased their employment by 3 per cent per annum in the 1980s, and these also provided growing employment in Turkey, Sweden, the United States, Portugal, Finland, Ireland, Norway and Austria. The contribution to the growth of employment of foreign-owned companies has been predominantly favourable while, in the 1980s, the general international tendency was for the employment provided by domestically-owned companies to decline.

Figure 4.8a Trend in employment by foreign affiliates in manufacturing industry, 1980–90

(a)

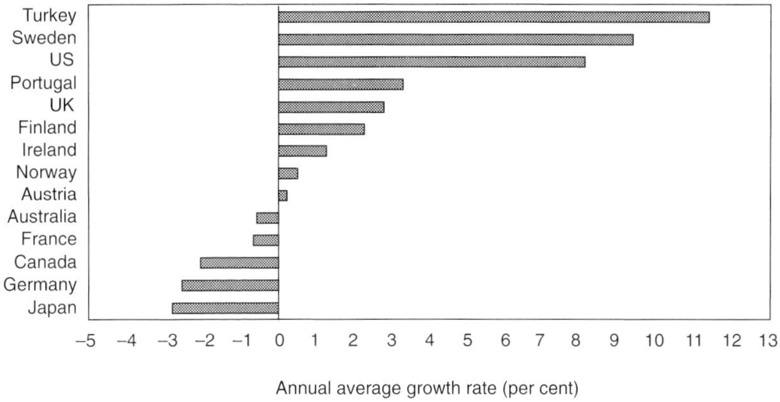

Figure 4.8b domestically owned firms,* average annual growth rate

(b)

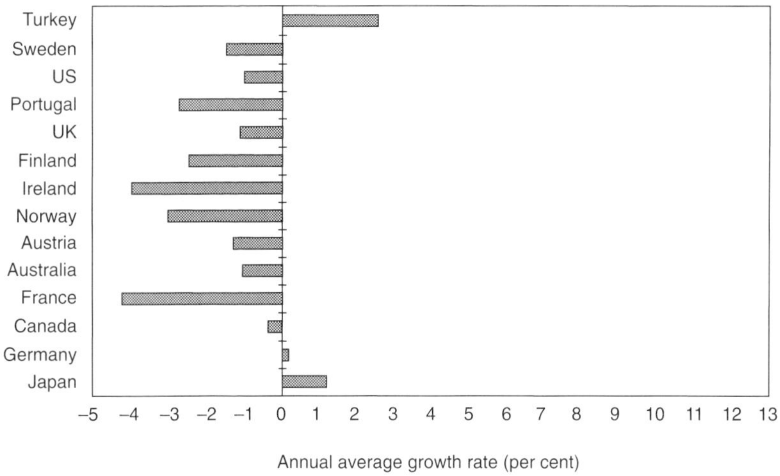

Notes:
* Total number of firms *minus* foreign affiliates.
The change is calculated over the period 1980–6 for Australia and Canada, 1983–8 for Ireland, 1981–4 for Portugal, 1985–90 for the United Kingdom and 1986–90 for Turkey.
Source: OECD, EAS Division, Industrial Activity of Foreign Affiliates data bank

Figure 4.9 Level of wages per employee of foreign affiliates in manufacturing industry, 1980–90
National Firms = 100

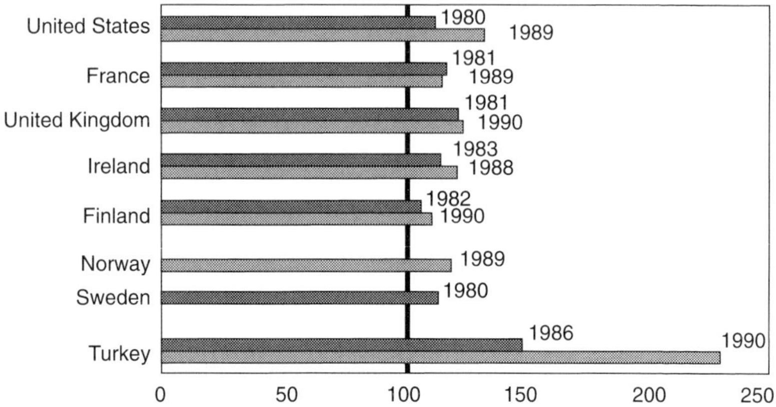

Source: OECD, EAS Division, Industrial Activity of Foreign Affiliates data bank.

Table 4.6 Labour productivity of foreign affiliates in manufacturing industry, 1980–90

	Growth rate 1980–1990 (1985 prices)		Level of foreign affiliates affiliates in 1990 (when level in domestic firms = 100)
	Foreign affiliates	Domestic firms	
United States	4.0	–	–
Japan	0.2	4.1	210
Germany	2.7	2.2	197
France[a]	1.2	3.7	127
United Kingdom[b]	5.3	2.7	173
Finland	5.0	3.7	90
Ireland[c]	6.9	4.8	153
Norway	1.9	5.2	144
Sweden	10.8	3.8	109

[a] 1980–9.
[b] 1985–90.
[c] 1983–8.
Source: OECD, EAS Division, Industrial Activity of Foreign Affiliates data bank.

Foreign-owned companies in Britain pay higher average wages than British-owned companies, but Figure 4.9 shows that the same is true of the United States where foreign-owned companies pay about 30 per cent more, France where they pay 10 per cent more, Ireland where they pay 15 per cent more, Finland where they pay 7 per cent more, Norway and Sweden where they pay 10–12 per cent more and Turkey where they pay 130 per cent more. In Britain in 1990, foreign-owned manufacturing companies paid wages which were about 20 per cent higher on average than those paid by British-owned manufacturers. In Britain and in several of the other countries, the margin by which the wages paid by foreign-owned companies exceed those paid by domestically-owned producers widened, which suggests that their competitive advantage was growing. In every case, the presence of foreign-owned companies was beneficial for pay.

They were able to pay higher wages because, in most cases, their productivity was higher. The information the OECD presented found that in 1990 foreign-owned affiliates had a 73 per cent productivity advantage in the United Kingdom, a 97 per cent advantage in Germany and a 27 per cent advantage in France (Table 4.6). The United Kingdom data presented in Table 4.2 (p. 77), derived from the 1992 CSO Census of Production, shows an advantage of 40 per cent against the OECD's 70 per cent, but both sets of statistics find that foreign-owned manufacturers achieved far higher productivity. They also achieved faster growth in productivity in Germany, the United Kingdom (where British-owned companies achieved 2.7 per cent productivity growth and foreign-owned companies 5.3 per cent), Finland, Ireland and Sweden.

The international evidence indicates that British experience was similar to that of other leading economies. Companies with something special to contribute produce in several countries and they raise productivity, employment, wages and investment wherever they produce.

Britain's competitiveness as a base for international production

The countries which have succeeded in attracting multinational companies have gained substantially and since the Second World War Britain has been more successful in attracting the investment of the world's technological leaders, Japan and the United States, than either France or Germany. 40 per cent of the Japanese and the United States investment which has come to Europe has come to Britain, and there are several reasons why the United Kingdom has been especially successful in attracting this.

First, and most obviously, English is the first or second language throughout most of the world, and this is of great advantage to the executives who live and work in the countries in which they invest. But Britain has also had the advantage that its labour costs have been far lower than those in France and Germany (Figure 4.10), including labour with specific computer and IT skills (Table 4.5, p. 81).

Taxation has also been far lower in Britain. (Table 3.3 on p. 68 above and Figure 4.11). In 1997, the current receipts of general government, virtually all taxes *plus* social security contributions, were 39.0 per cent of GDP in the United Kingdom and averaged 45.9 per cent in the European Union. The overall tax advantage of producing in Britain therefore averaged nearly 7 per cent of GDP. Tax receipts totalled 45.1 per cent of GDP in Germany, 6.1 percentage points more than in

Figure 4.10 Hourly labour costs for production workers in manufacturing industry in 1993

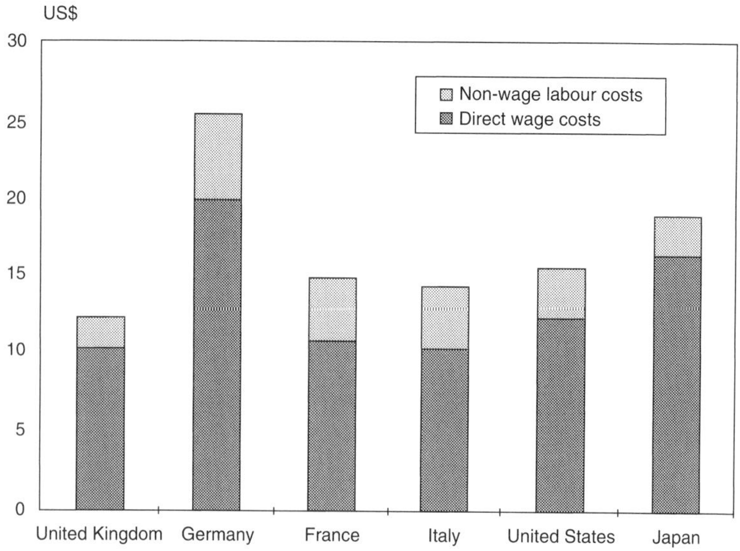

Note: Measured at 1993 market exchange rates.
Source: US BoL.

Figure 4.11 Total taxes on business as a proportion of GDP in 1992

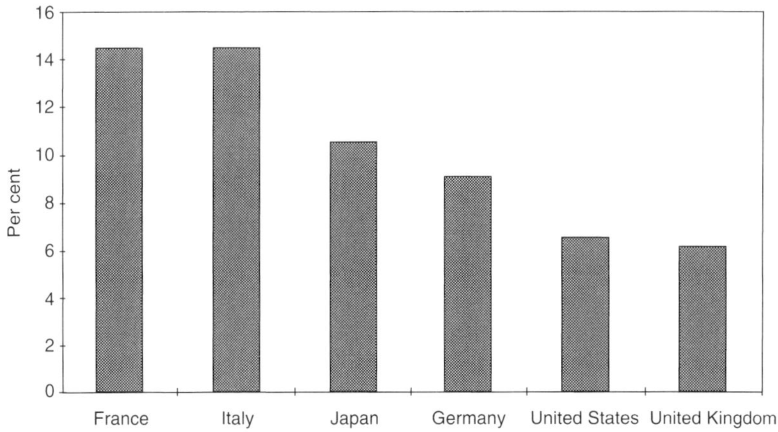

Note: Taxes on business defined as corporation tax, payroll taxes and employers' social security contributions.
Source: OECD.

Britain, and 50.3 per cent in France, 11.3 percentage points more than in Britain. Many of the higher taxes in France and Germany fall directly on business, and Figure 4.11 shows that in 1992 business taxes averaged about 14 per cent of GDP in France, 9 per cent in Germany and 7 per cent in Britain.

An additional advantage which Britain has offered has been the lowest telecommunications costs in Europe: these were at about two-thirds of the French level and half the German level in 1994 (Figure 4.12). Telecommunications have become highly competitive in Britain while monopolistic producers are still protected in France and Germany. This is another area where those with the specific skills required are available in Britain and far cheaper to employ than in France or Germany.

A further advantage Britain enjoys as a magnet for international investment is the way in which this has enjoyed the total support of government. The advantages of international investment have been entirely understood in Britain, all barriers have been removed, and those who lead foreign companies have been in no doubt that their presence in Britain will be welcome, and that British-owned companies would at no point receive preference in the awarding of government

Figure 4.12 Telecommunications costs in the European Union in 1994

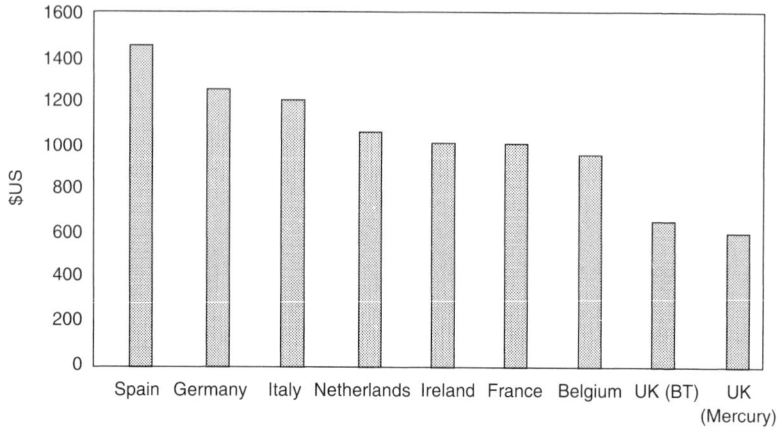

Source: Tarifica 1994, as per Invest in Britain Bureau, *Britain the Preferred Location*, (2nd edn).

contracts or in any other way. Britain has a tradition of transparent administration, and it has provided an excellent and attractive environment for international companies.

Inward investors also speak of Britain's world-class scientific base, its regulatory regime which has encouraged innovation, making Britain a centre for high-technology industries such as pharmaceuticals and biotechnology, its now excellent labour relations, and its cultural heritage which makes Britain an attractive place in which to live and work.[2]

Doubts have been expressed as to whether Britain will continue to be a magnet for international investment if it remains outside EMU. The *Financial Times* commissioned a poll from MORI prior to the November 1998 CBI Conference in which 753 companies were questioned. This included the question:

> If the UK decides not to join the euro for the foreseeable future, do you think that it will make your company more likely to invest in Britain, less likely, or that it will make no difference to your company's plans?

The responses of the 10 per cent of companies which were foreign-owned divided as follows:

	(per cent)
More likely	1
Less likely	11
Make no difference	86
Don't know	2

The overwhelming response that British non-membership of EMU would 'make no difference' underlines the significance of the fundemental factors which have been outlined, which have favoured overseas direct investment in the United Kingdom in comparison with the other leading European economies.

There have been a variety of reasons why the United Kingdom has been the most attractive base in Europe for international capital, and why a high fraction of US and Japanese companies which wish to produce and sell in the EU's single market have chosen Britain as their productive base. These will survive Britain's EMU decision.

The long-term implications of foreign direct investment

Up to now the impact of foreign direct investment has been described as unambiguously favourable to the host country, with the result that Britain has apparently benefited more than any other leading European economy. Is this indeed what economic theory indicates, and if Britain is benefiting so greatly from inward investment, is the economic impact on the economy of its still greater outward investment similarly beneficial?

Economic theory suggests that anything which increases a country's capital stock in quantity or quality will have a favourable impact on the marginal productivity of labour, and that this will be associated with both higher real wages and higher employment. Britain's greater attractiveness to international capital should therefore have an unambiguously favourable long-term impact on workers' living standards and employment opportunities. It is possible to conjure up assumptions where the capital stock is increased in a peculiar way which reduces the demand for labour. David Ricardo and Karl Marx argued that this was a possibility in the books they published in 1821 and in 1867, but their arguments require very peculiar assumptions. Ricardo, for instance, arrives at the result that machinery will reduce the demand for labour only if its introduction *reduces* manufacturing output. Marx's conclusions require that capital expenditures grow far faster than the outputs they produce.[3] Late nineteenth- and twentieth-century economic development has not been associated with the far faster increases in capital than in output which Ricardo and Marx predicted. As a consequence, the economies with the highest investment have tended to be those with the fastest rates of increase in the demand for labour. It can therefore be concluded that inward investment which raises a country's capital stock will generally also raise real wages and the demand for labour, and by making employment more attractive, reduce an economy's equilibrium (or 'natural') rate of unemployment (NAIRU).

British trades unions have fully recognised the advantages of inward investment which they have warmly welcomed, and they have worked extremely well with the international companies which have come to Britain. They have especially supported Japanese and German companies, which have approaches to management and labour relations which involve more consultation than in many British-owned companies and less distance between managers and workers. Ford has been here so long that its managerial style and labour relations came to resemble those in the more conservatively managed British-owned motor vehicle manufacturers; its transformation in the late 1980s and the early 1990s may also owe something to the standards established by the new inward investors.

Japanese and German entrants have often preferred to locate in greenfield sites where there is no experience of the inefficient working practices which were allowed to become endemic in traditional manufacturing areas. The general reaction of British employees to inward investment has been extremely favourable, and most have wished that there was more of it, because it has been widely appreciated that it offers prospects of more jobs and better pay.

Economic theory predicts an entirely different outcome for the owners of British capital. It suggests that an increase in the capital stock will generally reduce the marginal product of capital, and therefore the profits of British-owned businesses which are likely to be adversely influenced by the entry of international capital. But this unfavourable prediction has not been borne out. Many UK producers, faced by competition from highly efficient international entrants (and Table 4.6 showed that inward investors generally produced with higher productivity) have been stimulated to raise their own productivity, and UK producers have learned work habits from inward investors which have proved extremely favourable. Many British-owned companies have benefited from the pressure to reduce what economists describe as their 'X-inefficiency', the extent to which their productivity falls short of best practice, and foreign-owned producers have often established new UK bench-marks. British producers used to utilise their resources less efficiently, but as a result of inward investment, they are now performing closer to their technical potential. Their workers have also learned much from the example of the inward investors, and appreciated that a similar level of performance by their own companies would produce higher pay. There are, of course, examples where inward investors damaged the relative profitability of British producers, cut their markets and forced some into bankruptcy.

Individual companies used to be irritated by government grants to potential inward investors to persuade them to come to Britain. They believed that as a consequence they would have to compete without government subsidy with newly subsidised foreign producers. In the 1980s government grants to inward investors were wholly phased out and only regional development grants remain, which are equally available to British-owned producers. While individual companies have opposed particular inward investments, there has been no significant tendency for British employer organisations to express any general hostility to the unambiguous welcome from successive governments for new inward investors. It may be that managements in general have appreciated the advantages from the wider establishment of best practice in Britain. In addition, so far as the performance of British capital depends on the overall success of the economy, managements have welcomed developments which offered so much to the balance of payments and to the general level of economic performance.

When I was Director General of the National Economic Development Office (NEDO) from 1988 to 1992, the 80 company chairmen and chief executives and the 400 directors of leading companies who served on the National Economic Develoment Council's industrial sector groups were profoundly concerned that the British economy as a whole should perform more effectively. There was an overwhelming realisation that the performance of British companies had to improve. As individuals they welcomed developments which offered new examples of best practice and strengthened the general performance of the British economy, even when in their capacity as directors of individual companies they faced stronger competition from new inward investors. Since Britain's workers fully recognised that they stood to gain from inward investment, while those who controlled British-owned companies did not oppose it, the case for attracting as much as possible has become uncontroversial.

In contrast, the level of outward investment which is far greater has proved controversial. In 1987–97 Britain spent far more on direct investment overseas than came into the country: £219.5 billion went out and £146.2 billion came in. (Table 4.1, p. 75) Whether this level of outward investment has been beneficial is the final question which will be considered.

Outward investment raises the capital stock and therefore employment, wages and profits overseas. It is sometimes suggested that if the same sums were invested here, British instead of foreign workers would benefit. Outward investment is therefore controversial and its merits are not always supported.

Overseas investment by multinational companies often serves precise business purposes such as producing closer to markets, and exploiting opportunities to mine raw materials and to manufacture necessary components. Many world-class companies seek to maintain a presence in every leading economy to enhance their international standing and their world-wide sales. Multinational companies hedge against exchange rate movements by producing components in currency areas where the majority of their final sales occur: aircraft manufacturers produce in North America to reduce the vulnerability of their final profits. International investment by British-owned companies is therefore often complementary to home investment and it enhances profits and employment at home as well as overseas. Outward investment exceeds inward investment for the Netherlands, Switzerland, France, Sweden, Italy, Germany, Spain and Japan as well as the United Kingdom (Figure 4.1, p. 76). It fell below inward investment only for the United States, which has a far larger and a more self-sufficient economy. The general economic tendency for the world's leading economies to have far more outward than inward direct investment reflects the general tendency for outward investment to be complementary to home production. If a preference for outward over domestic investment was a sign of economic weakness, then the evidence of Figure 4.1 would indicate that Japan, Germany and Switzerland have inefficient economies. Britain's tendency to have more outward than inward direct investment is entirely in line with the experience of other leading economies.

While outward investment is generally complementary to domestic investment, there is a well known line of argument which suggests that where foreign investment is a clear alternative or substitute for home investment, companies may choose to invest abroad when the benefits to the national income would be greater if they invested at home. Companies will invest overseas instead of at home if they expect to earn higher net-of-tax profits, so such decisions should always be in shareholders' interests. But if a British-owned company invests abroad, its contribution to the UK's national income will be limited to its profits net of all foreign taxes. If it invests at home the national income benefits to the extent of both its net of tax profits and, also, the taxes it pays to the British Exchequer. British taxes add to the national income and companies disregard this consideration when they decide where to invest. Hence a decision to invest abroad could be the right decision for a company's shareholders and the wrong decision for the aggregate incomes of the country's citizens. If governments could view such decisions in isolation, they might be tempted to restrain companies' decisions to invest overseas instead of at home.

But governments cannot 'cherry-pick' and encourage international investment when they judge it to be beneficial and stop it when they prefer home investment. Free international capital movements now generally prevail, so multinational companies produce in the areas of the world where they expect to earn the highest profits, and it is no longer possible for governments to tell them where they should invest. It is not even possible to oblige a British-owned company to maintain its headquarters in the United Kingdom. During the early 1990s Jardine Matheson decided to become a Bermuda- instead of a Hong Kong-based company because of what it then regarded as the political risks of remaining in Hong Kong. If British governments told companies with UK headquarters where they should invest then, like Jardine Matheson, they could decide to manage their UK activities from a Dutch or Swiss base, and gradually shift production out of the United Kingdom, if producing here became irksome. The world-class companies at the heart of some of Britain's most successful industries already produce in several countries, and they decide all the time where to expand and where to contract. It is precisely because British governments do not interfere in such decisions that so many maintain their headquarters in the United Kingdom.

Thus while outward investment will not always be as advantageous as equivalent investments at home, there is no possibility of intervention to persuade British-owned companies to exercise a bias in favour of investing in the United Kingdom. British governments can best bring this about by creating a business environment with low taxation and a minimum of regulation so that companies themselves choose to produce here. Creating conditions for business that are unpredictable is one of the greatest potential turn-offs to the international companies which are considering Britain as a productive base. Knowledge that governments will allow companies to make their own decisions without interference has been one of the strongest elements in the British strategy to encourage inward investment.

The world's leading governments have created conditions where capital can choose its country and companies can decide where they will produce. It is greatly to Britain's advantage that an attractive environment has been created for both UK companies and for international capital.

Notes

1. Cantwell and Hodson (1990), Table 5.20, p. 175.
2. These are outlined in HMSO (1995) Chapter 12.
3. I have analysed Ricardo's argument from the third edition of *Principles of Political Economy and Taxation* that the introduction of machinery may reduce employment and Marx's from *Das Kapital* in Eltis (1985).

Part II
Europe

5
Europe's Unemployment Crisis *

Introduction

Unemployment in the European Union averaged 9.4 per cent in May 1999 compared to 4.2 per cent in the United States and 4.7 per cent in Japan. It was 16.2 per cent in Spain, 12.0 per cent in Italy, 11.2 per cent in France and 10.5 per cent in Finland, and it exceeded 8 per cent in Belgium and Germany, which was far higher than in the United States and Japan. Why do most EU economies now have much higher unemployment than the United States and Japan?

There is a historical element in the explanation. In both Europe and the United States unemployment was driven upwards by the oil shocks of 1973–4 and 1977–8, but it then fell back in the United States but not in Europe (Figure 5.1). Monetary policy was governed by the independent central banks of Frankfurt and Washington, and neither permitted dearer oil to produce a sustained increase in inflation. The consequent monetary tightening brought inflation down to pre-oil price levels on both sides of the Atlantic and unemployment rose in consequence. Employment recovered in the United States, but not in Europe.

What needs to be explained is why European unemployment failed to come down again. After the oil shocks, European investment and growth, which were both higher than in the United States, astonishingly failed to generate any new jobs in the private sector (Figure 5.3). A 1993 statement from the European Commission (1993 p. 141) summarises Europe's comparative failure:[1]

---

* This is a revised and up-dated version of *European Competitiveness and Employment Generation* (European Policy Forum, 1995).

Figure 5.1 Unemployment rates in Europe, the United States and Japan, 1980–98

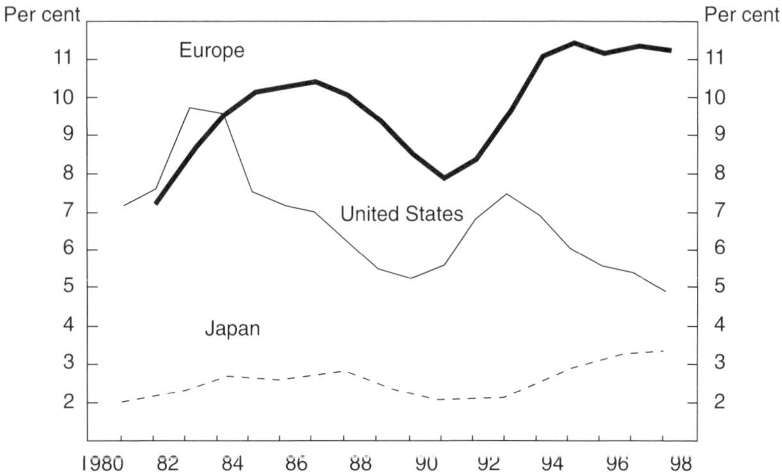

Source: OECD.

Figure 5.2 Employment participation rates in Europe, the United States and Japan, 1980–98

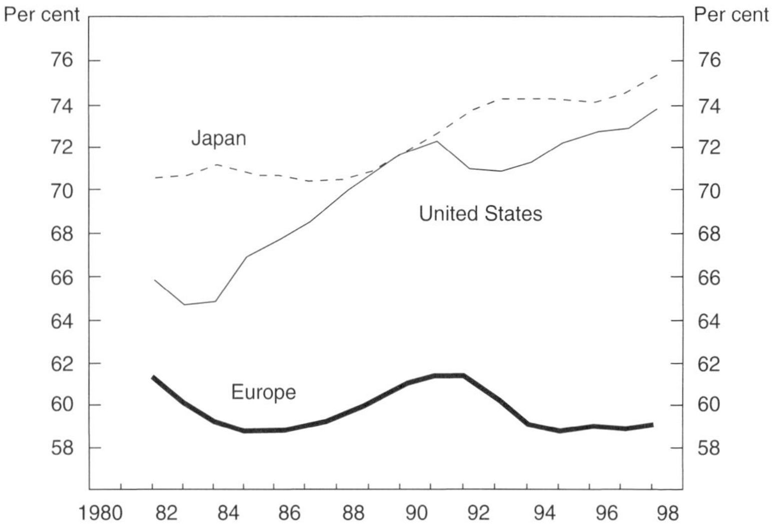

Source: OECD.

> Between 1970 and 1992, the US economy grew in real terms by 70% – somewhat less than Community growth of 81%. Yet employment in the USA rose by 49%, *compared with only 9% in the Community*. In Japan, where the economy grew by 173% from its 1970 level, employment grew by 25%.
>
> In most European countries the proceeds of economic growth have mainly been *absorbed by those who remained in employment*, and there is a large pool of unemployed who have been excluded.

Any solution of Europe's unemployment problem must now lie with Europe's private sectors because extra public sector jobs can be financed only through higher taxation or borrowing, and neither of these can be raised. Average taxation in the European Union is already higher than in Japan and the United States by more than 12 per cent of GDP, and the creation of a substantial number of additional public sector jobs would raise European taxation further if they were tax-financed. Additional taxes might fall on corporate profits and weaken the inducement to invest. Alternatively they might fall on the cost of employing labour, which would increase the labour-saving bias in new investment.[2] If extra taxation mainly fell on personal incomes, it would narrow the gap between the earnings of those at work and the levels of social benefit available to the unemployed, which would reduce the incentive to work and increase the equilibrium or 'natural' rate of unemployment (NAIRU).

If extra public sector jobs were financed by borrowing, European levels of public debt would rise further. These already averaged 77 per cent of GDP in the European Union as a whole in 1977, and therefore substantially exceeded the 60 per cent maximum agreed in the Maastricht Treaty. Still higher debt to GDP ratios would raise interest rates in Europe in relation to those in the United States and Japan which would add to the inability of Europe's private sectors to generate new employment.

Europe's only solution is to seek to re-create the conditions where widespread private sector job-creation used to occur. This would call for reductions in average levels of taxation towards the lower levels of the 1950s and 1960s and greater flexibility in Europe's labour markets. Europe, where (outside Scandinavia) less than 60 per cent of the population of working age is employed, makes far less use of the productive potential of its populations than either the United States or Japan where more than 70 per cent are in employment[3] (Figure 5.2). Europe needs to create conditions where the less talented and skilled can be more easily priced into the labour market.

Figure 5.3 Public and private sector employment creation, 1974–92

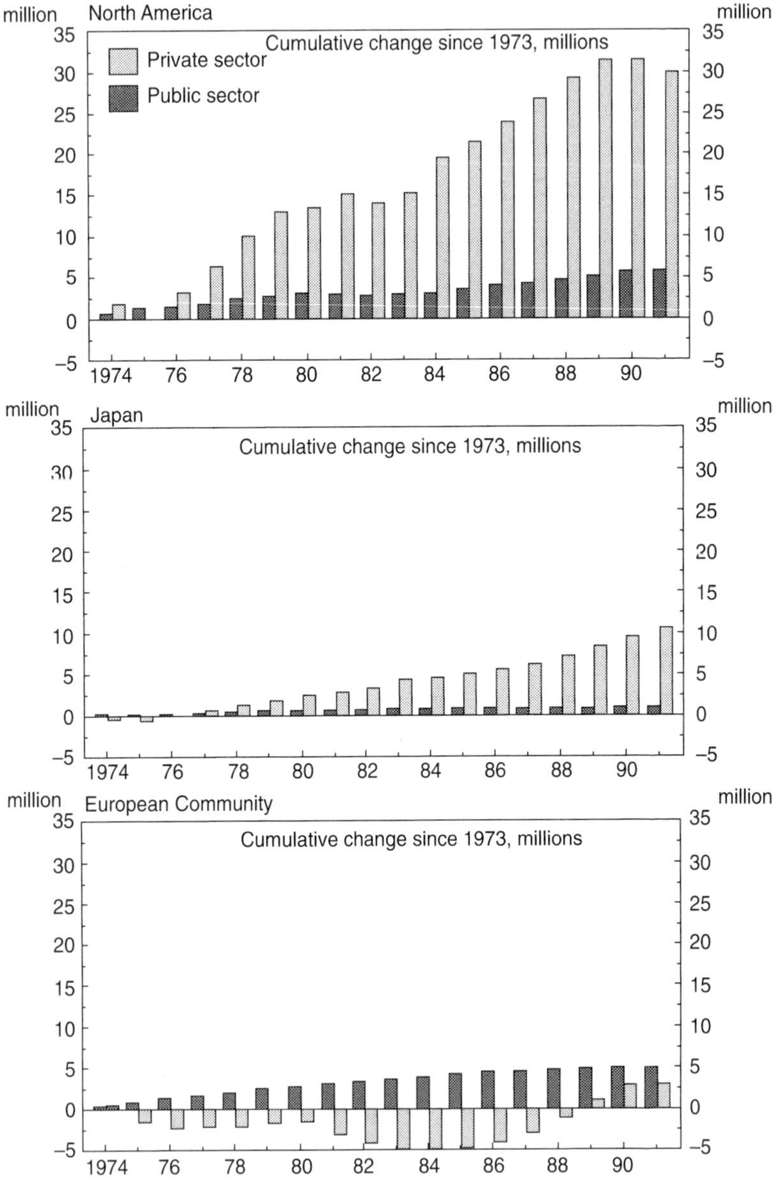

Source: OECD.

In 1993 the Commission addressed the causes of the continual rise in underlying European unemployment in its White Paper, *Growth, Competitiveness, Employment,* which the 1995 Commission updated and reviewed in *The European Employment Strategy: Recent Progress and Prospects for the Future.*

This opened with the statement that the European Union could create 11 million additional jobs by the year 2000 if it succeeded in achieving a rate of growth of 3–$3^1/_2$ per cent from 1995 to 2000. Growth in the European Union actually averaged 2.4 per cent from 1995 to 1998, with the result that underlying unemployment failed to fall. The average growth rate of the fifteen members has exceeded 3 per cent in only two of the eighteen years from 1980 to 1998, so the Commission's 1995 projection of 3–$3^1/_2$ per cent growth was heroically optimistic. The question Europe needs to address is why the growth rates it actually achieved, which are comparable to those of the United States, entirely failed to create private sector jobs.

The policies which the European Commission recommended for Europe in 1993 and in 1995 are very different from those which led to massive job creation in the United States. They will be examined in detail below. Before this, an account will be presented of the experience of one of the EU's newest members, Sweden, which pushed the European trends for increased spending on social welfare and on public sector job creation further than any other country. Its subsequent predicament shows what might occur in the rest of Europe if the trends to expand government expenditure which have been powerful in the last three decades are not halted and reversed. An account of the Swedish welfare model will therefore be presented to demonstrate the risks to Europe if its response to its present unemployment crisis becomes similar to the one which undermined the Swedish economy. Some of the European Commission's proposals repeat errors which produced great damage in Sweden. Their failure in Sweden underlines why they could do similar damage in the European Union as a whole.

The Swedish errors Europe must avoid

Until 1990, Sweden's unemployment rate was one of the lowest in the world, lower even than Japan's in all but three of the years between 1975 and 1990. In 1991 Swedish unemployment started to rise and in 1998 it reached 8 per cent. Sweden's public debt to GDP ratio soared from 44 to 77 per cent beween 1990 and 1998. From 1990 when its financial collapse began until 1998, its GDP rose only 8 per cent in comparison with increases of 15 per cent in the European Union and 21 per cent the United States.

In earlier decades the reaction of Swedish governments to unacceptable unemployment would have been additional public expenditure, but this was already at its political limits. General government outlays were boosted from 59 per cent of GDP in 1990 to 71 per cent in 1993 and even the 62 per cent to which this was reduced by 1997 was the highest in the European Union.

The assumptions on which Swedish economic policy used to be based were set out with great clarity by two Swedish economists, Hans Söderström and Staffan Viotti in 1979. The model they set out corresponds in several respects to the Bacon and Eltis model which we first set out in full in 1976,[4] and restated in Chapter 1 above.

Söderström and Viotti assumed that Swedish workers had the power to pass tax increases on in higher money wages in the annual wage negotiations which are a feature of Scandinavian wage bargaining. The private tradable sector of the Swedish economy could not pass these wage increases on in higher prices, because Sweden is a small open economy where its goods have to compete with foreign ones: at the time Söderström and Viotti wrote, the Krona was not devalued regularly as Swedish wages increased. Since the tradable sector had to pay higher wages whenever taxes were increased without being able to charge higher prices, it had to cut employment.

In Figure 5.4, the schedule *PP* shows the number of workers the private sector can employ at a profit. When the real cost of labour is *OW*, the workers who can be employed profitably are *ON*. After higher taxes which are passed on raise the real cost of labour to *OW′*, the workers who can be employed profitably fall to *ON′*. There is therefore a reduction in private sector employment which is shown on Figure 5.4 by *N′N*.

So the initial effect of higher social spending is to raise taxes, which go on to increase the real cost of labour which companies in the private sector have to meet, and this reduces the number of workers private sector companies can employ. Söderström and Viotti then go on to bring another element in the Swedish model into their argument. Since the publication of Keynes' *General Theory* in 1936 and the important contemporary work of distinguished Swedish economists, all political parties subscribed to an understanding that government had an obligation to act as employer of last resort. Anyone the tradable private sector could no longer employ therefore had to be found alter-

Figure 5.4 A higher cost of labour reduces private sector employment

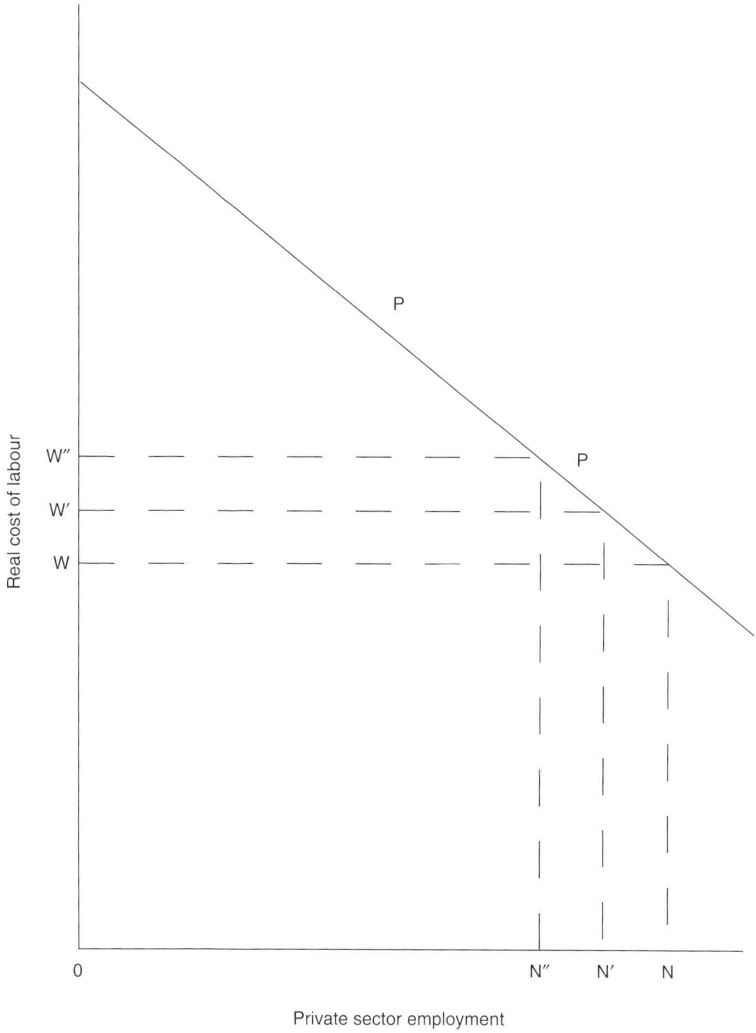

native work by the government. This forced up public expenditure and taxes yet again, and after workers had passed the extra taxes on, the real cost of labour rose above *W′* to *W″*. This reduced private sector employment further to *ON″*.

This additional reduction in private sector employment obliged governments to create still more public sector jobs which caused government expenditure to rise again. This caused a third increase in taxation, raised the real cost of labour a third time and the whole process was repeated, and continued to be repeated.

Robert Bacon and I outlined a similar process in the 'Declining Britain' articles which we published in *The Sunday Times* in November 1975, developed in *Britain's Economic Problem: Too Few Producers* in March 1976, and restated in Chapter 1 of this volume.

The more detailed Söderström–Viotti statement of the same dynamic process has been present in the Swedish economy and it has produced successive escalations in taxation and a continual decline in employment in the private tradable sector of the economy. The maintenance of full employment in Sweden involved ever-rising public expenditure and a continual increase in the ratio of public to private sector employment.

Figure 5.5 shows the extent to which this has actually occurred. In 1975 the United Kingdom, Germany and Sweden had similar ratios of general government expenditure in GDP. Since then both the leading political parties in the United Kingdom have abandoned the assumption that the government has an obligation to act as employer of last resort. British unemployment was less than 3 per cent of the labour force in 1975 but the inflation rate was 24 per cent and the budget deficit 10 per cent of GDP so British policy had to change and in 1976 James Callaghan, Harold Wilson's successor as Prime Minister made his famous statement (supposedly drafted by Peter Jay, then Economic Editor of *The Times*) that:

> We used to think that you could spend your way out of a recession and increase employment by cutting taxes and boosting government spending. I tell you in all candour that the option no longer exists, and that in so far as it ever did exist, it only worked on each occasion since the war by injecting a bigger dose of inflation into the economy, followed by a higher level of unemployment as the next step.[5]

Margaret Thatcher, who succeeded Callaghan as Prime Minister in May 1979, had already said on 15 September 1975 as Leader of the Opposition that:

> The private sector creates the goods and services we need both to export to pay for our imports and to provide the revenue to finance

Figure 5.5 Ratio of government outlays to GDP in the UK, Germany and Sweden, 1965–93

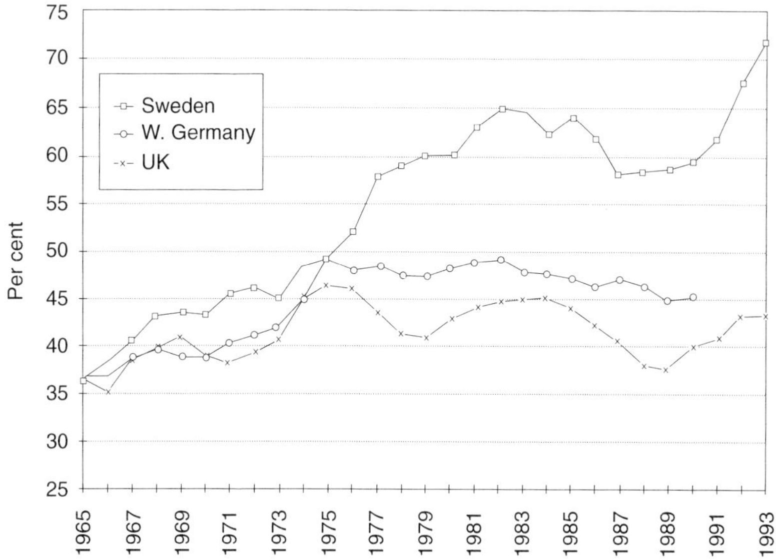

Source: 1978–93, *OECD Economic Outlook*, December 1994; 1965–77, *Economic Outlook*, December 1991 and earlier issues.

public services. So one must not overload it. Every man switched away from industry and into government will reduce the productive sector and increase the burden on it at the same time.

Therefore in 1975 and in 1976 the leaders of both the principal British governing parties adopted policy approaches which precluded further increases in government expenditure and public sector employment. Figure 5.5 shows how after 1975 the trend in UK public expenditure ratio has been downwards although it rose for well known cyclical reasons in the recessions of the early 1980s and the early 1990s.

Germany's public expenditure ratio fell after 1975 until the extra costs of reunification raised it by 4 percentage points from 1990 to 1994, with the consequence that in 1997 it had returned to its 1975 level. Because there have been no overall expenditure cuts comparable to those in Britain, German general government expenditure was $5^1/_2$ percentage points above the British ratio in 1997. Reunification raised taxation in the former West Germany and some of the extra taxes may have been passed on and reduced private sector employment in the Swedish manner.

Figure 5.5 shows how, from 1975 until 1983, the Swedish public expenditure ratio soared out of control as the government continued to act as employer of last resort in the manner which Söderström and Viotti predicted. Figure 5.6 shows how the continuation of that policy approach raised Sweden's ratio of public to private sector employment from 53 per cent in 1975 to a peak of 75 per cent in 1983, and in 1993 it was still 73 per cent. In Britain, the ratio of public to private sector employment peaked at 41 per cent in 1975 and fell back to 30 per cent by 1993, mainly as a consequence of the privatisation of several state-owned industries.

The relentless increase in Sweden's public expenditure from 36 per cent of GDP in 1965 to 43 per cent in 1970, 49 per cent in 1975, 60 per cent in 1980 and 64 per cent in 1985, after which the economic and political model broke down and public expenditure was cut for a few years, before it was allowed to rise further to 71 per cent, underlines that a persistent process was at work. This raised the public expendi-

Figure 5.6 Ratio of Public to private employment in the UK and Sweden, 1965–93

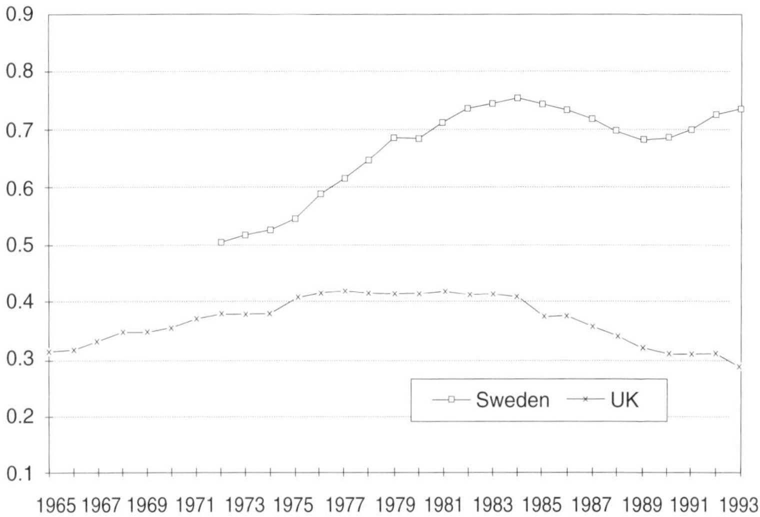

Sources: *Statistical Abstract of Sweden* and *UK National Income and Expenditure*.

ture ratio by between 4 and 11 percentage points every five years, with an average increase of 5 percentage points in a half-decade. The Söderström–Viotti formulation which is close to the Bacon–Eltis one of 1975–6 predicts precisely that outcome.

There is the same three-stage progression that we set out in the appendix to Chapter 1:

(i) *Tax increases are passed on and raise the cost of labour* If we assume, as in Sweden when taxation peaked in the mid-1980s and the model broke down, that employer and employee taxes together average approximately two-thirds of the cost of labour, and taxes are raised by 1 per cent of the cost of labour, the full passing on of that 1 per cent of extra taxation would actually raise the cost of labour 3 per cent.

An example can illustrate that surprising proposition. If labour costs per head are initially 300 Krona, of which employer and employee taxes are 200 Krona, an employee actually receives 100 Krona net of tax. If taxes are then increased by 1 per cent of total labour costs – that is, by 3 Krona per worker, and workers – themselves bear the full increase in taxation, employees will receive 97 Krona in place of the former 100 so their real living standards will fall 3 per cent. If they then obtain a *real* pay increase of 3 per cent, this will restore their real *net-of-tax* incomes to their former level.

It is interesting that in 1979 when Sweden's ratio of taxation to GDP was 60 per cent, Assar Lindbeck actually said that Swedish workers required a pay increase of between 2 and 3 per cent to compensate for an increase in the ratio of taxation in the national income of 1 per cent.[6]

If alternatively only two-thirds of employer and employee taxes are passed on when the ratio of taxation in GDP is 67 per cent, an increase in taxation by 1 per cent of GDP would raise the real cost of labour 2 per cent instead of 3 per cent.

(ii) *A higher cost of labour reduces private sector employment* If labour is more expensive, capital will be substituted for it. A 1 per cent increase in the real cost of labour reduces the amount of labour used to produce an unchanged output by between $^1/_2$ and 1 per cent or by perhaps something like 0.67 per cent.[7] Hence with the peak Swedish tax ratio of 67 per cent where an increase in taxation of 1 per cent of GDP raised the real cost of labour by around 2 per cent, private sector employment could be expected to fall by two-thirds of that, or by about 1.33 per cent.

(iii) *A reduction in private sector employment will cause government to create extra tax-financed public sector jobs which will force taxation up further* A 1.33 per cent fall in private sector employment would reduce the economy's tax base by less than 1.33 per cent because the marginal workers squeezed out will have a level of productivity which is less than the average productivity of the whole labour force. If their productivity is three-quarters of the average, the 1.33 per cent fall in Swedish private sector employment consequent on the 1 per cent (of GDP) increase in taxation would go on to reduce the Swedish economy's tax base by three-quarters of that, or by 1 per cent of GDP. Public sector employment which has to be financed through taxation would then have to be substituted for the jobs lost in the private sector. If the newly employed public sector workers were paid at the same rate as those in the jobs in the private sector which were replaced, and equipped with capital of equivalent cost, total employment and total pay in the economy would be unchanged, but 1 per cent less of the economy would be tax-paying so the level of taxation on the diminished tax-paying fraction that remained would need to rise by 1 per cent of GDP, the same as the increase in taxation which initiated the process.

The sequence of ever-rising taxation

With these estimates, which are intended to represent the peak Swedish predicament in the mid-1980s, an initial increase in taxation of 1 per cent of GDP would go on to force taxation up by a further 1 per cent of GDP. The same process would then be repeated. The second increase in taxation by 1 per cent of GDP would again raise the cost of labour, reduce private sector employment and oblige the government to produce equivalent extra public sector jobs because of its obligation to act as employer of last resort. This second increase in taxation would lead to a third and taxation would continue to increase by 1 per cent of GDP in each successive cycle: taxation would increase indefinitely and private sector employment would fall indefinitely.

With different assumptions, each Söderström–Viotti/Bacon–Eltis cycle could be less severe than the one before. If the series opened with the 50 per cent tax ratio of France or Germany, and workers succeeded in passing on only one-half of tax increases because trade unions were weaker there than in Sweden, the initial 1 per cent increase in taxation would raise the real cost of labour 1 per cent instead of 2 per cent, which would go on to cut private sector employment by two-thirds of this, or by $^2/_3$ per cent. That would cut the tax base by three-quarters of this or by just $^1/_2$ per cent instead of by the full 1 per cent of the Swedish cycle at its peak. With these weaker assumptions therefore, the Söderström–Viotti/Bacon–Eltis sequence would produce a second cycle which was half as severe as the first, a third cycle which was half as severe as the second and eventual total tax increases which were only twice the initial increase. The sequence of cycles could also be explosive, with each tax increase and employment reduction larger than the one before.[8]

In 1965, when the process began, Sweden's tax ratio was only 36 per cent of GDP, and the Söderström–Viotti/Bacon–Eltis sequence will certainly have been damped. Other considerations will have played a part in the relentless increase of Swedish public expenditure and taxation. By 1980 the cycle may well have become strong enough to almost repeat itself and this process alone will have sufficed to give a constant momentum to the upward trend in Swedish public expenditure and taxation. From this point onwards no further government decisions of any kind will have been needed to set Swedish public expenditure and taxation on a relentless upward course.

By the mid-1980s the situation had become intolerable, and Sweden first abandoned the balanced budget policy which had obliged governments to raise taxation in line with public expenditure. In 1990 it could no longer persist with the principle that the government would act as employer of last resort, with the result that Sweden then abandoned full employment. In consequence by 1998 its unemployment had risen to a level close to the EU average. At the same time its small, weak and unprofitable private sector lost the power to create new employment. The 25 largest Swedish-owned companies employ only 25 per cent of their labour in Sweden. By 1995, three-quarters of their employment and production had moved away from Sweden, largely because taxation of every kind was lower elsewhere.[9]

The impact over decades of the Söderström–Viotti/Bacon–Eltis cycle explains much of Sweden's regress to an unsustainable economy by the mid-1980s. Its private sector (with many of its most efficient companies largely producing overseas) could no longer provide a sufficient level of employment to sustain the standard of living in the form of public and private consumption to which its population had become accustomed.

The experience of Sweden is an object lesson for the countries which currently have 50 per cent public expenditure ratios and which will drift in a similar direction if their political majorities begin to expect the state to act as employer of last resort. The European Commission is well aware of Sweden's example, and there are powerful passages in the 1993 White Paper which speak of the need to hold taxation and social costs down. But there are other passages which call for large increases in European public expenditure. The European Commission's 1993 and 1995 analyses of Europe's unemployment will now be examined, including tensions between exhortations to prevent further increases in taxation and detailed proposals for a variety of additional expenditures.

The Commission's analysis of European employment

The European Commission's 1993 White Paper includes several powerful passages which underline the damage caused by Europe's comparatively high levels of taxation and social expenditure, and how these undermine Europe's private sectors' potential to create employment. For instance (p. 152):

> Between 1970 and 1991 statutory charges [the sum of taxes and obligatory social security contributions] rose in the Community from 34 to 40% of GDP. Over the same period they remained stable in the United States of America, at slightly below 30%. In Japan, statutory charges have increase appreciably since 1980 but in 1991 stood at 31% of GDP, i.e. the same level as in the USA and a quarter lower than the average level recorded in the European Union.

By 1993 general government receipts in the fifteen countries of the present European Union averaged 47.2 per cent of GDP while in Japan and the United States the ratios were still far lower at 33.3 and 31.6 per cent of GDP. Britain's ratio was 35.8 per cent, 11.4 percentage points below the EU average and only slightly higher than taxation in Japan and the United States. The Commission stated unequivocally that Europe's higher levels of public expenditure and taxation had damaged employment (p. 54):

> The current levels of public expenditure, particularly in the social field, have become unsustainable and have used up resources which could have been channelled into productive investment. They have pushed up the taxation of labour and increased the cost of money. At the same time, the constant rise in the labour cost – affecting

> both its wage and non-wage components and caused, at least in part, by excessively rigid regulation – has hindered job creation. As a result, the level of long-term investment has fallen and the lack of confidence among those involved in the economic process has caused demand to contract.

The 1995 Progress Report reiterated (p. 51) this concern:

> Financing a developed social protection system has been one of the reasons behind the growing financial needs of the public sector. Meeting these extra needs of public receipts has resulted in an increased overall tax wedge on labour's income.

The 1993 Commission's White Paper even had passages which contained a good deal of the Söderström–Viotti/Bacon–Eltis hypothesis of a vicious circle in which rising public expenditure and consequent tax increases diminish the tax-paying private sector, thus reducing the tax base, and forcing still greater tax increases on the declining fraction of the private sector that survives (p. 154).

> The high level of non-wage labour costs is prejudicial to employment, exerting a dissuasive influence: it encourages the substitution of capital for labour and promotes the parallel economy; it particularly affects employment in Small and Medium Enterprises; finally, it leads to relocation of investment or activities.
>
> Faced with inadequate demand, firms attempt first and foremost to reduce their costs by laying off workers, labour being the adjustment variable. The rise in unemployment pushes up contributions and reduces the number of contributors: labour costs increase, and so forth; and a kind of vicious circle is established. A firm which, by laying off workers, reduces its own costs also passes on the cost of unemployment to other firms in industries which cannot lay off workers as easily, and they too see their situation deteriorate.
>
> **Highly labour-intensive firms**, whose labour costs and social security budgets are relatively high, are then in turn compelled to lay off workers, to relocate or to resort to the underground economy, either directly or through subcontracting.

The European Commission's vicious circle is weaker than the one outlined to represent the Swedish case because it is initiated only by non-wage labour costs instead of by the taxes paid by both employers and employees since both may be passed on. The Commission also assumes that workers who lose their private sector jobs become unemployed and/or join the 'black economy', which the Commission estimated at 5–20 per cent of Europe's GDP and which the legal sector even subcontracted from. In the Söderström–Viotti/Bacon–Eltis vicious circle, those who lose employment in the private sector are re-employed in an expanding public sector which is fiscally more expensive than financing their unemployment through the state which increases the possibility that the vicious circle will be explosive. Unemployment benefits average about 70 per cent of earnings at work in the European Union, so paying these in place of a full wage to workers in extra tax-financed jobs which are created for the unemployed dampens the extent of each successive complete cycle of job loss, and consequently increased taxation, by about one-third.

But these powerful passages by the Commission were not matched by specific proposals to bring European public expenditure down towards the far lower levels of the United States and Japan. Instead, there were a number of proposals which would have increased European public expenditure.

The Commission recommended that, over six years, Europe should invest ECU 220 billion (now 220 billion Euros) in new trans-European transport and energy projects, ECU 150 billion in telecommunications information highways, and ECU 174 billion on large environmental projects, or ECU 534 billion in all on infrastructure investments (that is approximately £350 billion, or $568 billion, in September 1999 exchange rates). It believed that so far as possible these should be financed by private investors through European capital markets, but that the Commission should be prepared to support these projects through loan guarantees, interest rate subsidies, and the provision of a new facility of 'Union Bonds' (p. 34):

> 'Union Bonds' for growth would be issued on tap by the Union for long maturities to promote major infrastructure projects of strategic interest covering the trans-European networks plus cross-border projects with EFTA, Central and Eastern Europe and North Africa. The beneficiaries would be project promoters (public sector agencies, private companies) directly involved in the trans-European networks. The European Investment Bank would be invited to appraise and advise the Commission ... and act as agent for individual loan contracts.

In addition, a European Investment Fund (EIF) would be established which would guarantee the interest of loans of long maturities issued by the private or public companies promoting a project. In return for these guarantees, the loans would have a convertible facility, so in the case of commercially successfully projects, the European Investment Fund would acquire an equity stake.

The Commission wrote: 'The new instruments are needed for projects specifically included in the Master Plans' [*sic*] and complement the lending of the European Investment Bank, which is more general. The European Investment Bank would itself make loans as it already has for the Channel Tunnel a highly important trans-European project.

These new expenditures and loan guarantees would need to be provided through borrowing by the European Commission, something it was not allowed to do in 1993 and which is still outside its competence in 1999. An indication of the possible outcome of many of the projects in the 'Master Plans' can be judged from the financial progress of the Channel Tunnel, a magnificently engineered trans-European project where the promoters have ceased to pay interest on their £8 billion debt which includes almost ECU 1 billion (now £640 million) it owes to the European Investment Bank.

Capital projects which do not cover their costs are as much a drain on European government finances as current expenditures, and they will ultimately have to be financed from taxation levied by European governments. The proposed trans-European networks are described in detail in the 1993 White Paper, and the 1995 Progress Report (p. 16) recommended the acceleration of their 'realisation'.

The Commission also wished Europe to spend considerably more on social welfare (pp. 15–16):

> If only one proof were needed that our economies have not yet reached maturity and that there are still needs to be met it would be the existence in Europe of some 50 million people below the poverty line ... We need a comprehensive policy, preventive as well as remedial, to combat the poverty which so degrades men and women and splits society in two. The areas of action are familiar: renovation of stricken urban areas, construction of subsidized housing, adaption of education systems with extra resources for children from disadvantaged backgrounds, and an active employment policy which attaches high priority to the search for an activity or training accessible to everyone.

These are admirable Swedish policies and, as in Sweden, they can become very expensive. The adoption of humane social policies always calls for increased expenditures.

The Commission said much about the potential for employment creation through industrial policy. An interesting example concerned its analysis of the Audiovisual sector (pp. 119–20). While the European market has been 'among the fastest growing in the world', it emerges that the United States has 'benefited most from growth in Europe increasing its sales of programming in Europe from $330 million in 1984 to $3.6 billion in 1992. In 1991, 77 per cent of American exports of audiovisual programmes went to Europe', nearly 60 per cent to the Community. The EU's annual deficit with the United States in audiovisual trade was $3.5 billion in 1993. The Commission predicts that the growth of the audiovisual sector will accelerate, and that if, 'the growth is translated into jobs in Europe and not into financial transfers from Europe to other parts of the world':

> job creation could be of the order of 2 million by the year 2000, if current conditions prevail. Furthermore, bearing in mind that, if proper resources are deployed, there is a clear potential ... for an increase in our share of the market, it is not unrealistic to estimate that the audovisual services sector could provide jobs, directly or indirectly, to four million people.

The Commission emphasised that:

> The sector intrinsically provides many high-level 'grey-matter' jobs, like technicians, performers, script-writers, directors, and so on. It is thus potentially less vulnerable to competition from low labour cost markets.

The Commission concluded:

> It is vital that the predicted growth in the European audiovisual market be translated into jobs in Europe. Given the intrinsic nature of audiovisual products (i.e that they need to be amortized on large domestic markets) concerted national policies at Community level are needed to achieve this objective. The aim must be to establish a growth–employment relationship that is positive within the European audiovisual sector and to prevent increasing resources from being diverted to job creation in other parts of the world, with

> Europe becoming a passive consumer of other countries' audiovisual products and with both its economy and culture depending on others.

So European money would be deployed to protect European culture and employment.

The Commission had a number of proposals which would have involved increased public expenditure and therefore higher taxation, but at the same time it argued strongly that Europe's private sectors would benefit from lower taxation, though because of its proposals to increase public expenditure it could not propose clear tax reductions. Its final chapters therefore focused on proposals to switch away from taxes which reduced employment to those which might increase it. The Commission's object was to find a new tax structure which would raise the same revenue, and damage employment less.

It found that switching from taxes on employment to higher value-added taxes would have a neutral impact on employment. Its recommendation of a policy switch which could raise employment was consequently the replacement of part of the employment taxes paid by employers with a new carbon tax on energy. The Commission believed that this would simultaneously reduce pollution, protect the environment, preserve energy supplies for the future, and encourage the development of European energy-saving and environment-protecting technologies.

In the Commission's proposed example (which it repeated unamended in the 1995 Progress Report (pp. 22, 34)) employment taxes paid by employers were reduced by 1 per cent of GDP with the reduction concentrated on the low paid: their employment taxes were supposedly reduced by four-tenths. Equivalent tax revenues were to be found from a new CO_2/energy tax of $10 a barrel. On the basis of economic modelling, the Commission concluded that if the revenues which resulted from the consequent increase in European growth were all invested in employment creation, European employment could be increased by almost 3 percentage points, and the European unemployment rate reduced by 2.7 percentage points.

If the huge carbon tax was solely imposed on Europe's consumers (as implied in the calculations on p. 158) the cost of electric light and heating to Europe's families (apart from the minority, mainly French, who rely on nuclear energy) would rise and the impact of this would be regressive. The rich spend a lower fraction of their incomes on light and heating than the poor, so the tax would hit the poorest most. In the United Kingdom it created a political storm in 1992–3 when the government attempted to impose a value-added tax of 8 per cent followed by one of $17^1/_2$ per cent on domestic electricity and home heating; John Major's government failed to get this $17^1/_2$ per cent proposal through the House of Commons, and had to substitute extra taxes on alcohol and tobacco. Consumers would react similarly in the rest of Europe if governments sought to implement the Commission's 1993 and 1995 proposals of the far larger tax, a $10 levy on a barrel of oil equivalent on all European families.

If such an 'energy tax', as most would call it, was imposed instead on Europe's producers it would especially damage the energy-intensive industries headed by chemicals and steel, where energy costs can be as high as one-quarter of total costs. To attempt to solve Europe's unemployment problem by imposing a massive new tax on fuels which constitute up to one-quarter of the costs of Europe's steel and chemical industries would be a remarkable proposal, and the Commission nowhere estimated how many jobs would be destroyed in Europe's energy-using industries by an energy tax which fell on producers.

It avoided having to make such calculations because it assumed that consumers would pay its proposed carbon tax, but Swedish experience and the Swedish model suggest that a considerable fraction of extra taxes which reduce workers' living standards will be passed on. Real industrial and commercial costs will increase throughout Europe if a heavy new tax is imposed on consumers which workers then succeed in passing on. That would increase the cost of labour and go on to reduce private sector employment in the manner of the Söderström–Viotti/Bacon–Eltis model. The Commission nowhere considered the possibility that employees might pass the $10 a barrel carbon tax on if their families were expected to pay it. Up to now, Europe's governments have entirely ignored this central proposal in the Commission White Paper which their parliaments, like the British Parliament, might reject. The 1995 Commission actually singled out the United Kingdom Government for praise because (p. 33), 'VAT is now levied on energy ... coupled with a reduction in employers' social security contributions'. No other country has moved in any way in the direction it recommended, but the formation in 1998 of a German government which includes the Greens may lead to a renewed advocacy of European energy taxes.

Other proposals such as work-spreading by reducing hours of work are equally vulnerable to passing-on effects. Europe's workers would seek to maintain their living standards so they would expect to be paid the same for a 35-hour week as for a 38- or 40-hour week. That would raise real costs of production in Europe's private sectors, and go on to cut employment and increase the number of workers Europe's governments had to support through either government-funded jobs or unemployment benefits, as in Sweden.

The European Commission acknowledged that Europe's high structural unemployment, far greater than in the United States or Japan, was increased by a variety of labour market rigidities. Youth unemployment was raised by minimum wage regulations, there was a lower participation of women because they could not work part-time in several countries: in the 1995 Progress Report priority was attached to encouraging greater part-time employment, but it was emphasised (p. 31) that 'more flexible working conditions may not, however, be achieved at the expense of the level of social protection of workers'. Europe also has higher long-term unemployment because of its comparatively high and longer-lasting unemployment benefits: in the 1995 Progress Report the Commission recommended their review by each country.

The Commission baulked at the policies which would remove most rigidities because of the increasing social inequality which would result. It remarked (pp. 55–6):

> the Community's economy, with the exception of the period 1986–90, has always been characterized by low employment creation ... the origin of its unemployment problems go back to the beginning of the 1970s, when it proved unable to increase its rate of job creation to match the increase in the number of people seeking employment.
>
> By contrast, the USA has been able to respond to an even larger increase in the number of people looking for jobs with a strong increase in employment creation. Japan has also managed to increase its rate of job creation. The increase was less substantial than that recorded in the USA, but was more or less in line with the rate of increase in the country's active population.

But the Commission considered seeking to emulate the United States by achieving a greater 'employment intensity of growth' and rejected that approach, because it would require, 'the implementation, on a large scale, of measures increasing the willingness of employers to hire workers'. Wages would have to become more unequal 'to reintegrate those market activities which at present are priced out of it'. In addition, there would need to be, 'a reduction in all other costs associated with taking on or maintaining labour, e.g. social security rules'. Remarkably the Commission wrote (p. 60):

> Since more employment would be created for a given rate of growth, the apparent productivity of labour (real GDP per person employed) would by definition be lower. As a consequence, the room for real wage increases would also be smaller ... budgetary consolidation might lead to a decline of average net real wages ...
>
> there may be some unwelcome social aspects of the specific measures leading to a more employment-creating growth. In particular, the downward widening in the wage distribution would result in a substantial real decrease in the lowest wages. This would not be possible without a lowering of unemployment compensations and social protection schemes. Combined with the expansion of part-time work, this would also, *ceteris paribus*, widen the existing income distribution towards larger inequality and, at the limit, could create 'working poor' unable to survive decently from their wages and thus lead to a form of exclusion just as damaging as unemployment.

The Commission was thus unwilling to consider many of the social changes which would have a significant impact on the equilibrium or natural rate of unemployment. It regarded the market adjustments which would allow European employment to grow when output grew as less acceptable in the last resort than Europe's exceptional unemployment. It reiterated this position in its 1995 Progress Report (p. 4):

> This report concludes that a European approach to the job crisis does not mean that we have to make a choice between persistently high unemployment and growing inequality and poverty. It is possible to combat unemployment and to improve the overall employment situation without creating a new class of working poor and without giving up our high ambitions for social protection.

The 1995 Progress Report added (p. 8), 'the main features of the European social protection systems and the high level of protection which they offer must be maintained'. The 1993 Commission provided excellent explanations of the continual growth in Europe's underlying unemployment, but the 1995 Commission still denied Europe the fundamental solutions associated with pricing the unskilled into work. It did however propose (p. 21) some limited reforms 'targeted at the low end of the wage scale':

> These measures include special entry wages for new entrants into the labour markets, a review of social benefit systems acting as implicit wage floors and reductions in non-wage costs, either temporary (e.g. for the unemployed) or permanent (e.g. to compensate for disabilities), and especially for the low end of the wage scale.

It added that several of these measures would have 'significant budgetary consequences'. Because the Commission could not propose lower public expenditures it could only suggest tax-switching of a kind which is politically impractical (the recommendation that a CO_2/energy tax be substituted for employment taxes on the low paid) and which would quite possibly raise European unemployment further.

Reducing the high equilibrium level of Europe's unemployment will actually require a reversal of the policies which created it.

Towards a reduction in European unemployment

There are three principal ways in which European unemployment can be reduced. First, Europe requires labour market reforms to reverse the continual rise in structural unemployment which has become far higher than in the United States and Japan. Second, Europe requires a reversal of its escalating public expenditure and therefore in European tax levels which are now far above those in the United States and Japan. Lower European taxation would reduce the cost of labour to Europe's private sector companies, expand the number of workers they could profitably employ and so reduce the number the state had to support which could produce still further reductions in taxation by reversing the Söderström–Viotti/Bacon–Eltis cycle which undermined the Swedish economy. Third, the declining international competitiveness of European industry and commerce needs to be reversed. European industry has been losing world market share outside Europe to both the United States and Japan to an extent which goes far beyond the effects of real exchange rates. Improved European competitiveness would increase the number of well-paid jobs in industry and commerce.

A higher demand for labour would reduce unemployment for a time, but unless the equilibrium unemployment rate below which inflation accelerates was reduced, the reduction in unemployment could not be sustained. As soon as inflation accelerated the European Central Bank would raise interest rates until inflation was brought back to its target rate, and this would be reached only when unemployment had returned to its equilibrium rate. Therefore all policies to reduce unemployment will fail if the natural rate of unemployment is not reduced at the same time. The European Commission fully recognised this in its 1995 Progress Report, and it had many detailed recommendations aimed to reduce Europe's high 'natural' rate of unemployment (NAIRU).

The OECD estimate of the non-accelerating wage rate of unemployment in the EEC and subsequently the European Union was less than 3 per cent in 1970, about 6 per cent in 1980 while it was 9.7 per cent in 1995. The IMF estimated in 1997 that of Europe's then 11 per cent unemployment, between 8 and 9 per cent per cent was structural[10] – that is, that the natural rate was then close to 8–9 per cent. It must be a European objective to gradually bring the equilibrium unemployment rate back down from the 8–9 per cent of the 1990s towards its original 3 per cent.

There are elements in the equilibrium rate which have a significant social content. Until the 1970s there had been low unemployment in the leading European economies for two decades and social attitudes adjusted to the knowledge that almost everyone had a job. It was therefore possible to regard living off state benefits as aberrant social behaviour on which few were tempted to embark. Because jobs were universally available, those who administered Europe's social benefit systems could apply them rigorously.

In the 1990s, in contrast, as most European countries have become accustomed to unemployment of close to 10 per cent, it is widely appreciated that, as in the 1930s, many with the strongest personal desire to work will actually be unemployed for long periods. Living off state social benefits has therefore become inescapable to many European families, and those who administer social benefit systems have become fully aware of this. In the knowledge that little work was available, they became increasingly uncritical of benefit, applicants, so more and more workers settled into unemployment as a way of life and joined the long-term unemployed, many of whom almost ceased to look for work, or expect to find it again.

An economy can therefore settle at very different rates of unemployment and behave as if these are long-term equilibria, when they are merely temporary equilibria which can be transformed by reversing the changes in attitude and behaviour of the 1970s and the 1980s.[11]

But the transitory unemployment equilibria can be changed only slowly and gradually. Perhaps one-half of Europe's 10 per cent unemployment is long-term. If 5 per cent of European families are accustomed to living off benefits, and economic conditions change so that half of these can move back into remunerative employment, some will leave the benefits system to which they have adjusted their lives only if the financial rewards for returning to work are very considerable. Others will eagerly take jobs if they again become available. If unemployment falls significantly, the attitudes of those who make no effort to find employment will gradually appear less acceptable to Europe's electorates, to those who administer social welfare systems, and within the social milieux in which the unemployed live. Changes in attitude are achievable, and unemployment will become less acceptable the less of it there is.

Much can be achieved to facilitate this process by 'churning' unemployment so that fewer of those who are unemployed have the opportunity to settle into perpetual unemployment. Temporary jobs and occasional periods of training encourage those who participate to adjust their attitudes and skills so that they will be available for long-term work as soon as this becomes available.

Several of the detailed proposals of the Commission's 1993 White Paper and the 1995 Progress Report would have the effect of churning, and the Progress Report specifically proposed that more should be spent on 'active' policies to help the unemployed to find work, 'to give every unemployed person an incentive – especially financial – to look for work and, given more efficient employment services and greater geographical mobility, a better chance of finding one'. At the same time, less should be spent on 'passive' policies which involve financial payments to the unemployed whatever their actions (p. 35). The Commission added (p. 38):

> Despite the progress which has been made, *the balance between passive and active expenditure* is far from ideal. Efforts to activate employment policies without jeopardising high social protection standards must be stepped up (emphasis in the original).

But the Commission was reluctant to recommend some of the changes which would reduce the numbers in Europe's labour force in voluntary long-term unemployment because of its judgement that social equality and solidarity were higher objectives. Europe can rationally prefer greater equality and social solidarity to lower unemployment, and that is precisely the choice the Commission appeared to make in the 1993 White Paper. The social protection policies which have been reinforced in successive decades, and which the Commission continues to defend, must inevitably add to the residual of the apparently unemployable. Because there are far fewer families able to remain entirely outside the labour market in the United States and Japan, their equilibrium unemployment rates are far lower than those in most of Europe.

The adoption of some of the policies which the Commission recommends can produce a reduction in Europe's equilibrium unemployment levels, but more will be needed if actual unemployment is ever to be reduced to the levels in the world's other leading economies. Employment opportunities need to be created for those among the long-term unemployed who are prepared to seek work, and this is inhibited in many ways by the impact of Europe's far higher public expenditure and taxation than North America.

Continental Europe's average public expenditure ratios of almost 50 per cent, in contrast to the 30–35 per cent of the United States and Japan, are a severe handicap. Reductions in public expenditure would begin to substitute a virtuous circle for the 'vicious circle' of the 1970s and the 1980s which the Söderström–Viotti/Bacon–Eltis cycles describe.

If public expenditure ratios can be cut, tax ratios can also be reduced, and the 1995 Commission set out admirable prospective tax cuts which would especially assist the supply side of European economies. These would then create conditions where companies would employ more labour, because it had become cheaper relative to capital, and because companies expanded faster. Such lower taxation would gradually increase the financial rewards from employment relative to living off social benefits, so the supply of labour would rise at the same time as new employment opportunities were created. With more private sector output and fewer unemployed to finance, tax rates could be reduced further to produce a 'virtuous circle' in the period over which this process could be sustained.

It is often said that public expenditure ratios cannot be reduced because government spending is already at an irreducible minimum. That is never true. Britain faced a financial crisis in 1976, and in the following two years James Callaghan's Labour government cut real public expenditure by 8 per cent, a larger cut than any achieved by the Conservative governments which followed. Several European countries faced debt crises in the 1980s and the 1990s and succeeded in introducing very large public expenditure cuts to bring their budgets under control. Italy, one of Europe's most indebted economies, cut its public expenditure ratio by 6.8 percentage points, from 57.4 to 50.6 per cent of GDP, between 1993 and 1997. Ireland, one of Europe's most indebted economies in 1986, cut its public expenditure ratio by a staggering 10 percentage points from 50.7 per cent of GDP to 39 to 41 per cent from 1989 onwards. The Netherlands cut by $5^1/_2$ percentage percentage points from 1993 to 1997. Sweden cut by 8.7 percentage points between 1993 and 1997. Countries close to debt traps have had to do this. What Europe now needs is a similar will to cut public spending in periods when the immediate need for this is less extreme. That would introduce the possibility of creating a 'virtuous circle' with consequent scope for further public expenditure cuts which would be less painful and which would reinforce growth. If governments with tolerable budgets and public debt such as France and Germany which already meet the Maastricht conditions were to cut public expenditure as if they were in crisis, they could at the same time reduce taxation and recreate the conditions for faster growth in employment and output. This would produce the revenues for still further tax cuts.

Perhaps the most powerful beneficial effect from lower European taxation would be upon the investment potential of companies and their ability to finance research and development which the Commission all the time emphasises. In addition it would bring more of the world's leading companies to Europe and reduce the tendency for West European companies to transfer production to Eastern Europe, Asia and North America.

Britain has achieved much which Continental Europe could attain if it adopted similar policies. British structural unemployment was close to the European level of 10 per cent in the mid-1980s, but it was successfully reduced to about $6^1/_2$ per cent in 1998, which is close to the 5 per cent level of the United States. This has been achieved through a variety of policies which Continental Europe has not yet adopted.

The British ratio of taxation in GDP was not reduced in the 1980s and the 1990s, so Britain did not enjoy the benefits of a 'virtuous circle' of falling taxation and rising supply-side incentives. Taxation was, however, far below average European levels, tax increases were avoided and the tax burden was shifted so that employment-creation was especially assisted. Corporation tax was brought down to far below the EU average, and especially the rate at which small businesses are taxed. The reduction in the maximum rate of income tax to 40 per cent assisted the creation of new businesses and the growth of small firms which are taxed as persons and not as companies. Continental Europe has failed to shift the marginal tax burden away from the potentially job-creating profits of small businesses – and, indeed, from company profits in general.

British structural unemployment was especially reduced after 1992, when departure from the ERM created a renewed opportunity for sustained growth, and this was not immediately thrown away in an unsustainable boom. The consequent period of non-inflationary growth permitted the continual creation of additional job opportunities, while the policies of 'churning' which have been described brought many of the long-term unemployed back into the labour market. The development of these policies in Britain has been admirably described by Sir Alan Budd, the Government's Chief Economic Adviser in 1992–7.[12] Continental Europe expects to achieve similar non-inflationary growth in the early years of EMU, but it is questionable whether the conditions for successful churning will be in place if there are insufficient low-cost jobs to bring the long-term unemployed into the labour market. The Commission's labour market proposals are constrained by the need to avoid any changes which would increase inequality or reduce social solidarity, which precludes many of the policy reforms which could actually allow the unskilled unemployed to be priced back into productive work. Continuing resistance to the inequalities associated with low-paid employment could stand in the way of a process where the long-term unemployed first move into unskilled low-paid work and then move on to well-paid work after they have demonstrated that they have the necessary skills and application. The possibility of moving from unemployment into well-paid work via a period of low-paid work has been especially important in Britain and the United States.

Continental Europe is also inclined to seek to throw money into job creation rather than in the creation of the conditions where it will actually occur. British governments, unlike most in Continental Europe, have ceased to believe that they have the knowledge and strategic overview to take better investment decisions than the private sector. While European governments continued to believe that they could predict the most promising areas for future investments more successfully than capital markets, British governments have increasingly stood aside from strategic long-term investment decisions, and markets have performed far better than the governments of the 1950s and the 1960s which took responsibility for up to one-half of total British investment.

With entire freedom to act and to reap the potential rewards, private sector companies invested large sums to develop oil and gas extraction from the North Sea from which they derived no return for a decade or more. After that they made vast profits for their shareholders and for the British taxpayer. Private investors declined to finance the Concorde supersonic airliner and the UK nuclear energy programme and events proved them right: neither the capital nor the interest from the large sums governments invested in these projects have ever been recovered.

Two sayings encapsulate British experience with government efforts to direct industrial investment. Derek Morris and David Stout, two Economic Directors of the UK National Economic Development Office remarked perceptively that: 'An Industrial Policy where Ministers pick winners soon becomes one where losers pick Ministers.' A second comment comes from a senior Minister in the British Labour government of 1974–9: 'We created an industrial zoo of lame ducks and white elephants.' The wreckage of derelict state investments which litter the Italian landscape underlines that this has been the experience of other European economies. France's experience from strategic state investments has been less disastrous and there have been far-sighted initiatives in nuclear energy and aircraft but the extent of the losses of Crédit Lyonnais, with a need for the state to take over £15 billion of its debts, underlines that even énarques are fallible.

Thus while the Commission and all European governments agree about the need to raise the competitiveness of European industry and commerce, there are key differences in approach. Britain seeks to create conditions where workers price themselves into jobs while the Commission rejects all approaches to the labour market which weaken social solidarity. Britain prefers to allow those who control companies to take the strategic investment decisions while the Commission still hankers after 'Master Plans' and strategic policies about which industries (such as the audiovisual industry) are most likely to succeed in the twenty-first century.

If post-EMU Europe now achieves a decade of 3 per cent growth, equilibrium unemployment will fall significantly and there will no longer appear to be an unemployment trap. But that is extremely unlikely in an international environment replete with over-extended banks, weak governments in emerging countries and inflated stock exchanges. It is far more probable that Europe will need to reduce its unemployment in an international environment where sustained growth of no more than $1^1/_2$–2 per cent is achievable. In these conditions, the European Commission will need to recognise that if taxation remains too high to permit private sector job creation, and the labour market remains over-rigid, growing numbers will be condemned to an unemployment trap from which there is no apparent escape. There are European governments and official employers' representatives in the other fourteen countries of the European Union who share the British preference for lower taxation, more flexible labour markets and less preoccupation with Master Plans. These are all questions which will need to be debated within Europe, and with growing urgency, if long-term unemployment continues to grow.

Notes

1. European Commission (1993).
2. Cf. Herbert Giersch (1991).
3. European Commission (1993), p. 141.
4. Söderström and Viotti (1979), Bacon and Eltis (1976). Lindbeck (1979, p. 38) draws attention to similarities between our analysis and Söderström and Viotti's.
5. Callaghan (1987).
6. Lindbeck (1979), pp. 21–2.
7. Sato (1970) and Arrow, Chenery, Minhas and Solow (1961) found values for the elasticity of substitution between labour and capital, 'the decrease in the quantity of labour which is employed (relative to capital), divided by the relative increase in the cost of labour', of between 1/2 and 1.
8. The precise conditions where the Söderström–Viotti/Bacon–Eltis cycles are damped or explosive are set out in detail in pp. 24–8 of the Appendix to Chapter 1.
9. *The Economist* (18–24 February 1995), p. 47.
10. IMF (1997b), p. 64.
11. Economists describe the tendency for the 'natural' rate of unemployment to track actual unemployment upwards and downwards as 'hysteresis', and this has been discussed in a large European literature which is surveyed in C.R. Bean (1994).
12. Budd (1996).

6

The IT Revolution and European Employment

The IT revolution has far-reaching implications. In 1975 it cost $1 million to purchase the hardware required to process 1 million instructions a second. Just twenty years later in 1995 this cost had fallen 50 000 times to $20 (Table 6.1). A degree of computer power which was restricted to medium-sized businesses a generation ago is now available to whole populations.

While very small businesses and self-employed individuals have been able to purchase ever-more powerful programmes at a rapidly diminishing cost, the optimum scale for the production of computers and the microchips they incorporate is all the time increasing. The cost of

Table 6.1 Computer price deflation, 1975–95

Year of Introduction	Device	MIPS*	Price	Price per MIP
1975	IBM Mainframe	10	$10 000 000	$1000 000
1976	Cray 1	160	20 000 000	125 000
1979	DEC VAX	1	200 000	200 000
1981	IBM PC	0.25	3000	12 000
1984	Sun 2	1	10 000	10 000
1994	Intel Pentium	66	3000	45
1995	Intel Pentium Pro	300	6000	20

* Millions of instructions per second.
Source: PC Graphics & Video.

* This is a revised and up-dated version of *The IT Revolution and European Employment* (London: Foundation for Manufacturing and Industry, 1998).

establishing the most efficient plant to manufacture microchips has doubled every four years, and it reached $1.5 billion in 1998. There have been similar developments in the manufacture of computers. Thus while IT hardware and software is becoming universally available at ever-diminishing prices, its development and manufacture is dominated by a handful of very large corporations, mainly in the United States, Japan and Korea. This has significant implications for Europe.

In this chapter, some of the factual evidence on the extent of the IT revolution in North America and in Europe will be presented. After that, various economic implications of the new investment opportunities it has created will be set out. These have aspects which are entirely dissimilar from previous waves of investment. Finally implications for European public policy will be discussed.

After a number of false starts, Europe has removed virtually all the tariffs and anti-dumping duties which have been holding back its ability to take full advantage of the IT revolution. But the previous culture in which less efficient producers were protected from the full rigours of international competition has left the possibility of acquiescence in disguised protection which could still prove damaging.

The dimensions of the IT revolution in the United States and in Europe

The 50 000 times reduction in the cost of IT power achieved in North America in the 20 years from 1975 to 1995 amounts to 72 per cent per annum. High-tech capacity in the United States is expanding at 40 per cent per annum compared to an expansion rate in the rest of the business sector of $1^1/_2$ per cent. Moore's Law (named after Gordon Moore, the co-founder of Intel), claims that raw computing power doubles every 18 to 24 months, an annual rate of increase of 41–59 per cent.[1] This has been based on the number of transistors a micochip can contain, which has doubled every two years in the last decade.

The continuing trend for microchips of a given size and cost to offer ever-greater performance all the time widens the nature of the operations the new IT technologies can be designed to execute. The ability of computers to understand oral instructions and to convert verbal commands into actions is a widely predicted next step which will greatly advance their potential to take over routine work now performed by relatively unskilled labour. They are also being programmed to design highly sophisticated medical instruments, and they have come close to superseding Gary Kasparov's personal domination of the chessboard, at least when the speed of moves at which computers excel is allowed to take precedence over strategic depth where human genius still has an edge. In addition to performing routine tasks of the less skilled, computers are rapidly acquiring the potential to outperform those with the highest skills.

These are examples of the qualitative changes which the astonishing rates of progress associated with Moore's Law are enabling the world's high-tech research departments to bring on stream. New applications for microchips are discovered every year and the hardware and software to exploit them then comes to be marketed almost immediately by the world's highly competitive high-tech companies, each desperate to remain at the forefront of technology because otherwise their products will rapidly become obsolete.

In economic terms, the extraordinary rates of growth associated with the continually advancing power and scope of the microchip technologies is rapidly converting small numbers into very large ones. Until 1980 less than 10 per cent of US business investment was concerned with information processing. By 1998 this proportion had risen to 43 per cent (Figure 6.1), so more than two-fifths of US invest-

Figure 6.1 Composition of US business investment, 1980–98

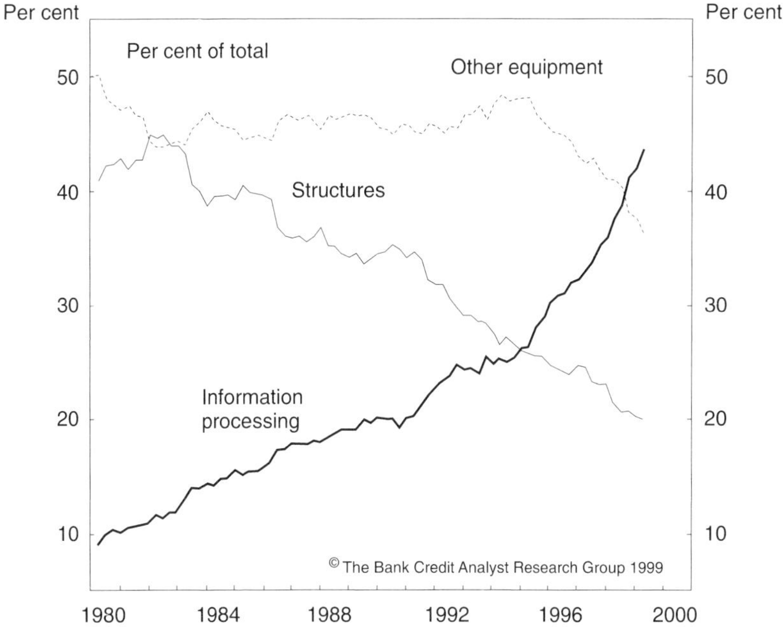

ment in plant and machinery, amounting to about 4 per cent of GDP is now IT related. In addition to investment in hardware, businesses spend heavily on computer software, and national statisticians do not even include such expenditures in their totals for investment. Software spending by US businesses has risen from $7 billion in 1983 to more than $110 billion in 1998 (Figure 6.2), so this now amounts to about 1.2 per cent of GDP. The total of combined US expenditures on computer hardware and software (all clearly business investment) therefore now amounts to more than 5 per cent of GDP, and it is rising.

The IT revolution is having far-reaching effects on pay and employment. By 1995 the average US white-collar worker had more than $16 000 of IT hardware at his or her disposal and this has doubled

Figure 6.2 US business purchases of software, 1983–98

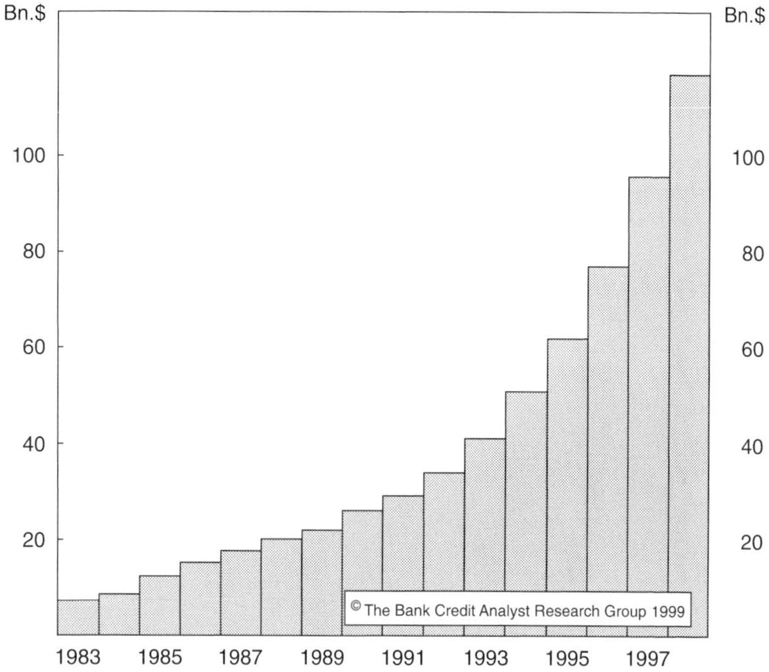

Source: Sentry Market Research (WWW.SOFTWAREMAG.COM)

since 1982 while non-IT equipment per head has risen only 25 per cent. Those who design and manufacture IT equipment are highly rewarded. The 4 million workers in US high-tech manufacturing and telecommunications and computer-related services were each paid an average of $47 000 in 1995 compared with $27 000 in other sectors. The high-tech sector's aggregate payroll rose 30 per cent to $189 billion between 1990 and 1995. The pay advantages of those with the ability to take full advantage of IT equipment is a considerable factor behind the growing inequality of pay in the United States. In 1980 the best paid tenth of workers in employment were paid 3.3 times as much as the lowest-paid tenth. By 1995 the advantage of the best-paid had risen from a multiple of 3.3:1 to 4.3:1. Numerous technology firms in Silicon Valley are reporting shortages of highly skilled workers, high-tech salaries there are almost twice the national average.

GDP in US high-tech grew by 10.2 per cent per annum between 1988 and 1997, while in the remainder of the economy its rate of growth was no more than 2.0 per cent (Figure 6.3). Because IT equipment has been becoming continually cheaper, a given rate of GDP growth has represented far more considerable capacity growth which has averaged 18 per cent per annum. Most of the extra growth in the high-tech sector has been due to extra productivity. Employment has grown just 2.5 per cent per annum against 1.7 per cent in the remainder of the US economy.

In 1997, total EU and Japanese expenditures on IT had reached 51 and 58 per cent of the US level expressed as shares of GDP; so Japan was 42 per cent behind the United States, while the European Union as a whole was 49 per cent behind (Table 6.2). The proportion of European households with a personal computer was 38 per cent of the US level and the United States had four times the number of households on-line and almost twice as many personal computers per 100 white-collar workers. There is wide variation within Europe. Among the IT leaders, Sweden spent 76 per cent of the US level, the UK 74 per cent, Switzerland (outside the European Union) 70 per cent, and the Netherlands 64 per cent. France, Belgium-Luxemburg and Germany at 55, 53 and 47 per cent of the US level were close to the EU average, while Italy at 32 per cent, Spain and Portugal at 31 per cent and Greece at 20 per cent were far behind.

Europe's share of the world market for IT equipment has been declining in relation to that of the United States. This means that the benefits from the IT revolution are emerging more slowly in Europe.

Figure 6.3 Measures of the US high-tech economy, 1988–98

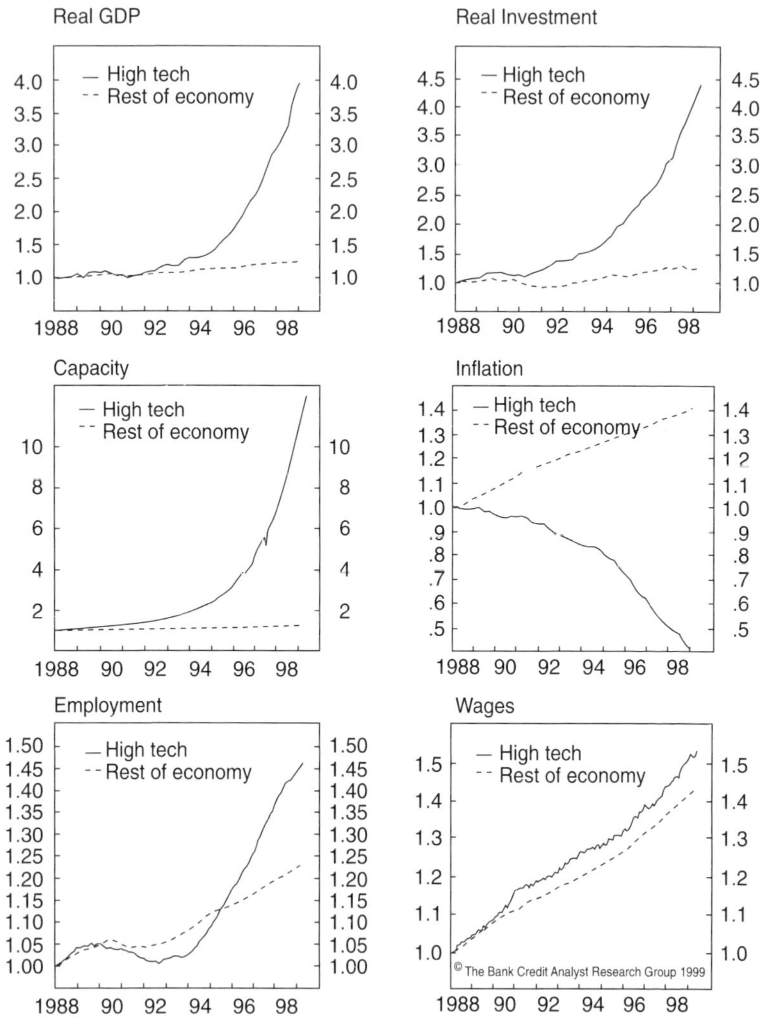

Note: All series are indexed to 1988 = 1

Table 6.2 Expenditure on IT in 1997

	Per cent of GDP	Per cent of US
United States	4.53	100
Japan	2.61	58
European Union	2.31	51
Sweden	3.45	76
United Kingdom	3.36	74
Switzerland	3.19	70
Denmark	2.96	65
Netherlands	2.92	64
Norway	2.65	58
Finland	2.64	58
France	2.51	55
Belgium/Luxembourg	2.38	53
Germany	2.13	47
Austria	2.08	46
Italy	1.45	32
Portugal	1.41	31
Spain	1.41	31
Greece	0.88	20

Source: European Information Technology Observatory, 1999.

According to the European Commission:

> Of particular concern is the fact that since 1990 Europe's share of world-wide IT markets has declined from 35 to 28 per cent. In the same period US IT markets have grown from a similar starting point to represent 41 per cent of the world-wide market in 1996.[2]

The true gap may be considerably larger than the data indicate because US purchasers have been able to pay lower prices for the same hardware and software.

This is partly because the European market has been protected by tariffs and extensive anti-dumping duties. The self-defeating nature of these is now widely recognised and it was agreed during 1997 that the tariffs, generally ranging from 7 to 14 per cent on imported IT hardware and software, would be removed by the year 2000. In December 1997 the European Commission also took the decision to withdraw anti-dumping duties on semi-conductors which were previously as high as 60 per cent. Europeans have become accustomed to paying higher prices so suppliers may fail to pass on the full benefits from the elimination of tariffs. There is moreover agreement between the semi-conductor producers of Europe, Japan and Korea to exchange pricing information. This may facilitate the establishment of a pricing structure where they agree to charge higher prices in Europe.

Very little hardware and software is now manufactured by European owned companies and US purchasers of IT are therefore located closer to the original producers which offers the opportunity to negotiate keener prices than those paid by Europeans obliged to shop at a distance. It is notable that personal purchasers of IT pay lower prices for the same hardware and software in New York than in London, Frankfurt or Paris. Typically IT hardware and software which is sold for $1million in the United States, is marketed for £1million in the United Kingdom, so British purchasers pay about two-thirds more for the same equipment. This is a Europe-wide handicap.

In consequence the EU's expenditure, at 51 per cent of the US level expressed as a ratio of GDP, represents real expenditures which are some two-fifths less with the consequence that average real European IT expenditures are at only about 30 per cent of the US level. In real terms IT expenditures in the United Kingdom, Sweden and Switzerland are at perhaps 45 per cent of the US level, while France and Germany spend 30–35 per cent as much, and Italy, Spain and Portugal 20 per cent.

With these far lower real expenditures, employment in the high-tech computer-oriented industries has risen considerably more slowly in Europe than the United States. In the United States, total employment grew 15 per cent between 1988 and 1997 while employment in the high-tech economy grew 25 per cent. In Europe total employment grew 8.0 per cent between 1980 and 1994 while employment in the Information and Communications Technology (ICT) industries grew 7 per cent. Employment in the manufacture of computers and computer components fell 20 per cent, while employment in the provision of software and computer services rose 171 per cent. Europe has been missing out on the growing global opportunities to manufacture computers and computer components but it is gaining from the vast job opportunities offered by their application in the whole range of user industries.

In April 1997 the European Commission drew particular attention to the significance of the IT revolution for European employment. It referred to a 1996 study by the IFO Institute in Munich, which indicated that over the next decade Europe could gain as many as 6 million jobs as a consequence of the rapid diffusion of the opportunities offered by ICT, or lose up to 3 million in a negative scenario where the European diffusion of these technologies was restricted. The analysis distinguishes three kinds of impact on European employment. The first, and most limited, is the direct effect on employment in the European ICT industries themselves. The second is the far-reaching impact on employment in other industries as a result of advances in their productivity and products as a consequence of the application of the new ICT technologies. The third is the impact of the new ICT technologies on the tradability of various services and the growing tendency for the provision of these to be located in areas of the world where the opportunities presented by the new ICT technologies can be most effectively applied.[3] The extent of these potential gains or losses in employment underline how important it is that Europe's gap in computer use should be closed.

The European Commission estimates that the European Union requires an overall growth rate of 2 per cent to prevent employment from falling and considerably more than this if employment is to grow.[4] The EU's rate of growth from 1990 to 1998 (1.9 per cent) was slightly below the Commission's critical 2 per cent rate. The extent by which Europe succeeds in exploiting the far-reaching opportunities offered by the IT revolution will have a considerable impact on the growth it achieves in the next decade in a world where others are bound to exploit the full economic potential of the new technologies.

The IT revolution offers precisely the kind of investment opportunities which Europe most needs to reduce the structural unemployment which afflicts some of the leading economies. Some fear that the new developments may raise productivity in a manner which will be job-destructive: it will be shown below that the impact on employment of the new IT-related technologies will generally be extremely favourable. The IT revolution involves radically new kinds of investment, with effects which depart markedly from those of previous technical revolutions. How the benefits differ, and the potential advantages from their exploitation in Europe, are the subject of the next part of the argument.

A different kind of investment

One of the most striking features of the IT revolution has been the manner in which everage computer prices have fallen in relation to every other kind of capital equipment, and to prices in general. From 1980 to 1998 US investment equipment in general became 10 per cent more expensive – that is, it rose in price by about 0.5 per cent per annum. In the same period the information processing price deflator *fell* more than 98 per cent, or by over 19.5 per cent per annum. The cost of information processing equipment therefore fell 20 per cent per annum in relation to the cost of other kinds of capital equipment (Figure 6.4). The state-of-the-art computers illustrated in Table 6.1 above fell in cost considerably more.

The sharp and continuing fall in the prices of computers and of related capital equipment has had a striking impact on investment. Throughout the last two decades companies and self-employed individuals have been able to replace computers with new models which offered superior performance at a diminishing real cost. An author using a personal state-of-the-art word processor and printer and uprating every few years now has a less expensive but immeasurably more

Figure 6.4 The falling price of US technology, 1980–98

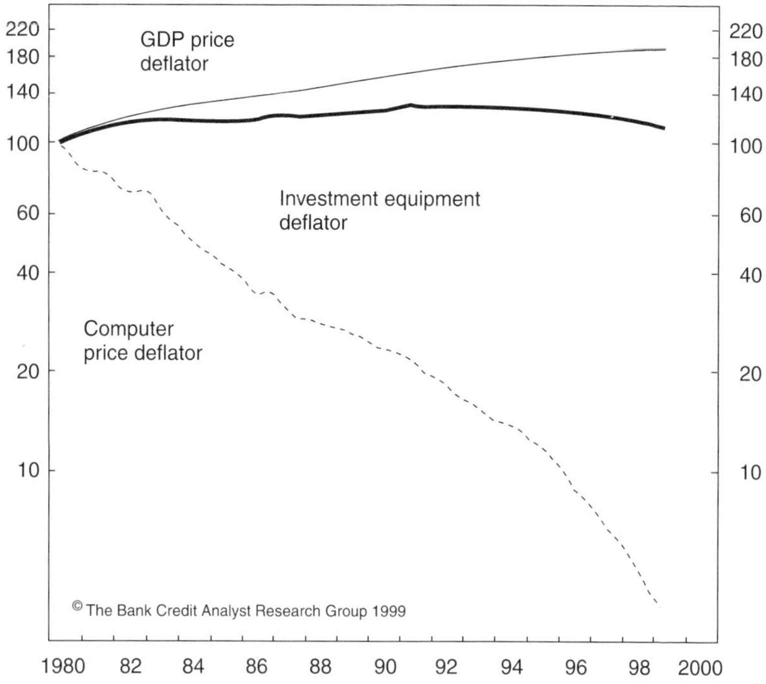

Note: Series are indexed to 1980 = 100.

powerful capital investment in his place of work. The same improvements have been available to companies.

In 1998, an author based in the UK can get all the word-processing and printing facilities he can use for about £2500, whereas he had to spend about £4000 for technically inferior equipment in 1980. The money value of the fixed capital with which he works has therefore fallen $37^1/_2$ per cent, but its real book value has fallen considerably more because prices in general have risen 150 per cent between 1980 and 1998, so the cost of the author's computer equipment, which has fallen $37^1/_2$ per cent in money terms, has actually fallen 75 per cent in relation to the general price level. His computer capital has therefore fallen to 25 per cent of the real money value of the equipment he was using in 1980. The author therefore now makes use of a far lower capital stock measured in *real money values*.

Because net investment is the change in the *value* of capital, the author's aggregate net investment between 1980 and 1998 has been negative. But if the author's capital equipment is measured in terms of its power to perform, today he is endowed with a much improved stock of capital. Measuring personal capital in efficiency units, in so far as this is possible, the author's real capital stock has grown with each replacement of an item of equipment by its technically superior successor. Each succeeding purchase of equipment has permitted faster operations, additional options, higher quality printing, greater ease of printing and higher standards of reliability, with a consequent reduction in maintenance costs in both time and money. Measured in efficiency units these items of capital stock have immensely improved since 1980, so the author has made a substantial net investment over the last two decades.

The more than two-fifths of US business investment which is now concerned with information processing will be enhancing the economy's productive power through precisely the same developments. Companies have been able greatly to improve the effectiveness of their IT equipment, while at the same time economising in the investment funds they need to commit to obtain it. They have had the same option as the author with his continually improving word-processor and printer, of reducing the real money value of capital equipment while at the same time continually increasing its power and effectiveness.

The combination of negative real investment, when this is measured in real money values, and positive investment, when it is measured as capital's power to perform, is an economic development with startling implications. It is not entirely new. Karl Marx, whose theory of the inevitable collapse of capitalism does not read well in this final decade of the twentieth century, was a brilliant innovator of economic concepts. He was the first to distinguish carefully between the *value* of capital; the cost of erecting it (his cost measurements were all expressed as labour costs) in relation to the cost of the wage goods it then produced; and the *technical composition* of capital, its physical power to perform. Marx emphasised capitalism's superb performance at the technical level where the *technical composition* of capital advanced all the time. Marx showed how pin factories had become vastly more productive than in the time of Adam Smith, so that the level of pin production which had required 120 men in Smith's famous pin factory of 1776 could be achieved by one woman or even a girl in Marx's 1867.[5] However this massive advance in capital's technical composition would fail to produce a higher financial rate of return for capitalists: historical movements of *values* within capitalism would often oblige companies to accept a falling rate of return on their capital investment. The value of capital expressed as a cost would keep rising in relation to the financial value of the aggregate output for which capitalists could sell their products. Businesses would have to incur ever-rising expenditures on investment for returns which would all the time be squeezed by competition. So however successful capitalism might be in the creation of growing productive power, it would eventually fail critical profitability tests which would depend on values and not on the growing quantity of pins which modern machinery enabled a single woman or girl to produce.

Marx's prediction of an inevitable squeeze on profit rates has so far proved erroneous, but the conceptual separation of capital's technical power from the sales values it could generate was far ahead of its time.

A highly positive aspect of the twentieth-century IT revolution is that, unlike Marx's pessimistic projection, it represents a favourable development in terms of both capital's technical power and the financial values which determine its profitability. Marx's nineteenth-century capital investments and the vast present-day investments in IT involve greater productive power and therefore massive improvements in the technical composition of capital; but Marx's investments created financial problems for entrepreneurs because these had to commit growing expenditures to take advantage of the new technical opportunities and their necessary capital costs grew faster than the profits they could earn. In contrast, much of the IT revolution can be exploited without any necessity for new net financial expenditures, as in the example of the UK author. The financial implications for the economy are therefore immensely favourable because, where companies invest to upgrade their IT, the financial commitments they are obliged to incur to service their new investments do not need to rise correspondingly.

At a given level of IT capacity, they have the option, like the UK author, of continually reducing their financial commitments. The response of most companies to the opportunities offered by the falling cost of new IT equipment has however been greatly to extend their capacity and to channel some of their potential cost savings into up-grading the range of functions in which IT plays a part. The result has been the great increase in expenditures on IT to reach 43 per cent of all business investment in the United States, despite the continuing fall in the cost of each item. The technical total of the IT stock in the United States is indeed growing, both to the extent of the increase in its money share in investment and additionally through the falling trend in the cost of each unit. The entire advance in the technical composition of capital in the United States is potentially productive.

These benefits have been conferred on US industry and commerce to three times their extent in Europe, and they have produced a considerable addition to US profits. They have raised the output of the US economy, and reduced what it had to spend on investment to attain it. To be able to spend less on new capital equipment which produces more is bound to be highly favourable to the real rate of return on capital. Because capital-augmenting technical progress raises the performance of capital without adding to its real money cost, its enhanced power to perform is omitted from conventional measurements of the capital base of US companies, so these significantly under-estimate the growth of the productive base and the real rate of return on capital that US industry and commerce is actually achieving.

Those who have sought to measure the growing physical capital of US corporations in relation to their soaring stock exchange valuations in the late 1990s have overlooked this development. Wall Street's rise may have exceeded US corporations' growing power to perform, so that share values required some correction, but there has also been considerable under-estimation of the true value of the US capital stock (measured in relation to its real earning power) because the capital-augmenting element from the IT revolution has not been taken into account.

Some have been concerned that the IT revolution may have job-destructuive implications, since many of the functions which used to be performed by routine labour are now effected through IT programmes. To some, IT is perceived as a contributor to the rising level of European unemployment. That is not what either the evidence or economic theory indicates. So far as evidence is concerned, the United States, where real expenditures on IT are more than three times Europe's, is the G7 economy with the greatest gains in employment and far lower unemployment without any accompanying acceleration of inflation. The IT revolution has had the most pronounced impact on the provision of financial services, and on telecommunications. Employment has risen faster in these than in the economy as a whole in all G7 economies. There are many detailed examples of job destruction within the world's banks and finance houses, but employment in the sector as a whole has universally grown. The clear inference is that, while some routine work has been eliminated, challenging additional tasks have emerged, often in smaller businesses in the same sector, which have provided extra job opportunities which have exceeded those eliminated in larger businesses.

So far as economic theory is concerned, the core of the analysis that the introduction of machinery would reduce employment was introduced by David Ricardo in 1821,[6] and developed by Marx in 1867. What is occurring now is precisely the opposite of the technical developments which produced structural unemployment in their analysis. Ricardo was eloquent about machinery's potential to destroy employment when he wrote in a letter to J.R. McCulloch in June 1821 (from his estate in Gatcomb Park, Minchinhampton, until recently, the residence of the Princess Royal) that:

> If machinery could do all the work that labour now does, there would be no demand for labour. Nobody would be entitled to consume any thing who was not a capitalist, and who could not buy or hire a machine.[7]

In May 1823, he told the House of Commons (the social reformer, James Mill had advised him to use some of the £800 000 he had made in the City to buy 'the rottenest of rotten boroughs': his seat cost him £4000 at each election) that:

> his proposition was not that the use of machinery was prejudicial to persons employed in one particular manufacture, but to the working classes generally. It was the means of throwing additional labour into the market, and thus the demand for labour, generally, was diminished.[8]

Marx echoed Ricardo's prediction that machinery could render much of the population redundant, and the displaced workers would then have no role in a modern society except as a revolutionary force:

> A development of productive forces which would diminish the absolute number of labourers, i.e., enable the entire nation to accomplish its total production in a shorter time span, would cause a revolution, because it would put the bulk of the population out of the running.[9]

For the strikingly similar technological developments which they predicted, Ricardo and Marx each assumed that the mechanisation of production would always involve a proportionately greater increase in expenditure on capital equipment than in the output it subsequently produced. The displacement of labour was invariably accompanied by an increase in the capital-to-output ratio. Without that assumption machinery would not displace labour, and Ricardo even said that if the introduction of machinery increases a country's gross output of commodities, 'then the situation of all classes will be improved'.[10] In Marx, it is the growing ratio of fixed capital to output that displaces labour and creates 'a reserve army of the unemployed' which prevents mechanisation from raising real wages. In reality, after the early decades of the nineteenth century mechanisation unquestionably raised the demand for labour and therefore real wages, and it greatly increased real output to create the conditions where Ricardo stated that it would benefit all classes.

To produce the socially disastrous results which Ricardo feared and Marx expected, the capital-to-output ratio had to rise continuously; but it has had no tendency to do so since the early decades of the nineteenth century. Ricardo and Marx showed how mechanisation could destroy employment; but the economic conditions required to create their conclusions have never prevailed.

Like mid- and late nineteenth-century capitalism, which continually raised the demand for labour, and therefore real wages, the IT revolution's general tendency has been to reduce the capital-to-output ratio; so its impact on employment has been the opposite of the malevolent consequences which Marx and Ricardo anticipated.

There is indeed a general risk of structural unemployment in Europe, because real wages are rigidly high, especially in Germany, and aggregate investment is insufficient to provide employment for all who wish to work at Europe's very high levels of pay and social provision. But because the IT revolution continually cuts the cost of providing capital equipment for newly employed workers, it acts to spread new investment over more workers and therefore to ease the degree of structural unemployment. Because IT investments tend to reduce the capital-to-output ratio, they are predominantly job-creating. Where there is a powerful trend for IT equipment to become ever cheaper, as in the United States, massively more jobs are created, but these are predominantly skilled jobs requiring the high levels of education at which much of continental Europe excels.

Recent inter-country studies indicate that the United States achieves lower scores in international mathematics and numeracy tests than France, Germany, the Netherlands, Sweden and Switzerland. A director of Du Pont Europe has remarked that instructions to the company's US workers have to be pictorial because they cannot be expected to understand written directions. The United Kingdom scores similarly to the United States, so its overall level of mathematical attainment is also below continental Europe's.[11]

On both sides of the Atlantic, an educational culture emerged in the 1960s which acquiesced in reductions in the detailed technical content of the mathematics taught in schools, with the result that a variety of qualifications came to represent a lower level of attainment. This trend has apparently eluded continental Europe. It was partly driven by the belief that social justice was advanced through greater equality within the educational system, and that this was a more significant objective than the technical levels which were in the end achieved.

The reductions in mathematical standards within the United States and the United Kingdom which international comparisons indicate are now arousing a significant reaction, especially because those who leave school semi-literate and semi-numerate are often condemned to low incomes and above average unemployment. In previous generations skill and dexterity in the performance of manual tasks often commanded high pay, but the market for such work has declined, while employment for those with the ability to perform intellectually challenging work has grown. There are therefore intensive efforts in both the United States and the United Kingdom to restore mathematics and literacy standards, and to familiarise the new generation of school leavers with the extensive potential opportunities which are being opened up by the new computer-aided technologies. Those who attach the highest priority to egalitarian objectives and those who seek high technical standards are now far more closely aligned because of the evident connection between weak levels of academic achievement and unacceptably low personal incomes, received either as unemployment benefits or low pay.

Continental Europe's avoidance of the Anglo–American trend which has been described should have enabled it to take more advantage of the IT technologies. But despite the superiority of its general level of mathematical and technical education, it has so far exploited them far less than the United States.

It will be shown below that Europe's failure to take full advantage of the opportunities created by the IT revolution has been especially associated with weaknesses in its approach to trade policy, which are only now being corrected. This has led to higher European prices for IT hardware and software.

How European IT policy has up to now acted as a brake on the rate of adoption of the new technologies is the subject of the final part of this chapter.

The European policy response to the IT revolution

The European Commission's reaction to the IT revolution has been driven by two contradictory cultures. Those who believe that all necessary steps should be taken to establish European industry among the world's technical leaders have offered a ready ear to the needs of European producers of IT hardware and software, and been prepared to offer these a degree of protection from competition from lower-cost North American and Asian competitors. At the same time, those who fear that the whole range of European industries is becoming less competitive, with a consequent loss of employment and world market share, have focused on the needs of Europe's users of IT components and equipment, and it has been in the interests of every manufacturing and service industry other than the IT producers themselves to obtain the computers and semi-conductors they require at internationally competitive prices. The inherent tension between the needs of the *producers* and those of the industrial and commercial *users* of IT equipment has had far-reaching implications.

International trade theory distinguishes between positive protection which assists producers, and negative protection which undermines them. An industry receives positive protection when tariffs or anti-dumping duties place it in a more favourable situation in relation to international competitors than would prevail in conditions of free trade. Negative protection arises when tariffs and anti-dumping duties place an industry in a less favourable situation than in conditions of free trade.

There is widespread awareness of the implications of positive protection, and a comparative ignorance of the potential damage to industrial competitiveness from negative protection. All recognise that interference with free trade through tariffs, import quotas and anti-dumping duties assists producers, especially in manufacturing industry, by limiting the degree of foreign competition they must overcome, but that it at the same time damages the short-term interests of final consumers required to pay higher prices. What is often lost sight of is that the final consumers of many industrial products are other manufacturing businesses whose power to compete is undermined when they have to pay more than the world market price for the components and materials they incorporate in the products they manufacture.

In 1997 there were European protests from manufacturers of 'unbleached cotton cloth' which is sold on to textiles manufacturers who design and market the clothes which reach the shops. The European manufacturers of plain unbleached cotton cloth, mainly located in Southern Europe, were suffering severe competition from Asia so they pressed the European Commission for anti-dumping duties. They requested these specifically from the Directorate concerned with trade policy which was then headed by Sir Leon Brittan. The manufacturers who develop unbleached cotton cloth into wearable clothing are mainly located in Northern Europe, and they wished to obtain this as a semi-finished material at world market prices, so they were profoundly opposed to the protection of the Southern European manufacturers of this vital material.

In 1997, and again in 1998, Northern Europe (including the United Kingdom) achieved majorities in the Council of Ministers, who are, when anti-dumping disputes are on the agenda, the trade ministers of the Fifteen. In 1998, they denied successive proposals from the Commission to offer protection to Southern Europe's manufacturers of unbleached cotton fabrics, by eight to six, the narrowest of margins. The United Kingdom, and the EU's three Scandinavian members together with Germany, Luxembourg, Ireland and the Netherlands, outvoted France and Austria (which on this occasion voted with Southern Europe), and the so called 'club-Med' (Greece, Italy, Spain and Portugal). Belgium abstained. This illustrates how there are inevitable tensions between manufacturers of industrial inputs, who benefit from the protection of their markets from lower-cost Asian and US competition, and manufacturers of the final goods which incorporate these inputs, whose competitiveness is undermined by the protection of the former group.

This is an example out of many of an inevitable conflict of interest between manufacturer and manufacturer. These receive positive protection when this enables them to sell at higher prices. They receive negative protection when they must pay more than their international competitors for vital inputs. What is positive protection for some is negative protection for others, and what assists some undermines others.

Such conflicts proliferate in the IT industries. Virtually every electronic product, however limited, nowadays incorporates microchips, semi-conductors and more sophisticated devices such as 'distributed random access memory chips' or D-Rams and the still more complex 'erasable programmable read-only chips' or Eproms. D-Ram chips are at the heart of every intelligent electronic device ranging from video recorders to scientific instruments and computers. If those who manufacture these devices are protected, every European electronic product, and the motor vehicles and the aircraft where sophisticated electronic instruments proliferate, becomes more expensive and less profitable to manufacture than in Asia and North America where these vital IT components are obtainable at world market prices. But tariffs and anti-dumping duties on these components assist European manufacturers of semi-conductors and D-Rams and Eproms such as Siemens. There is therefore conflict between producer and producer.

There is even conflict within the IT industries themselves. There are companies which manufacture IT components and companies which manufacture computers and the sophisticated hardware which incorporates them. Manufacturers of computers need to obtain components as cheaply as their Asian and North American competitors so their interests contradict those of the manufacturers of semi-conductors and D-Rams. US computer companies which manufacture in Europe have warned the European Commission that excessive European D-Ram prices could make it uneconomic to manufacture personal computers in Europe.

Europe's IT trade policy has been a battlefield. Until 1996 there were European tariffs which ranged from 7 to 14 per cent on virtually all electronic components. This had the support of electronic component manufacturers, but it undermined the many European manufacturers of final electrical goods. These were continually losing market share, and during the 1990s it was gradually agreed that the tariff protection of electronic components should be eliminated. Throughout the negotiations, the United Kingdom was among those who pressed for the removal of tariffs on IT equipment and components and it won increasing support. It was finally agreed in 1996 that all tariffs on IT components would be removed by the year 2000. This agreement was arrived at as part of the Information Technology Agreement (ITA) on the removal of trade barriers in the IT industries, and it was negotiated in Geneva during 1996 between all the countries in the World Trade Organisation (WTO). The European Commission negotiated as the official representative of the EU's fifteen member countries. The agreement was concluded during 1996 as soon as countries which represented 90 per cent of world IT trade were on board. The Union and the United States agreed to remove half their tariffs on semi-conductors and on other IT equipment by July 1997, a further quarter by January 1998 and the final quarter by January 1999.

But there has been a further threat to the users of electronic equipment in the form of anti-dumping duties which do not come within the Information Technology Agreement.[12] The IT component manufacturers of D-Rams and semi-conductors argued for many years that Japanese and Korean companies were selling D-Rams and Eproms below cost so that their competition was 'unfair'. Evidence on the costs of overseas producers is never complete or decisive. Evelyn Cronin, a senior semi-conductor analyst at Dataquest, has commented that: 'Accurate cost data would require close analysis of every D-Ram production line.' Moreover, the approach to accountancy which is required to establish a just price used to be a question which medieval monarchs allowed subtle theologians to determine, it is nowadays decided by those who advise the Cardinals of the European Commission. These judged during 1997 that the prices of imported personal fax machines weighing up to 5 kilogrammes were unjustly low and therefore deserved tariff protection of 89 per cent (Philips had complained about low-cost Asian competition). In 1998, Brussels investigated whether in-car laser optical reading systems were being sold at unjustifiably low prices by the Asian economies which had 65 per cent of the market (Blaupunkt and Grundig had complained). The price of imported D-Rams has been continually on the Commission's agenda.

Between 1983 and 1990 Japanese manufacturers increased their share of the European D-Ram market from 25 to 70 per cent. This led the European Commission to investigate a claim by leading European manufacturers of D-Rams, in particular Siemens, and those well known 'European' manufacturers, Texas Instruments and Motorola, that leading Japanese manufacturers were dumping D-Rams in Europe. In 1990, the Commission imposed minimum selling prices within Europe on eleven Japanese manufacturers including Toshiba, NEC, Hitachi, Mitsubishi, Sharp, Uki, Sanyo, Minebea and that well known Japanese company, Texas Instruments Japan. That Texas Instruments Europe should have invited the European Commission to impose minimum selling prices upon Texas Instruments Japan underlines how these disputes lie principally between producer and producer. After 1990 the eleven Japanese D-Ram manufacturers were asked to provide the European Commission with quarterly data on their costs of production, with the object of allowing their selling prices to fall in line with the rapid technical progress all were achieving, to establish a continually falling 'just price' within Europe. Any Japanese producer who failed to provide detailed quarterly evidence which satisfied the Commission would pay a 60 per cent anti-dumping duty instead.

The difficulties of European manufacturers were not confined to Japanese competition, and in 1993 minimum selling prices were also imposed upon three leading South Korean manufacturers, Goldstar, Hyundai and Samsung (with greater sales in Europe than any Japanese supplier) and a general anti-dumping duty of 24.7 per cent on all other imports from South Korea.

These anti-dumping measures against Japanese and Korean manufacturers were suspended in 1995 when world D-Ram prices rose as a consequence of a temporary shortage. But D-Ram prices fell by 80 per cent in 1996 and the European manufacturers, represented by their trade association, the European Electronic Component Manufacturers' Association (or EECA) pressed for a return of protection. During 1996 the Commission was negotiating to create the world-wide Information Technology Agreement, while there were at the same time pleas from the manufacturers represented by the EECA for renewed protection. The Japanese and the Koreans protested somewhat unrealistically that if this occurred they would establish a sellers' strike and decline to supply D-Rams to the European market, within which their share had risen from 75 per cent in 1990 (when price controls against them were first imposed.) to 80 per cent in 1996.

In April 1997 the European Commission succumbed to this EECA pressure and reimposed minimum prices and anti-dumping duties, saying that it had no alternative because these had been suspended only temporarily, and European law permits such extensions for only twenty-one months in the absence of detailed new research which had not yet been undertaken. An interesting development was simultaneously occurring. The EECA which represents Europe's D-Ram manufacturers was negotiating directly with the Electronic Industry Association of Japan and the Korean Semi-conductor Industry Association, to agree that the three trade associations would jointly monitor D-Ram prices. As soon as this was agreed, the EECA was able to recommend to the

European Commission that the anti-dumping duties it had up to then requested could be removed. The Commission accepted the EECA's advice and anti-dumping duties on D-Rams and Eproms were withdrawn on 1 December 1997. It therefore now appears as if Europe has removed all protection from its semi-conductor producers.

The European industry may, however, be receiving implicit protection through arrangements between its own trade association and those of its Korean and Japanese counterparts. It may emerge that the Japanese and the Koreans will sell in Europe at prices acceptable to the European producers. Should that prove the case, the European D-Ram manufacturers will remain protected and Europe's microchip users will be correspondingly handicapped. But this is being arranged in a manner which lacks the transparency of anti-dumping duties and minimum prices openly imposed and administered by the Commission. These are challengeable in the Council of Ministers, where the unbleached cotton case shows that those who vote to remove anti-dumping duties are capable of achieving a majority. Europe's manufacturers of semi-conductors may, in contrast, have organised implicit protection in a manner which is politically unchallengeable. As regards the Japanese and the Koreans, they already have 80 per cent of the market, and they may now have the opportunity to share this at prices higher than they can obtain in the world's more competitive markets.

These will include Singapore, Hong Kong, and perhaps also China, and in all probability the United States, where D-Rams and Eproms cost less than in Europe, giving their users of microchips a competitive edge over their European counterparts. European manufacturers of scientific instruments, electronically controlled machinery, robots, computers, televisions, video recorders, high-fidelity sound equipment, sophisticated car components and the washing machines and other household goods which are becoming increasingly 'intelligent' may therefore be handicapped in relation to their Asian and US competitors. The world's semi-conductor market totalled $140 billion in 1998, and it is vital that it be kept tariff-free and that Europe's IT users obtain their semi-conductors at the same prices as those who exploit the new technologies in the United States and Japan.

The prices of the most basic semi-conductors collapsed during 1998 because of the impact of Asian over-capacity, and there have been widespread plant closures, but higher prices could return as soon as world markets recover. When they do, it is vital that the falling costs and improvements in performance of Asia's component industries, boosted by lower currencies, are fully reflected in falling prices in Europe.

Europe has failed to exploit the opportunities of the IT revolution to the same degree as the United States. IT hardware and software have not been as cheap in Europe as in North America which is one reason why the extent of its use has been less. It is to be hoped that the European Commission regards it as a first priority to monitor European prices in relation to those of similar hardware and software in Asia and North America, and that Europe will on no account revert to anti-dumping duties. The supporters of free trade in this vital area will need to remain vigilant, so that the gains they have apparently established are sustained.

This chapter has shown that the Council of Ministers is capable of voting down anti-dumping duties. The Commission's decisions require the endorsement of a majority of governments and in the case of anti-dumping duties to protect unbleached cotton cloth, the United Kingdom was part of a majority which prevented their imposition. These debates have the highest significance for future European prosperity, but whether there is a majority for the imposition of anti-dumping duties on a wide range of manufactures rarely receives significant attention.

European employment will be undermined wherever the prices for IT hardware and software are significantly higher in Europe than in Asia and North America. The argument of this chapter has shown how a continual cheapening of IT equipment can be immensely favourable to employment, and this is a development which Europe especially needs. Moreover, a greater level of utilisation of the continually advancing IT technologies also has a significant influence on overall levels of profitability and on capital requirements for growth.

Even if there is no backsliding on trade policy, Europe is likely to continue to face a degree of price handicap because much of the IT hardware it uses is imported and virtually none is produced by European-owned companies. It fell behind at the start and the advances which are achieved by the leading companies have become so rapid that there will now be few areas where Europe can catch up. In aerospace it jumped in late with Airbus with vast government support to achieve a market share which is beginning to approach Boeing's. The rate of technical advance in the development of IT is considerably faster, so a late European catch-up is improbable, Europe's vital interest is therefore that of a vastly significant user and exploiter of IT systems.

Notes

1. Some of this information and the data which follow is derived from data published in the *Bank Credit Analyst* in 1997 and 1999.
2. European Commission (1997a), p. 3.
3. European Commission (1997a), p. 5.
4. European Commission (1997b), p. 6.
5. The startling level of productivity achieved in 1776 in Adam Smith's original pin factory is outlined in the first chapter, 'Of the Division of Labour', of *The Wealth of Nations* (Smith, [1776]1976). Smith's example is up-dated to 1867 by Karl Marx in the fifteenth chapter of *Das Kapital*, 'Machinery and Modern Industry' (Marx, [1867]1974, vol.1 pp. 432–3).
6. In 1821, David Ricardo added the chapter, 'On Machinery', to the 3rd edition of *Principles of Political Economy and Taxation* (Ricardo [1821]1951–73, I, pp. 386–97).
7. Ricardo, *Works and Correspondence*, VIII, pp. 399–400.
8. Ricardo, *Works and Correspondence*, V, p. 303.
9. Marx ([1867]1974), III, p. 263.
10. Ricardo ([1821] 1951–73), I, p. 392.
11. See, ONS (1997), OECD/Statistics Canada (1995) and Keys, Harris and Fernandez (1996).
12. The account of the European Commission's imposition of minimum prices and anti-dumping duties on D-Rams in 1990 and in 1993, and their subsequent removal, re-imposition and removal in December 1997, owes much to articles by Neil Buckley in the *Financial Times*.

7
The Lessons for Britain and for Europe from the Success of German Counter-inflation Policy*

In 1945 there was no reason to anticipate that post-war Germany would achieve more successful control over inflation than Britain or the United States. Its macroeconomics had been catastrophic in the inter-war years when the hyper-inflation of the 1920s was followed by mass unemployment and the collapse of orthodox financial policies.

How Germany learned to control inflation

Herbert Giersch, the first Chairman of the German Committee of Economic Experts, 'The Five Wise Men', made a crucial contribution to the establishment of post-war German economic policy on a sound basis and he has provided an account of how he developed an approach to policy which established the D-Mark as a far stronger currency than the pound or the dollar.

He served in U-Boats in the Second World War, and in his words 'the journey with the Navy, at the end of the war on a submarine boat, ended in a prisoner of war camp in England' (Giersch, p. 1986). He continues, 'reading Adam Smith's *Wealth of Nations*, one of the few books of the camp library, was to become crucial for my view of the world' (1986, p. 255). He then found Keynes' *General Theory* in another prisoner of war camp (are British prison libraries still like this?), but this impressed him far less.

* This is a revised and greatly extended version of *The Lessons from the Success of German Counter-Inflation Policy* (London: Economic Research Council, 1995).

On his return to Germany he became a Lecturer in Economics at the University of Münster where he heard British and US economists who came to advise the Germans on how to rebuild their economy. He was disappointed to hear Joan Robinson, one of Keynes' greatest Cambridge collaborators, 'expound a vulgar Keynesianism ... like Hamlet without the Prince of Denmark: a theory and a policy of full employment without wages' (1986, p. 257) Leading American visitors 'recommended expansionist policies, erroneously assuming that we had Keynesian unemployment rather than the classical kind arising from the influx of refugees and the physical destruction of the capital stock' (1986, p. 257).

Giersch went on to evolve a view of the world which was very different from Anglo–American Keynesianism and it had three characteristics which have since become orthodox in the leading OECD economies. He came to believe, first, after his disillusionment with the economics of leading British and US Keynesians, that inflation depended upon the growth of the money supply. In the early 1950s few economists in Britain or the United States believed this, and none who were influential. The second element in Giersch's new view of the world was that employment depended upon the real wage, and that if this was too high unemployment would result (1986, p. 269). Keynesianism had greatly under-estimated the impact of high real wages upon unemployment, and the new textbooks universally attributed this to an inadequacy of effective demand which could always be corrected through the appropriate degree of deficit financing. Giersch's third new broad principle was that the object of government budgetary policy should be to strengthen the supply side of the economy by not absorbing private saving into public expenditure and budget deficits, while the tax system should be used to create incentives to foster long-term growth (1986, p. 270)

This was the opposite of British economic orthodoxy in the early 1960s. Government investment was more than one-half of total investment, and even Conservative governments had failed to reduce the top rate of income taxation below 75 per cent. Keynes believed that the families which mainly ran British industry (through nepotism and inheritance) were too short-sighted to get investment decisions right, and it was generally believed by his followers that governments would take far better investment decisions than the private sector. Sufficient net of tax profits to finance investment therefore had a low priority in Britain. As for saving, Keynes had declared with numerous illustrative examples in *The General Theory* that throughout most of human history, saving had been too high. These fallacies formed the background for the economic policies which contributed to Britain's relative economic decline in comparison with Germany in the 1950s and the 1960s.

After a series of distinguished appointments in Germany, at OECD in Paris and at Yale, Giersch was appointed by Ludwig Ehrhardt to be the first Chairman of the German Council of Economic Experts in 1964. The new committee faced a crucial problem: since Bretton Woods, the exchange rate between the D-Mark and the dollar had been fixed, and this meant that Germany automatically imported US inflation. If Germany was in effect within a dollar zone, and prices rose at 4 per cent per annum in the United States, the prices of those goods and services which were internationally tradable – perhaps half the national income – would also rise at about this rate in every country with an exchange rate tied to the dollar. From the mid-1980s until their incorporation in the Euro in January 1999, the Austrian schilling and the Dutch guilder were pegged to the D-Mark, with the consequence that Austrian and Dutch inflation and interest rates were largely determined by decisions taken in Frankfurt. Their D-Mark pegs transmitted the success of German counter-inflation policy to Austria and the Netherlands. But the D-Mark's own dollar peg in the 1960s had the opposite effect.

The leading US economists were still strongly influenced by Keynesianism (Paul Samuelson, the celebrated MIT Nobel-Prize winning economist remarked that he didn't mind who determined economic policy so long as he got to write the textbooks), and their impact on policy was inflationary so if the D-Mark continued to be subject to a fixed exchange rate with the dollar, US inflation would automatically influence German inflation.

In 1964, Giersch and his colleagues offered the startling advice that the D-Mark should be detached from the dollar. This outraged the German business community which believed that upward revaluations of the D-Mark would destroy the profitability of their exports. Ehrhardt, who had become Federal Chancellor, remarked that the Wise Men were offering 'stones to a public in need of bread' (1986, p. 264) By an extraordinary process of political persuasion in 1968, the Committee of Experts achieved the vital separation of the D-Mark from the dollar, which made it possible to establish it as a far stronger currency.

From the D-Mark's initial revaluation in 1968 to its incorporation into the Euro at the end of 1998 it rose 142 per cent in relation to the dollar, or at an average rate of 3.0 per cent per annum. The dollar was worth 4.0 D-Marks in 1968 and 1.65 in December 1998. From 1968 until December 1998 the D-Mark rose 245 per cent in relation to the pound sterling, or at an average annual rate of 4.2 per cent. The pound was worth 9.65 D-Marks in 1968 and 2.80 in December 1998 so from 1968 to 1998 sterling lost 71 per cent of its value in comparison with the mark.

Despite the relentless rise of the D-Mark in relation to both the dollar and the pound, Germany's share of world trade in manufactures was more than sustained in comparison with the US and UK shares. There was continual apprehension by the German business community that the rising D-Mark would price German manufactures out of world markets, but this did not occur. German exports were so well made that they continued to grow strongly, and the current account of the German balance of payments was in almost continuous surplus from 1968 until 1998. This was influenced by macroeconomic considerations in addition to the exchange rate (including, especially, Germany's high savings ratio in comparison with Britain and the United States), but its continual rise evidently proved no obstacle to a strong export performance.

The crucial significance of Germany's 1968 decision is that without it the Bundesbank would have been all but irrelevant to inflation in Germany. If the D-Mark had continued to be pegged to the dollar, the United States would have taken the principal monetary decisions which influenced the German economy, and the Bundesbank would have had no more influence over German inflation than the central banks of Austria and the Netherlands had over inflation in their countries in the 1990s.

Because the D-Mark rose 3 per cent per annum in relation to the dollar, average German inflation has been about 3 per cent less than US inflation. Because it rose more than 4 per cent per annum in relation to sterling, German inflation has averaged around 4 per cent less than UK inflation.

The benefits to Germany from lower inflation

One of the most beneficial consequences for Germany from its lower inflation has been a generally lower level of interest rates. Portfolio holders, including the world's banks and insurance companies and international fund managers, can choose the country in which they will invest their assets. Countries with faster inflation and falling exchange rates such as the United States and the United Kingdom have to pay higher interest rates to compensate for the fall in the value of their currrencies which the world comes to predict as it sees it happening time after time. Because the pound fell more than 4 per cent per annum relative to the D-Mark from 1968 to 1998, UK interest rates had to be about 4 per cent higher than Germany's. The gap narrowed in the later 1990s with UK inflation only $1^1/_2$–2 per cent above Germany's, and in December 1998 the interest rate on ten-year government bonds was 4.0 per cent in Germany and 4.8 per cent in the United Kingdom, an advantage to German borrowers of just 0.8 percentage points.

In addition to the benefits to the German business community from lower interest rates, there have been further advantages because the lower German inflation rate has required less correction over the decades. German businesses have been less inconvenienced by the need to deflate in order to balance the macroeconomy.

When I was Director General of the National Economic Development Office (NEDO) from 1988 to 1992 the fifteen chairmen of the industrial sector groups produced a paper addressed to the Council chaired by the Chancellor of the Exchequer. These included senior industrialists (Sir David Barnes, Sir John Cuckney, Sir Ivor Cohen, Sir Ian Gibson, Sir Ronald Halstead), and senior trade unionists (Bill Jordan and Eric Hammond). They agreed that a principal difference between British and and German industry was that those who led German companies could concentrate on production. They had more predictable macroeconomies and lower interest rates so they could focus on engineering, product design, research and development (R&D) and marketing. They did not need to divert attention all the time to finance. In contrast, many of those who ran leading British companies were preoccupied with questions involving their bankers and the City of London in their perpetual need to control the financial flows on which the survival of their companies depended. Because of this fundamental difference, British companies were far more often led by accountants, while German companies were far more often led by those with particular expertise in production with a strong science and engineering background at the start of their careers (Eltis, Fraser and Ricketts, 1992).

Because of the United Kingdom's comparatively unstable macroeconomy and its far higher interest rates, business leaders with expertise in accountancy have often had to veto far-reaching proposals to expand and develop new product ranges. In Germany's climate of lower interest rates and financial stability, the arrangement of finance had a lower ranking.

Another advantage to business of low interest rates from which German manufacturers benefited is most readily illustrated from the housing market. Britain had an average inflation rate of 7 per cent in the 1980s and the 1990s, while Germany's was 3 per cent. Home owners therefore paid average interest rates of perhaps 10 per cent in Britain and 6 per cent in Germany. If a family had to pay 10 per cent interest in Britain, while house prices were four times an employee's earnings (the average in recent decades), when an employee bought a house, 40 per cent of his income was required to pay interest. An employee with an income of £25 000 who bought a £100 000 house and paid a 10 per cent interest rate had to find £10 000 interest a year, a high proportion of his £25 000 income on which he also had to pay taxes and social security contributions of about £7000. Husbands and wives who were both working could find £10 000 interest to pay for their house from their combined incomes of perhaps £40 000, but if either ceased to work, they could no longer keep up with their interest payments, and their houses were then repossessed by the banks or building societies to which they owed £100 000. The situation of British companies has been comparable. If they were paying 10 per cent nominal interest rates and had to finance large investments through borrowing, their companies became vulnerable to repossession in the same way as a family home.

Consider, in contrast, the situation in Germany with 3 per cent inflation and 6 per cent interest rates. A German family which borrowed £100 000 and paid 6 per cent interest only had to find £6000 interest a year which was within the scope of a single earner with an income of £25 000, so when either a husband or wife ceased to work, a German family could still find the interest to service a loan of £100 000. Their houses were therefore less liable to be repossessed when the economy fell into recession. Because German interest rates were lower, the condition of businesses with large loans was similarly robust, so there were far fewer bankruptcies than in Britain where it was found that each 1 percentage point addition to the inflation rate has added 6 per cent to the number of bankruptcies (Wadhwani, 1985). This illustrates how the control over inflation which the Bundesbank achieved led to lower German interest rates, which helped to secure the financial independence of German companies and families.

German industrialists, who were better able to base business conditions on long-term considerations, enjoyed great advantages throughout the period in which German nominal interest rates were below Britain's as a consequence of lower inflation. Why did Britain fail to match these advantages?

Why Britain failed to control inflation

In the decades which followed the Second World War, British governments, and the economists who advised them, had the unreal belief that they could control the economic cycle, so after unemployment began to rise, the immediate political response was: 'this is intolerable – Why do we have this unemployment? The government should expand spending, it should cut taxes, it should lower interest rates.' With a continual focus on the short-term relationship between demand and productive capacity, far less attention was paid to inflation which rose in each successive cycle in the 1960s and the 1970s. Because of the underlying belief that the economic cycle was controllable, the British governments of the 1960s and the 1970s focused primarily on this and lost sight of the inflationary consequences of their counter-cyclical policies. They repeatedly believed that they could avoid the awkward short-term choice between inflation and unemployment through the negotiation of incomes policies which involved unions, employers and government; but these only reduced the pace of wage increases for two years, after which unions attempted to recover the pay increases they believed they had sacrificed. Partly as a consequence of the misjudgement that a future acceleration of inflation would be containable through incomes policies, governments repeatedly succumbed to the political pressure to end recessions early, and to renew expansion long before inflationary expectations had been significantly reduced. These premature boosts to demand then created the foundations for still faster inflation in the next cycle.

The British focus on counter-cyclical demand management precluded the creation of the conditions actually required to bring inflation down, which the Bundesbank repeatedly imposed on the German economy. It understood that there is no way in which inflation can be reduced without reductions in demand and in spending; price increases cannot be reduced without a weakening of business markets, and this always involves an increase in unemployment. Its approach is illustrated by the manner in which Germany handled its reunification crisis in 1990. German inflation was comfortably settled at 2 per cent before reunification, but after this it rose to more than $4^1/_2$ per cent. The former West Germans agreed to pay reunification taxes which caused an initial acceleration of costs and prices. The Bundesbank's response was to raise interest rates to 10 per cent, unemployment soared, Germans protested vehemently (and not only Germans, because other Europeans with currencies linked to the D-Mark had to pay similar interest rates) but two years after the Bundesbank's imposition of 10 per cent interest rates, German inflation was back from $4^1/_2$ to 2 per cent. By accepting the immediately unpleasant consequences of 10 per cent interest rates for more than a year, Germany avoided a sustained rise in inflation and in inflationary expectations from 2 to $4^1/_2$ per cent. During the oil shocks of the 1970s when British inflation was allowed to rise to 25 per cent, German inflation peaked at 8 per cent after which the Bundesbank pulled it back to its target range.

The Bundesbank became the institution which Germany used to control inflation once Ehrhardt and Giersch had freed the D-Mark from the inflationary dollar. Its president and its directors are bankers and its sole task is to control inflation. It has often caused immediate discomfort to German ministers and to German companies, who would have preferred a British policy of reacting with sensitivity to rising unemployment by cutting interest rates. Because of its legal independence, it was able to resist the unpopularity which its refusal to restore interest rates to their former levels caused, and it brought rates down only when excessive inflationary expectations had been truly eliminated. In consequence, the inflationary impact of unfavourable shocks such as the rise in the oil price in the 1970s and the higher taxation consequent upon reunification in the early 1990s was merely temporary: the Bundesbank always brought inflation back to its target range.

The British situation began to become comparable to Germany's in 1979 when Margaret Thatcher's government astonished the economics profession and the political community by attaching more significance to the control of inflation than to the amelioration of the vicissitudes of the economic cycle. Very high interest rates from 1979 to 1982 brought inflation down from the 10–25 per cent rates of the 1970s to about 5 per cent from 1983 to 1988, but this German policy was not persevered with. Inflation was allowed to rise again to an unacceptable $9^1/_2$ per cent in 1989. The government had remained responsible for interest rate decisions, and it misinterpreted the economic data in 1987–9 to a degree which allowed inflation to shoot upwards as in many previous cycles. The British authorities wrongly believed that inflation was quiescent and that the exceptional expansion of the real economy in 1987–9 was a consequence of the supply-side improvements which the government's microeconomic reforms had achieved. The Chancellor, Nigel Lawson, and the economists who advised him in no way expected to lose control over inflation, but the ever-changing economic data and the significant economic inter-relationships are always interpretable in a variety of ways.

There is a British temptation to prefer analysis which suggests that interest rates can be held lower with all the apparent short-term benefits this brings to companies and to families. Prior to 1997, British interest rate decisions were not merely consequent upon the economic judgements of chancellors: the consent of the prime minister was also required. Even Margaret Thatcher and John Major, the most anti-inflationary of prime ministers, sometimes delayed the implementation of proposals from the Treasury to raise interest rates, because of the immediate discomfort this would inflict on Britain's property-owning democracy where almost 70 per cent of families own houses financed through borrowed money. In Germany, interest rate decisions could be taken immediately on the basis of objective examinations of the economic evidence by the Bundesbank, free from any prior wish that this would justify lower rates. With the inevitable uncertainties of economic interpretation, it is always possible to read economic data so that it appears to justify the politically preferable option of lower rates, and the British authorities often read the data that way.

The inflationary surges in Britain in 1987–9 and in Germany in 1989–91 sharply illustrate the contrast between counter-inflation policy in the two countries. The postponement of interest rate rises in Britain in the later 1980s as a consequence of misinterpretation of the data allowed inflation to rise to $9^1/_2$ per cent, while reunification merely raised German inflation to $4^1/_2$ per cent. Both countries responded with the imposition of interest rates calculated to bring inflation down, but the economic damage in Britain was far greater because British inflation had to be reduced from $9^1/_2$ to $2^1/_2$ per cent, while German inflation merely needed to be reduced from a peak of $4^1/_2$ per cent to the Bundesbank's target range of 0–2 per cent. Because Britain lost control over inflation to a greater degree, it had to pay a higher price to bring it under control: the imposition of 15 per cent interest rates, when 10 per cent rates sufficed in Germany. The consequent recessions in the early 1990s were far longer and deeper in Britain because inflation had to be reduced by 7 percentage points against $2^1/_2$ in Germany as a consequence of Britain's less immediate response to accelerating inflation. Business conditions therefore became far more difficult for British companies as soon as it was recognised, as it always is in the end, that excessive inflation had to be squeezed out of the economy.

Because raising interest rates was a technical question outside the political process in Germany, the Bundesbank was entirely free to judge the moment to raise them. This prevented inflation from running away in the manner it so frequently did in Britain. It was able to raise interest rates whenever it appeared on a balance of probabilities that inflation would otherwise accelerate. British governments, with their political preference for lower rates, failed to act on a mere balance of probabilities. As with juries in a court of law, the chancellor and the prime minister required proof that the case for condemning the economy to higher interest rates was decisive. Proof that interest rates have to be raised is far more difficult to establish than a mere belief that the evidence points in that direction.

Germany's lesson for Britain

In May 1997 Tony Blair's newly elected Labour government with Gordon Brown as Chancellor immediately recognised the case for transferring responsibility for interest rate decisions to the Bank of England which, like the Bundesbank, could act independently of short-term political pressure. Germany had evolved an independent central bank which had proved extremely effective and conferred substantial benefits on German industry and commerce. It had created an institution which worked; the lesson for Britain was to achieve something similar.

The incoming government decided to achieve this by establishing a Monetary Policy Committee of nine with the power to determine short-term interest rates and a remit to maintain inflation within 1 percentage point of a $2^1/_2$ per cent target rate. It is a Bank of England committee, and five of its nine members are the Governor, the two Deputy Governors, the Chief Economist and another executive director of the Bank, while the remaining four are independent economists. In the first two years after its establishment, British inflation was brought to $2^1/_2$ per cent and held there in the German manner. The Chancellor is responsible for the initial appointments, but it is a well established British tradition that those who hold senior public appointments exercise independent judgement to fulfil their terms of reference. The nine members of the Monetary Policy Committee are therefore politically independent, like the directors of the Bundesbank. In Germany also, the initial appointments are by government, but most of the directors of the Bundesbank are appointed by the governments of the provincial Länder.

In Britain, the government has no direct influence on the Monetary Policy Committee's decisions, but its Chief Economic Adviser attends its meetings, and presents evidence so the government can make its analysis known without having a direct role in decisions. The chancellor has retained the right to vary the inflation target which the Monetary Policy Committee is asked to achieve, so if any government finds the consequences of the Bank of England's counter-inflation policies unacceptable, it can ask the committee to set interest rates in a manner which could accommodate an acceleration of inflation to higher rates.

It should gradually come to be understood that when British interest rates are raised or lowered, this is because the members of the independent Monetary Policy Committee are exercising their best judgements to control inflation. Interest rate decisions should gradually be taken out of politics and come to be judged on the technical question of whether they are sustaining control over inflation within the politically established target range.

The principal difficulty in political education towards this understanding is the need to overcome the initial belief that higher interest rates are harmful because they damage the finances of companies and families, and therefore destroy prosperity and employment. The economics profession in Britain, the United States and Europe widely accepts that any extra unemployment which follows demand reductions to diminish inflation will be eliminated, and that unemployment will return to its microeconomically-determined equilibrium rate. With this analysis, bringing inflation down does not damage long-term employment. In the language of economics, the long-term Phillips curve is vertical: short-term losses in output will be recovered and, indeed, if more effective counter-inflation policy reduces the degree of fluctuation in the economy, businesses will gain the advantages of more predictable markets and lower average interest rates.

Governments are always tempted to respond to short-term political lobbying for lower interest rates, even when these are certain to raise inflation in the medium term, because as Harold Wilson famously said, 'a week is a long time in politics'. The Monetary Policy Committee and the Bundesbank are not subject to such pressures, so they are able to focus on the long-term impact of interest rates on inflation. Britain acted on that German lesson in 1997.

Germany's lesson for Europe

This is also Germany's lesson for Europe. The European Central Bank (ECB) which will determine the interest rates of the eleven founder members of Economic and Monetary Union (EMU) was modelled on the Bundesbank. Each national government appoints a director, in the manner that the Länder each appoint a director of the Bundesbank, and the eleven governments unanimously agree on the appointment of the European Central Bank's executive board of six including the President and the Vice President, in the manner that the Federal Government appoints the President of the Bundesbank. The seventeen directors of the European Central Bank have been asked to set interest rates with the sole object of controlling inflation. By passing control over German interest rates to this newly created central bank, Germany's direct influence over monetary conditions in its own country has been reduced to two votes out of seventeen. Whether German inflation will now remain equally under control will depend upon whether directors appointed by governments which have achieved weaker control over inflation than Germany will attach the same priority to preventing it. If inflation edges upwards, will the European Central Bank immediately raise interest rates to reverse its acceleration in the manner of the Bundesbank?

The directors appointed by countries which have not learned Germany's lesson may prefer softer options. There may also be attempts by the governments of the eleven, which will meet regularly as the Euro-X Committee, to exercise political influence over the ECB's decisions. President Mitterrand of France foreshadowed this when he said, in September 1992 in a televised debate with Philippe Séguin on whether France should join EMU:

> One hears it said that the European Central Bank will be the master of decisions. It's not true! Economic policy belongs to the European Council [of Ministers] and the application of monetary policy is the task of the Central Bank. The people who decide economic policy, of which monetary policy is no more than a means of implementation, are the politicians. (Connolly, 1995, pp. 191–2)

The attitude of Mitterrand's successor as President of France, Jacques Chirac, may be similar. In May 1998 he vetoed the appointment of Wim Duesenberg as President of the European Central Bank for the full eight-year term the rest of Europe desired, and obtained agreement that he would be succeeded by a Frenchman after just four years. The tradition of acting independently of political pressure within terms of reference agreed on appointment guides office holders in Britain, but it is not the custom throughout Europe. It is often assumed that those initially appointed by governments retain an abiding obligation to respect their judgements. President Mitterrand continued the 1992 debate with the statement that 'members of the European Central Bank cannot help feeling a certain tenderness for the interests of their own country' (Connolly, 1995, p. 192). President Chirac's insistence on a French successor to Duisenberg indicates a similar assumption.

If governments actually acquire over-riding influence over the decisions of the ECB, as Mitterrand predicted, tacitly expressed behind the scenes, or else overtly exercised through exchange rate targets which the Bank is required to accommodate, Germany could lose the Giersch formula on which its post-war policies were based. He, as we have seen, believed that employment depended on the real wage, that inflation depended on whether monetary conditions were loose or tight and that economic growth depended upon successful supply-side policies including especially a tax structure and a level of public consumption which left room for adequate private-sector investment.

The European Commission's response to growing European unemployment as expressed in the Delors report of 1993 (which was discussed in detail in Chapter 5) included large European public investment projects financed through new powers to borrow by the Commission. Such ideas may now acquire the support of leading European ministers; they are precisely what Keynesian visitors misguidedly recommended to Germany in the 1940s and the 1950s. In Giersch's formulation, unemployment is mainly the consequence of an excessive real cost of labour, but many European ministers believe that conditions in the labour market should be agreed between the social partners, including the trade unions, and these will be strongly opposed to the reductions in public expenditure which will be needed if employment taxes are to fall. Moreover, if the European Central Bank is ever required to create monetary conditions compatible with a politically coordinated policy of Keynesian expansion, the use of of interest rates to control inflation will be sacrificed.

Britain has apparently learned the German lessons, but if it becomes a late entrant to EMU, it may be obliged to join new Keynesian initiatives of the kind it found so damaging in the 1960s and the 1970s. It will be less surprising if Britain reverts to former errors than if Germany itself abandons the policies which have proved so successful.

Whether Germany will find that it has replaced the Bundesbank with a European Central Bank which acquiesces in the approach to macroeconomics which it rejected in the 1950s and the 1960s has become one of the more interesting questions in European politics.

Part III
EMU

8
The Creation and Destruction of EMU*

Introduction

It is becoming clear that the United Kingdom will be fortunate not to be a founder member of EMU. All the countries which join will have the same short-term interest rates – yet the representatives of each country will only have the influence of a single vote in their determination.

Twice within the last decade attempts to align British with European interest rates to control the level of sterling produced catastrophic effects. In 1987–9 Nigel Lawson's policy of shadowing the D-mark produced interest rates which were far too low, leading to explosive monetary growth and an inflation rate of nearly 10 per cent. From 1989 to 1992 Britain's brief ERM membership produced interest rates which were far too high, an actual decline in bank lending and a deep recession with disastrous economic and political consequences.

The British economy is particularly vulnerable to inappropriate interest rates and exchange rates: the City of London is more deregulated than the financial sectors of France and Germany. As a result, too low or too high an interest rate does far more damage in Britain than in France or Germany. Real spending is more interest-elastic (sensitive to the rate of interest), so getting the interest rate wrong produces greater inflationary expansion or else contraction than in France and Germany.

The British exchange rate also has a markedly different impact because there is a far greater high-tech component in British than in

* This chapter was published as *The Creation and Destruction of EMU* (London: Centre for Policy Studies) in July 1997.

French or German trade. Britain's high-tech competitors are mainly US and Japanese, and partly for that reason sterling moves more closely with the dollar than the continental currencies. If Britain lost the flexibility to move with the dollar, British high-tech industries would be undermined whenever the dollar fell in relation to the continental currencies. The British economy will repeatedly pay a heavy price if British interest and exchange rates are again locked into those of France and Germany.

But there is now another reason why Britain is fortunate to be free of any obligation to participate in the Euro. It is beginning to be understood that this will be especially vulnerable during the 36 months between the start date of 1 January 1999 (when all the participating currencies will remain legal tender) and 31 December 2001 (when they will finally be superseded by the Euro). During these 36 months, French and Belgian francs and the peseta and the lira will all remain legal tender alongside the D-Mark and the Dutch guilder. During these three years the world's financial community will be able to arrange to owe French francs and peseta or lira and to be paid in D-Marks or guilder, in case any element in the 'irrevocably' fixed exchange rate structure of 1 January 1999 breaks.[1]

A collapse during the three years in which national currencies remain legal tender would create an opening for banks and hedge funds to profit hugely at the expense of participating governments. As in 1992, some of Europe's governments will have an inescapable obligation to defend with all the resources at their disposal the exchange rate structure agreed at the end of 1998, while George Soros and others who command international financial resources will be free to express a costless preference for the D-Mark or the guilder, over the lira, the peseta, or the French franc. A breakdown in the agreed exchange rates cannot possibly result in a rise in their value against the D-Mark. But if there is any breach in the EMU dykes, hedge funds will again make billions from the resulting fall of the lira, the peseta, the French franc, or the Belgian franc (or indeed sterling if it enters and is again allowed to collapse, despite all assurances). The creators of EMU have agreed to offer the world's financial community three complete years of costless one-way options.

The vulnerability of EMU to international speculation during this extensive transition period is beginning to be recognised. Martin Taylor, the highly regarded Chief Executive of Barclay's Bank, astonished a St Gallen bankers' conference at the end of May 1997 by declaring that if exchange rates for the start of EMU which do not reflect true convergence are politically imposed, it will become the duty of speculators to 'drive them apart'. Alan Greenspan, the Chairman of the United States Federal Reserve, also believes that the Euro will be vulnerable: he has been quoted as saying: 'The Euro will come but it will not be sustainable.' Niall FitzGerald, the pro-European Chairman of Unilever commented in a lecture on 12 June 1997 that:

> Starting rates and participants will have to be carefully judged to avoid political tensions that might in due course tear the currency apart ... if the Euro is set up on the wrong basis, the Single Currency could be blown apart within a few years – never to be seen again.

This condition, where the Euro will be extremely vulnerable to international speculation, has come about because it is essentially a political construct. Its creators believe, despite accumulating evidence to the contrary, that governments are more powerful than the foreign exchange market. As Pierre-Antoine Delhommais commented in a series of documents on, 'La guerre des monnaies', published by *Le Monde* in March 1997:

> The great majority of the French political class is persuaded that the actions and will of States are sufficient on their own to allow them to fix the course of exchange rates at the levels they desire.

Economists are aware of the power of the foreign exchange market, but some believe that this can be disciplined by governments. A so-called 'Tobin tax' (after James Tobin, the US Nobel prize-winner in economics) has been proposed on all dealings in foreign exchange to limit the power of speculators to destroy currencies. Even if, which would be astonishing, the governments of all the G7 countries and every member of the European Union agreed to impose such a tax, a currency which the international financial community regarded as vulnerable and which therefore offered vast profits to hedge funds, could be destroyed in Swiss markets (for Switzerland would scarcely agree to cramp the scope of its highly profitable banks by agreeing to tax financial transactions in Zurich or Basle) or in Singapore or Hong Kong (if China is willing to profit from 'capitalism's internal contradictions'). If vast profits become available from the destruction of the lira or sterling as in 1992, no commitee of Nobel Prize-winners, or Heads of State, or Finance Ministers could ring-fence them from the foreign exchange market's attentions. The distinguished Cambridge Professor, Wilhelm

Buiter, a member of Gordon Brown's new Monetary Policy Committee, commented that:

> foreign exchange dealers are moved by bandwagon effects and swept along on waves of euphoria or pessimism. Firmly held views are changed at the drop of a hat [and] it is important for governments not to stand too much in awe of the market;

but he adds perceptively that governments have to pay attention to dealers 'in the same way that adults have to pay attention to children armed with Uzis' (*Economic Policy*, April 1997).

This chapter will open with an account of how European politics is creating a list of EMU starters which will not converge sufficiently to protect them from the pressures of which Martin Taylor, Alan Greenspan and Niall FitzGerald have spoken. It will continue with an account of how international speculation may then destroy the Single Currency.

The Conservative Party in Britain has been undermined for almost a Parliament by the debate on the merits of British participation in EMU. This debate was mainly about the Single Currency's implications for national sovereignty, without any recognition of its potential vulnerability. Any temptation by the Labour government to seek to enter should be tempered by Martin Taylor's comment that no one presently knows at which point between 2.30 and 2.90 D-Marks the sustainable exchange rate of sterling lies. If the United Kingdom decides to participate, it could easily emerge that it has again entered a European exchange rate system at the wrong exchange rate. Prudence is likely to prevail, especially as there are some in the Labour government who are as suspicious of EMU as the most sceptical Conservatives.

If Britain remains outside EMU, the City of London will retain the same opportunities as Switzerland to be one of the world's leading financial centres. The Swiss franc is stronger than the D-Mark and it is likely to become far stronger in comparison with the Euro. Sterling's advantage could be similar if the Euro is weak while the Bank of England's new power to determine interest rates gradually raises Britain's anti-inflation credibility. The City of London has vastly more international financial business than Frankfurt and Paris combined and the advantages which have produced this will remain, and even grow if the Euro proves vulnerable.

On 24 June 1997, Eddie George, the Governor of the Bank of England, was asked about the single currency after his Mais lecture in the City University. His response was:

> I find it difficult to accept that if you see a precipice coming and you're running in a crowd, you say, 'We can't stop now because someone might fall over us.' (*The Observer*, 29 June 1997)

How EMU will be established

EMU is likely to proceed on the agreed start date, 1 January 1999. Many countries including Germany will find it difficult to meet the Maastricht criteria but the political will to go ahead is likely to overrule the economic realities, at least in the short-term.

The German government is taking the lead in the establishment of EMU. However, the majority of Germans do not wish to give up the D-mark, and many fear its replacement by a 'Palermo mark'. As a result, German money has flooded to Switzerland, despite the fact that Swiss interest rates are 2 per cent below Germany's (a reflection of the greater credibility of the Swiss franc). But there is a long-standing tradition in German politics that the opinions of the German people are a challenge for their leaders to overcome whenever they contradict the judgements of those who govern Germany. Bismarck set the scene with his description of universal suffrage as, 'government of a house by its nursery. But you can do anything with children'.[2]

Chancellor Kohl, and those close to him, were determined, for overriding reasons of state, that EMU would begin on time. Gerhard Schröder, a possible leader of the opposition Social Democrats, favours the retention of the D-Mark, but even if he wins the German elections in 1998 the German commitment to EMU will by then be unshiftable.

It is now certain that Germany will technically fail to fulfil the Maastricht criteria. Its budget deficit became uncontainable by orthodox means after unemployment shot up by more than 400 000 in a single month. During 1996, 40 billion D-Marks of investment by German companies was made outside Germany, and German labour costs are still, despite the recent fall in the D-Mark, far above those in any other country except Switzerland. Private sector employment has been falling in Germany and there is continuing job destruction while employment is exported East and West: more than 1000 German companies produce in Britain, led by Siemens which is investing £1.3 billion in a semi-conductor plant. German unemployment will continue to grow during 1997. Because unemployment destroys budgets, the deficit on which Germany's fulfilment of the Maastricht criteria will be judged may be substantially above 3 per cent.

Kohl would then have to acquiesce in the dilution of the criteria by which Germany's deficit and therefore everyone else's will be judged. The European Commission which is determined that EMU should go ahead takes technical advice from Eurostat, the statistical office of the Commission. Eurostat has agreed that all kinds of one-off payments may count towards the calculation of Europe's deficits, including the most notorious case of them all: the 0.5 per cent of GDP that France-Télécom paid the French state in return for a takeover of its future pensions liabilities. This will improve the French budget during 1997 and produce a budgetary deterioration in later years as the state has to pay pensions which would otherwise have been the responsibility of France-Télécom. France will require further tolerance as its Socialist government seeks to introduce new 'employment-creating' expenditures. Its first proposals are to raise substantially the taxation of profits. This will cut the deficit in the short-term – but go on to damage long-term employment, so after an initial improvement, France's budgetary situation will deteriorate.

There has already been agreement by Eurostat to regard Italian capital transfers as deficit-reducing within the current year, and to accept a one-off Italian Euro-tax as an indicator of long-term convergence. The Italian government has even promised to refund part of the Euro-tax to taxpayers in 1999 when its budget will swing back into larger deficit after entry into EMU is achieved: Albert De Michaelis, a senior Eurostat official, has said that this promise to reimburse the Italian taxpayer does not invalidate the Euro-tax as a deficit-reducing measure. The promise to pay the tax back in 1999 is not legally binding because it is no more than 'a political commitment' (*Financial Times*, 22 February 1997).

Germany's expedient to get its prospective deficit below 3 per cent was to have been a revaluation of the Bundesbank's gold reserves but this has been successfully resisted by the Bundesbank. It is likely that Kohl will now seek alternative capital account adjustments which will satisfy Eurostat without outraging the Bundesbank.

Kohl will also have to resist scrutiny by the German Constitutional Court which can declare that any dilution of the agreed criteria has invalidated Germany's signature of the Maastricht Treaty. If he can overcome this obstacle, an acquiescent Eurostat, a determined Commission and a qualified majority of the Council of Ministers will ensure that sufficient countries qualify for EMU, and that the project will go ahead. Because Germany will qualify only through acquiescence in a confusion of capital with current transactions or else a bending of the criteria, others whom Germany would prefer to exclude will also have to be admitted. A dilution of statistical scrutiny for Germany is bound to loosen the criteria by which the budgets of others are judged.

Belgium's debt to GDP ratio is still 130 per cent, more than twice the permitted maximum, and it is at the heart of the Commission's list of EMU starters. It already enjoys monetary union with Luxembourg, the most impeccable of candidates. But if Germany has to be finessed through the criteria and there is also acquiescence in Belgium's 130 per cent debt to GDP ratio, who can be excluded? Greece will fail on all the criteria and it does not expect to enter, while Denmark has the right to stand aside, and Sweden may prefer to retain its right to devalue which has figured so successfully in its economic policy in the last decade. Britain is entitled to keep well clear of EMU. It is probable, therefore, that the first wave of EMU entrants will comprise 11 members (that is, the fifteen members of the European Union, excluding Greece, Denmark, Sweden and the United Kingdom).

How can Italy be excluded if Spain and Portugal are admitted? France will favour the inclusion of Spain and Italy because French employment and tourism have been severely damaged by the devaluations of its southern neighbours. France would also welcome the presence of Spanish and Italian directors in Europe's central bank. It has not relished the domination of the Bundesbank over French monetary policy for more than a decade, and it hopes that the submergence of a single Bundesbank director within a board that includes many non-German directors will give France the opportunity to recover a degree of influence over its monetary policy. That is likely to remain the view of Lionel Jospin's Socialist government because it reflects the assessment of the nature of French interests of all Socialists and most Gaullists.

Europe's previous monetary union

Few remember France's previous leadership of a European Monetary Union. In 1865 France, Belgium, Italy and Switzerland formed a Latin Monetary Union and were soon joined by the Papal States (on their union with Italy) and Greece.[3] This used the French franc as its common unit of account, and silver coins of equal weight were minted in each country. These were called French francs in France, Belgian francs in Belgium, Swiss francs in Switzerland, lira in Italy and drachmas in Greece.

Difficulties arose in 1866 after Italy printed paper money in time of war and France also printed money in the débâcle of 1870–1. Later in the 1870s the Union's silver coins became seriously over-valued after a collapse in the price of silver in relation to gold. This meant that, like today's paper money, the Union's silver coins were worth more as legal tender than the metal they contained. Germany and Holland unloaded all the over-valued silver coins they could find on France in exchange for gold, which was worth more. Italy's small silver change disappeared overseas and Italian businesses had to use stamps as currency in place of coins. It was in the interests of each country in the Union to issue as many over-valued coins as possible to gain purchasing power at the expense of the others. They had to be restrained from doing so; exceptions were made for Greece and Italy which had special needs for extra resources.

Finally, the dissolution of the Union became a possibility and the other countries asked France for a guarantee that in that event, they would be repaid the gold value of their reserves of silver francs. France declined to give that exchange rate guarantee, Belgium walked out, and the Union dissolved in acrimony, but it had lasted, much diluted, from 1865 until the 1890s. Will a new European Monetary Union (EMU) survive as long?

Can it actually survive its critical three years of transition if it includes some of Europe's most financially vulnerable economies?

The vulnerability of EMU between 1999 and 2002

Europe's unemployment is high and rising. In 1997, Spanish unemployment exceeds 20 per cent while French and Italian unemployment exceed 12 per cent. In the short term, extra public expenditure can preserve jobs which are otherwise threatened by market forces, while tax cuts can be targeted on the costs of employing labour. This the European Commission supports as a means to raise employment.

There will be elections in Europe in 1999, 2000 and 2001 and electorates are desperately concerned to contain unemployment. European governments will want to introduce job-creating strategies which cost public money, and if they have gained entry to EMU through creative accounting, there will be still less resistance to its use afterwards. It is therefore certain that some budgets will move even more strongly into deficit. The sophisticated analysts of the world's capital markets will immediately understand what is happening; it is only Eurostat and a few of Europe's governments which will assert that all is under control.

As with the nineteenth-century Latin Monetary Union, the countries which succeed in running the largest deficits will attract real resources from others with sounder finance. Those with the soundest budgets will resent this, but there will not be a majority of directors in Europe's central bank to prevent it. With confused accounting, those continuing to run sound budgets will not even be able to establish the existence of anything untoward.

A further difficulty is that some of the exchange rates which will be 'irrevocably fixed' on 31 December 1998 will subsequently become inappropriate. The DM 2.95, at which sterling entered the ERM in October 1990, proved unsustainable. France will support the admission of Italy and Spain into EMU but it will exact the price of high initial exchange rates for the lira and the peseta to restore some of its lost competitiveness. Italy and Spain will accept that price to gain admission, but their companies will be embarrassed afterwards, as Britain's were between 1990 and 1992.

Italy held back growth during 1996 while it tightened its budget to qualify for EMU; now it is behind France and Germany in the economic cycle. That will give it all the more reason to expand during 1999 and 2000, and with its exchange rate almost certainly over-valued, its currency will come under pressure in the first years of EMU. Strains will then emerge within Europe. The old safety valve for these was a lower exchange rate, but that solution will no longer be available. The mechanism for redistributing employment within a single currency area, such as the United States, is falling pay in regions where jobs are lost, and rising pay where labour is scarce: such developments have produced great internal migrations. That cannot occur in Europe, which lacks a common language and where governments pay sufficient unemployment benefits to persuade many who lack jobs to remain where they are. According to Rudi Dornbusch, one of the world's most distinguished international economists:

> The United States has substantial flexibility in both wages and labour market institutions. With such arrangements it could conceivably enter a regime of fixed exchange rates. Europe has neither flexible wages nor functioning labor markets, but already has mass unemployment. EMU will add to it, both on the way there and once the system is trapped in fixed rates across divergent countries. If there was ever a bad idea, EMU is it.[4]

Much will be expected from Europe's fixed-currency bloc if it begins to operate in 1999. When Britain entered the ERM in October 1990, the Chancellor, John Major, was immediately able to announce a 1 per cent cut in bank base rates from 15 to 14 per cent. His successor, Norman Lamont, was able to cut them further to 10 per cent by May 1992, and inflation was reduced from 9.5 per cent in 1990 to 3.7 per cent in 1992. Much could be said in favour of the policy to join the ERM, and it was, but in September 1992 the world's foreign exchange markets demonstrated that continuing membership was unsustainable. The world's foreign exchange transactions exceed $1400 billion a day, while the aggregate reserves of all the world's governments total no more than $1400 billion. Governments are impotent where there is any lack of confidence in a politically engineered exchange rate structure. A week before sterling fell, Lamont obtained a 25 billion D-Mark loan. The chairman of one of London's merchant banks remarked: 'For a day everyone was very impressed. The next day they said, "thank you very much" and took the money'.

It took almost two years for sterling to encounter this insurmountable pressure and EMU might have an easy ride at first. But the political pressures to reduce unemployment will eventually strike one or more governments, and a continuation of fictitious budgets will arouse the suspicions of the international financial community. All who operate in a country's currency will take evasive action the moment critical articles on the budgetary policies of any European government begin to appear. The world's plethora of 'teenage scribblers' is paid to write striking articles each week. Journalists pick these up quickly.

Imagine it is Italy (it could just as well be France or Spain). Then all will be conscious of their exposure to the lira and they will not need to hold any. At the irrevocably fixed exchange rates, there will be no penalty in switching lira deposits into D-Marks. Even if the option of switching into Euros exists and the Euro is available as transactions money before 2002, most will prefer D-Marks. In the event of an EMU breakdown, it will prove more profitable to switch from the lira to the D-Mark or the Dutch guilder than from the lira to the Euro. That Italy will be behind Germany and Holland in the cycle will strengthen the case for holding Dutch or German currency if there is any possibility of an EMU breakdown.

There may be an initial agreement in 1999 to convert all the government bonds of EMU members into Euro-denominated bonds. In the absence of such an agreement, those who hold lira-denominated bonds

– and Italy's debt/GDP ratio is more than twice Maastricht's permitted 60 per cent so there are plenty of them – will prefer to have their wealth denominated in D-Marks. They will therefore sell Italian and buy German bills and bonds. Here they will sacrifice some interest: Canada has a single currency, and oil rich Alberta pays 0.60 per cent less interest than the resource-poor maritime provinces and more heavily indebted Quebec. The explanation of North American interest rate differentials within single-currency areas is the additional default risk in heavily indebted cities and provinces. If French Canada can be required to pay more interest than English Canada, more interest can also be required from Italian Europe than from German Europe if it follows less disciplined policies.

If suspicion falls on Italy or Spain, money will flood from Italian and Spanish debt and into the government debt of the rest of Europe. This will add to the interest rate differential against Italy or Spain which will be much discussed in the world's financial press.

All the money that leaves Italy or Spain from holders of bonds and bills, and from exporters and importers who manage to reduce their exposure to the lira or the peseta, will seek a home in bank deposits and in bills and bonds denominated in D-Marks or guilder. In principle, that vast monetary movement could be contained by an equivalent creation of D-Marks by the Bundesbank. The European Central Bank will be able to print Euros, but it will not be free to print D-Marks. Will it concern the Bundesbank if it has to keep buying liras or pesetas and selling D-Marks which it has to print in response to the flood of liras or pesetas which the world is seeking to unload at the irrevocably fixed exchange rates? If the Bundesbank is willing to be an unlimited buyer of liras or pesetas and issuer of D-Marks, the world will be able to change its liras or pesetas into D-Marks if that is what it desires, and the fixed exchange rate will be sustained. All the liras and pesetas and D-Marks will be due to become Euros in 2002, so where will the problem lie?

The difficulty is that a massive printing of D-Marks will leave most Germans, and not least the directors of the Bundesbank, more than unhappy. The situation would be containable if the European Central Bank gave an exchange rate guarantee to all holders of liras and pesetas including the Bundesbank that in 2002 these would unquestionably be exchangeable for Euros at the irrevocably fixed exchange rates. Professor Tim Congdon has pointed out that this guarantee has not been offered and it only can be by Europe's governments. Only they have the real resources to back up a guarantee that, in the event of an

Italian or Spanish departure from EMU, all liras and pesetas will be convertible at the previously agreed exchange rates. In the absence of such a guarantee, Germany and the Bundesbank, acting on its behalf, may be unwilling to flood the world with D-Marks in exchange for liras or pesetas. In the nineteenth-century Latin Monetary Union, France declined to offer an exchange rate guarantee in the event of dissolution. Germany may similarly decline to guarantee the currencies of countries which are allowed to slither into EMU during 1998.

The new European Central bank may have the legal authority to *instruct* the Bundesbank to print an unlimited quantity of D-Marks; but if that instruction is compromised by injunctions in the German courts, where the loss of the D-Mark will have many opponents, the Bundesbank could stall, as it stalled while sterling foundered.

As soon as the possibility of the departure of one or more countries from EMU between 1999 and 2002 is recognised, movement towards the D-Mark will not be confined to those who are exposed to weaker currencies through trade or holdings of debt denominated in their money. There will be staggering opportunities for profit at the expense of those who, like the British government in 1992, seek to hang on to exchange rates which they cannot in the end sustain. George Soros will be there. He has already written:

> In all likelihood the euro will be introduced in 1999 as specified in the timetable ... People will direct all their anger and resentment over unemployment at the single currency. There may well be a political revolt – particularly in France, notorious for such rebellions – and it would likely take a nationalistic anti-European direction ... mounting popular discontent would likely sweep away present policies, including the single currency.[5]

It is to be hoped that the warnings from Dornbusch and Soros and many others will alert Europe's leaders to the cliff-edge before it is too late. Many have warned that the project will end in disaster if the entry conditions are politically manipulated, as they are now bound to be if EMU is to go ahead. The Duke of Wellington remarked nearly two centuries ago: 'Any one can get 10 000 men into a square but it needs a real general to get them out again.'[6] Has Europe the real generals it will need to march eleven governments out of Maastricht?

But the creation of a Euro that survives into 2002 will still leave the task of reducing Europe's unemployment without the advantages that exchange rate flexibility now offer to individual European economies with high unemployment. Will the younger generation of Europe's politicians, which has already taken over in the United Kingdom, be willing to take the risks with employment that the Euro will inevitably create?

Notes

1. See Congdon (1996) for an account of the conditions which will prevail between 1999 and 2002 if EMU is established.
2. Madden (1981), p. 48.
3. This section draws heavily on the article, 'Latin Union' in *Palgrave's Dictionary of Political Economy (1894–1900)*, II, pp. 570–4. *The New Palgrave Dictionary of Economics*, edited by John Eatwell *et al.* in 1987, has omitted this article and failed to replace it with another which includes an account of the Latin Monetary Union: 'Those who forget their history are sentenced to repeat it.'
4. Dornbusch (1996) p. 124.
5. Soros (1996) pp. 10–11.
6. Longford (1972), p. 61.

9

Further Considerations on EMU: It will Create Instability and Destroy Employment*

Introduction

Gordon Brown has declared that: 'The decision on a single currency must be determined by a hard-headed assessment of Britain's economic interests.'[1] This chapter argues that there are fundamental *economic* obstacles to British membership of EMU which will need to be taken into account, even if convergence with the European economies is apparently achieved.

The UK economy is and will remain far more sensitive to interest rate fluctuations than the economies of continental Europe. In addition, the United Kingdom will often require different interest rates.

The UK economy has a very different structure of production from continental Europe. UK exchange rates therefore need to be sensitive to fluctuations in the dollar and the yen as well as the euro.

Despite widespread apprehension to the contrary, the supremacy of the City of London as the financial centre of Europe will not be damaged if the United Kingdom stays out of EMU. Its comparative international efficiency will ensure that it will prosper at least to the same degree as Switzerland, whether or not it continues to maintain an independent currency.

The euro will be especially vulnerable to financial strains during the transition period. International markets will be able to buy and sell

* This is a revised and up-dated version of *Further Considerations on EMU: it will create instability and destroy employment* (London: Centre for Policy Studies, 1998).

bills and bonds denominated in national currencies (where the responsibility to service them is unambiguously tied to their issuer). Interest rate differentials will widen against any country which is evidently finding its membership uncomfortable, and these may impose additional costs on its government.

European governments have so far found no solution to the underlying problem of growing unemployment. The pressures to find solutions may impose unsustainable strains on EMU. The countries with the most intractable unemployment difficulties may question the constraints of EMU membership.

Britain will prosper to a far greater degree outside EMU, and membership will prove especially uncomfortable if critical internal strains develop within the new Euro Area.

Britain will often require different interest rates

In Britain, a large number of banks and building societies compete to take deposits and to lend. In consequence, any family or company which can offer adequate security can obtain all the finance it needs at interest rates which are close to the base rate the Bank of England establishes. Because of the intense competition in the market for finance, this is allocated according to who can afford to pay the market rate of interest and not through administrative decisions by those who control particular banks.

In much of continental Europe, families obtain finance for home ownership or for personal consumption far less readily. Since would-be borrowers have a more limited range of banks and building societies to turn to, they are far more often denied loans. Families cannot finance 90 per cent of the cost of home ownership as in Britain. In consequence, aggregate mortgage debt is 60 per cent of GDP in Britain but only 40 per cent in Germany, 25 per cent in France and less than 10 per cent in Italy. The interest rates paid on these lower levels of personal debt are also less flexible than in the UK. The variable interest rate liabilities of the United Kingdom personal sector total 64 per cent of GDP. They are only 16 per cent in France, 3 per cent in Germany and 2 per cent in Italy.[2] Aggregate continental European bank and building society lending therefore rises and falls far less when interest rates change, both because there is less of it and because it is less sensitive to the rate of interest. This also means that in these countries the rate of growth of the money supply is considerably less sensitive to the rate of interest.

An independent committee chaired by Rupert Pennant-Rea (with a membership which included Sir Peter Gregson, Sir Tim Lankester, Charles Bean, David Begg, David Miles, Richard Portes and Martin Wolf) reported in May 1997 that: 'Simulations on macroeconomic models run by national central banks suggest that, for the UK, the impact of an interest rate change on domestic demand after two years is four times the EU average.'[3] They continued (p. 17):

> The implication of this is clear. Unless UK balance sheets become more European, inside EMU the UK would be more sensitive to changes in short-term interest rates. The impact of any change in European monetary policy would therefore be disproportionately channelled through the UK. As a result the UK economy would be disproportionately volatile.

The UK's share of the EU's GDP was 15 per cent in 1998. If the impact of an interest rate change is four times as great within the United Kingdom as in the remaining six-sevenths of the EU, approximately two-fifths of the total EU-wide impact on aggregate spending of a change in the rate of interest would arise within the United Kingdom and the remaining three-fifths in continental Europe. The United Kingdom would then become the EU's principal regulator of effective demand, with highly damaging consequences for its financial stability.

Past disasters when British interest rates were over-closely tied to those in Frankfurt are familiar. In 1987–9 Nigel Lawson's policy of shadowing the D-Mark had the consequence that London interest rates were inappropriately low. At these bargain rates the British personal and small business sectors rushed to borrow, and bank and building society lending exploded, with the consequence that house prices soared. Shortages of every kind of labour associated with construction developed, and pay accelerated first in construction and then in the remainder of the economy. Inappropriately low interest rates raised the rate of inflation in the United Kingdom from $4^1/_4$ per cent in 1987 to $9^1/_2$ per cent in 1989. There was no comparable acceleration of inflation in continental Europe.

In 1989–92, as a consequence of ERM membership, Chancellors John Major and Norman Lamont were again obliged to pursue a policy of shadowing Frankfurt interest rates. These proved inappropriately high for British conditions in the aftermath of German reunification. Bank and building society lending collapsed, together with house prices and the liquidity of small businesses. Bankruptcies and housing repossessions soared, and the consequent recession proved far deeper in Britain than in continental Europe.

In these episodes the British economy built up steam when the engine drivers in Frankfurt decided that the European boiler needed to be stoked up, while it had to be run down when Frankfurt decided that the European economy was over-heating. Within EMU, the Governor or Deputy-Governor of the Bank of England would become one of the European Central Bank's six executive directors, but one vote out of six (and two out of perhaps twenty in the Bank's broader directorate) would be insufficient to ensure that European interest rates were appropriate for British conditions.

If Britain had actually been among the EMU starters, British interest rates would have had to come down to $2^1/_2$ per cent in April 1999. With rates as low as this, everyone in Britain who wished to move upwards in the housing market would have rushed to take advantage of an apparently unique opportunity to borrow cheaply to purchase more expensive property. Bank and building society lending would have exploded and inflation, led by pay in building and construction, would have soared in relation to that in continental Europe. This would have gone on to undermine the competitiveness of production in the remainder of the economy and Britain would have rapidly become a high-cost area within the new monetary union.

Britain would of course seek to time its entry to coincide with a convergence of interest rates so that it would temporarily appear that the interest rates judged to be appropriate for Frankfurt and Paris were also right for London. But subsequent divergence would arise. When it did, British employees and companies would rediscover that they had been condemned to produce in markets which fluctuated disproportionately in relation to those in continental Europe, in the manner that the Pennant-Rea Committee predicted.

Some believe that the underlying structure of British and continental balance sheets is moving closer together and that these may converge; more British borrowing is now at fixed rates than used to be the case. There is none the less a fundamental difference in the finances of British and continental families. The British personal sector holds far more extensive financial assets, 288 per cent of GDP against 186 per cent in France, 140 per cent in Germany and 162 per cent in Italy. The extra British personal assets mainly consist of greater holdings of equity shares. Far more UK pensions are arranged through the private sector. British governments have correspondingly less liability to finance future pensions. The OECD estimates that in 1997 the net present value of France's future pensions and social security liabilities exceeded Britain's by 176 per cent of its GDP, that Germany's exceeded Britain's by 206 per cent of GDP and Italy's by 259 per cent of GDP. Since personally controlled UK wealth is more extensive, private expenditures will remain far more sensitive to interest rates. In addition to their direct effect on housing finance, they have a large and immediate influence on the equity market which will continue to have a disproportionate impact on consumer spending through the impact of stock market prices on apparent personal wealth in comparison with continental Europe.

There is therefore no realistic prospect of significant convergence between financial balance sheets in Britain and Europe. Within the single currency, the British economy would be destabilised from time to time by booms induced by inappropriate interest rates which produced highly inflationary property and share markets.

Britain will often require a different dollar exchange rate

Membership of EMU would fix the sterling exchange rate in relation to the European currencies, but not with regard to the dollar and the yen. Fixing sterling with respect to the D-Mark and the franc would increase its volatility in relation to the dollar and the yen. In the 1980s and the 1990s, whenever the dollar has risen in relation to the D-Mark, sterling has risen with it. When the dollar has fallen in Frankfurt, sterling has also fallen. Fixing the UK's exchange rate with continental Europe would actually increase its volatility with regard to the rest of the world.

There are fundamental reasons why the sterling exchange rate moves partly with the dollar and partly with the D-Mark. Britain, like the United States but unlike any other EU country, is a significant oil producer. Britain also resembles the United States in the extent of its high-tech industries such as biochemicals, aircraft, scientific instruments and telecommunications. In these the principal international competition comes from the United States and Japan.

The United Kingdom has a higher ratio of high-tech production than France, Germany and Italy. The details are set out in Table 9.1. France, Germany and Italy excel in the mid-tech manufacture of motor vehicles, washing machines, refrigerators, and mechanical engineering products. Britain excels in original research with far more Nobel Prizes than any country except the United States; but it generally requires others to help it to manufacture what it brilliantly designs and develops.

Table 9.1 Shares of high-tech and IT, 1993–1997

	High-tech as per cent of manufacturing (1993–4)		IT as per cent of GDP (1997)
	Value-added	Exports	Expenditure
United States	24.2	37.3	4.53
Japan	22.2	36.7	2.61
United Kingdom	22.2	32.6	3.36
France	18.7	24.2	2.51
Germany	20.1	21.4	2.13
Italy	12.9	15.3	1.45
Spain	13.7	14.3	1.41
Sweden	17.7	21.9	3.45

Sources: OECD and Morgan Stanley for High-tech ratios. European International Technology Observatory for IT.

In the high-tech industries such as pharmaceuticals, where Britain has some of the world's largest and most efficient companies, success in research and development (R&D) is far more significant than skill in the mechanics of production, and Britain has established a large comparative advantage. France and Germany in contrast enjoy a considerable comparative advantage in the mid-tech industries where skills in production are paramount. For UK high-tech production, the sterling–dollar exchange rate matters most.

It is often supposed that because between 50 and 60 per cent of UK trade is with other EU members, and only 15 per cent with the United States, sterling's exchange rate with the United States matters little in relation to its exchange rate with France and Germany. What such calculations ignore is that where Britain exports high-tech products to Europe its principal competition *within Europe* will often come from US companies. A Morgan Stanley survey of companies which enjoyed world-class competitive advantage found that more of these are located in Britain than in France and Germany combined.[4] When such companies sell in Europe, their principal competitors are often equally large and competitive US and Japanese companies.

With EMU membership, Britain's exchange rate would be locked into France's and Germany's, and the interests of UK high-tech production would become subordinate to the influences which determine the appropriate exchange rate for the predominantly mid-tech products of continental Europe.

The advantage of sterling's present flexibility with regard to both the dollar and the European currencies is that foreign exchange markets can take both kinds of influence into account. They do so in general by raising sterling less than the D-Mark when the D-Mark rises, and by reducing it less when the D-Mark falls. That takes account of the particular need to sustain the competitiveness of Britain's high-tech production. Between April 1996 and September 1999 when sterling soared, it rose 34 per cent in relation to the continental currencies, but only 11 per cent in relation to the dollar, so the competitiveness of British high-tech trade was far less undermined. In general, since 1992, sterling has fluctuated approximately half as much against the dollar as it has against the D-Mark.

With a different structure of production from continental Europe's, Britain often needs a different combination of exchange rates. The present flexibility of the sterling rate with regard to both the D-Mark and the dollar delivers this.

British membership of EMU would produce exchange rate stability for companies which compete mainly with European producers, but instability for those which compete mainly with producers based in North America and Asia. It would therefore create exchange rate stability for some multinational companies considering additional investments in the United Kingdom and instability for others. When, in November 1998, multinational companies with large investments in the United Kingdom were asked by MORI whether EMU membership would increase or reduce their investments in Britain, 86 per cent said it would make no difference, while just 11 per cent said they would be more likely to invest here.

The City of London will retain the same advantages as Switzerland

There is some apprehension by those who fail to recognise its comparative efficiency that the City of London will be damaged if Britain stays out of EMU. They assume that monetary union will produce a continental European zone of stability and economic strength: this is far from clear. They also fail to recognise the extent of the City of London's world-wide business: Frankfurt and Paris cannot match London's domination of international financial transactions.

The City of London has vastly more international business than Frankfurt or Paris. In 1998, daily foreign exchange market turnover exceeded $637 billion in the United Kingdom when it was less than

$100 billion in Germany and less than $80 billion in France.[5] Derivatives turnover was almost twice as great in Britain as in France and Germany combined.[6] In 1992 marine insurance was almost twice as great in Britain as in France and Germany combined, while aviation insurance was more than seven times as great.[7] In 1995 cross-border bank lending was greater in London than in France and Germany combined, and equity turnover was one-and-one-half times as great, while turnover in foreign equities was almost thirty times as great: markets for these scarcely existed in Frankfurt and Paris.[8]

Much of this business will be independent of whether or not Britain is part of a single currency area, and London's greater market share is based on its superior efficiency, which produces narrower dealing margins. London gains its exceptional profits through its competitive strength. London's efficiency could be weakened if banking regulations made in Frankfurt reflected continental rather than British interests. Larger capital adequacy ratios of the kind proposed in Germany would in effect tax Britain's already well regulated banks.

Switzerland offers an example of a country which does not maintain exchange rate stability with the currency of any other country, yet none the less sustains a highly prosperous and competitive financial centre. The comparative international efficiency of the City of London would ensure that it could prosper similarly if Britain continued to maintain an independent currency.

EMU's vulnerability

Those who argue that Britain should join EMU believe that this would enable it to enter a large new currency area of strength and stability. But doubts have been widely expressed about its sustainability if some of the countries which have been included have converged insufficiently with Germany. In September 1996 Professor Allan Meltzer told a US Conference: 'I have very little doubt that they will go ahead on January 1 1999. My question is, Will they still be there in 2001?'[9] His apprehension is even shared by Hans Tietmeyer, President of the Bundesbank until July 1999, who told a Karlesruhe audience on 13 October 1997 that: 'sustaining the monetary union may need perhaps more solidarity than beginning it.'

The European Commission has been aware of EMU's vulnerability and it anticipated and sought to prevent the full virulence of the potential for speculative attack which I described in detail in my 1997 Centre for Policy Studies paper, *The Creation and Destruction of EMU*, which is republished here as Chapter 8. In July 1997, the Commission announced that from January 1999 until 2002 when euro notes will actually be used, the D-Marks, French francs, Italian lire and Spanish pesetas which still circulate will be regarded as sub-divisions of the euro, and defined as quantities of euro cents, to be determined as soon as the irrevocably fixed exchange rates are established.[10] If the world's banks sell liras on an enormous scale and buy D-Marks in the manner I described in 1997, they will be selling euros and buying euros, and end up with exactly the quantity of euros they started with. If the euro breaks, the component currencies will not necessarily emerge with their former legal identities because these will all have become sub-units of the euro. That is the European Commission's defence against the potential threat of speculation.

It relies on conformity by the Bundesbank to obligations which require it to print unlimited euro-D-Marks in exchange for euro-liras. If, for any reason, it is slow to do this, a *de facto* premium of the euro-D-Mark over the euro-lira would emerge. Well informed observers are convinced that the Bundesbank will not hesitate in its obligation to print euro-D-Marks in exchange for euro-liras, and that it will then hold these in its balance sheet, or else convey them to the new European Central Bank.

But no defence can be absolute, and even if the Bundesbank acts in the manner that most now assume, EMU will still be open to pressure in the markets for bonds and bills: a significant element in my 1997 account of its vulnerability. Interest-bearing bonds and bills are always specific to the country or company which issues them. Canada has a common currency, but interest rate differentials between the bonds issued by the Canadian provinces have been as high as 150 basis points ($1^1/_2$ per cent) because of their different credit ratings. Differences between the long-term interest rates which Europe's governments pay will remain, despite their common currency, as they do between the Canadian provinces.

Alberta has no responsibility to service Quebec's debt, and the German government will accept no responsibility for debt incurred by the Italian, Spanish and Portugese governments: these will continue to be their legal responsibility. If there is any suspicion of the Italian government's ability to service its debt, whether in liras or euros, its credit rating will fall and the comparative long-term interest rate it has to pay will rise correspondingly. In September 1999, nine months after the establishment of EMU and the irrevocable fixing of exchange rates, the interest rates on the ten-year government bonds of the ten Euroland governments other than Germany were within 40 basis points of Germany's. They were not identically equal: on 28 September, Portugal's interest rate was 38 basis points above Germany's, Belgium's was 32 basis points higher, Finland's was 29 points higher and Italy and Spain paid 25 to 26 points more than Germany: the French government paid only 0.10 per cent more than the German government. These margins change from day to day and they reflect the relative credit ratings of Euroland's eleven member governments.

If EMU breaks, it is likely that German and Italian government debt will again be denominated in D-Marks and liras. But if what emerges from the euro is to be New-D-Marks and New-liras, there is no doubt that the ratio of the New-D mark to the New-lira will exceed that of the Old-D-Mark to the Old-lira which initially entered it. If there is a break-up, those who hold bonds for which German companies or the German government are responsible will gain to whatever degree the ratio, New-D-Mark/New-lira exceeds the Old-D mark/Old-lira ratio. Hence if EMU breaks and Italy in effect devalues by 20 per cent in relation to Germany, those who hold any German bill or bond will gain 20 per cent relative to those who hold any Italian bill or bond.

This will be a one-way bet because it will be known that the post-EMU Italian–German exchange rate can move only in one direction. In comparison, speculating against sterling within the ERM was risky. If sterling had survived in September 1992, it would have risen from the 2.78 D marks at which George Soros sold £1 billion to 2.85 D Marks, and he would have lost nearly £30 million.

If an EMU break-up ever becomes a genuine possibility, most who seek to exploit it will prefer to deal in bills or very short-term bonds so that their potential exchange rate gain will be maximised in relation to other influences. Many bills and bonds issued in the private sector will remain denominated in their present national currencies throughout the three-year transition period. Holding these will involve no shift into and then out of the euro. The proposed regulations which the European Commission published in July 1997 state that during the transition period beteen 1999 and 2002:

> Acts to be performed ... stipulating the use of or denominated in a national currency unit shall be performed in that national currency unit

and it is only in 2002 that 'where reference is made to national curency units, these references shall be read as referring to the euro unit'.

Those who wish to take advantage of a possible break-up and a new exchange rate structure will find no difficulty in discovering bonds and bills which have a continuing legal existence in D-Marks and liras throughout the transition period. They will not buy and sell cash, as in recent waves of speculation, because the European Commission appears to have removed the separate element between cash balances in different European currencies; but the Commission cannot succeed in the same way with bills and bonds where the responsibility to service them is unambiguously and inseparably tied to their issuer.

Hence, if there is an EMU crisis, the financial community will move heavily into bond and bill markets with the consequence that the interest rate differentials which are no more than 0.40 percentage points (and virtually zero with short maturities) will widen. Italian public debt is 120 per cent of the national income and it is mostly in short maturities. Each percentage-point increase in the interest differential against Italy would raise the cost of financing Italian public debt, and therefore Italy's budget deficit, by about $1^1/_4$ per cent of GDP. This would further weaken the market's perception of Italy's public finances, and throw additional costs onto employment in Italy.

The threat to EMU from Europe's growing unemployment

If there is a crisis which threatens EMU's continuation it is likely, as George Soros has intimated, to centre on the inability of the leading European economies to prevent unemployment from rising. Europe's unemployment failure, which was discussed in detail in Chapter 5, lies at the heart of scepticism about prospects for the single currency. Unemployment within the European Union rose from 7 per cent in the same economies in 1980 to $9^1/_2$ per cent in May 1999. In 1980 unemployment was similar in the United States and in Europe. By May 1999 US unemployment had come down to 4.2 per cent while European unemployment had risen to 9.4 per cent. More than 20 per cent of European men and women under the age of 25 who wish to work are unemployed. If European unemployment rises towards 12 per cent and above, with youth unemployment averaging more than 20 per cent, and with still higher unemployment among racial minorities and in inner-city areas, there will be growing threats to law and order in formerly stable societies.

The proportion of Europeans with jobs compares unfavourably with the United States and Japan. In 1998 fewer than 65 per cent of Europeans were employed, while more than 77 per cent of US and

Japanese men and women were in paid employment. Europe's private sectors have created no jobs since 1970 and such job creation as has occurred has been by government. In each economic cycle, no European jobs are created in the expansion phase, and this is followed by job destruction in the subsequent recession. From 1990 to 1993, when recession predominated, 4.4 million EU jobs were lost and unemployment in the eleven countries now in Euroland rose from 8.6 to 10.9 per cent. From 1993 to 1998 when the eleven Euroland economies expanded at an average rate of 2.4 per cent per annum, their average unemployment remained at 10.9 per cent. With this trend, their unemployment will rise to more than 13 per cent in the next recession which could come as soon as the deterioration of Asian markets weakens Europe's exports, or else when the world's stock exchanges suffer a significant correction of their historically high price–earnings ratios. French and Italian unemployment is above the Euroland average, so if in the next recession this rose from 10.9 to 13 per cent, unemployment in France and Italy could approach 14 per cent or worse.

There is a straightforward explanation for the failure of the continental EU economies to create jobs even in periods of economic expansion. European taxation was only slightly above the US level in the 1960s, but since then it has risen sharply, and taxation in Euroland now exceeds that in the United States and Japan by 14 per cent of GDP. Steven Englander of Smith Barney in Paris has produced a cross-country study of taxation and unemployment in OECD economies which suggests that each extra percentage point of taxation in GDP is associated with extra unemployment of 0.3 per cent (Figure 9.1).

The explanation is the principle of the wedge. Taxation of virtually any kind creates a wedge between the sales value which workers and companies create and the wages and profits they receive. The wedge reduces the extent to which workers and companies are rewarded for producing. The tax wedge in eleven-country Euroland now exceeds that in the United States and Japan by 14 per cent of GDP.

Herbert Giersch, the first chairman of Germany's council of economic experts, the 'Five Wise Men', which Ludwig Ehrhardt established in 1964, who made the substantial contribution to the control of inflation in Germany which is described in Chapter 7, has suggested an elaboration. Because taxation raises the real cost of labour, it leads to a substitution of capital for labour with the result that new technology acquires a labour-saving bias.[11] Since the 1970s, taxation has greatly raised the cost of labour in Europe in relation to other factors of production (Figure 9.2). This helps to explain why European

Figure 9.1 Taxation and unemployment rates in OECD economies in 1995

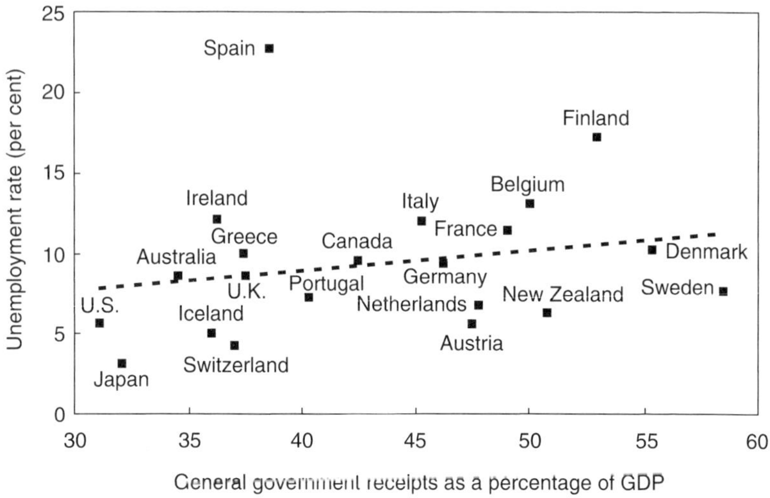

investment expenditures which considerably exceed those in the United States as a share of GDP create virtually no jobs.

In Chapter 6, it was shown that in the United States 43 per cent of all business investment is now concerned with information processing where Europe invests considerably less. (Table 6.2, p. 137). Since 1980 the real cost of IT equipment has fallen 98 per cent in relation to the cost of equipment in general, with the result that workers with the skills to exploit the new technologies can be equipped extremely cheaply with elementary equipment or else with higher-priced plant of extraordinary power and sophistication. This had an extremely favourable impact on job creation in the United States, but as was explained in detail in Chapter 6, for more than a decade Europe handicapped its potential to exploit the new technologies with tariffs and anti-dumping duties on the principal IT components to protect its own manufacturers. These duties will only be fully removed during 1999. European users of IT have hitherto been denied the opportunity to buy the latest equipment as cheaply as purchasers in the United States and Japan, which has placed a brake on purchases of this category of investment with vast potential for job creation. Instead, European producers have invested mainly in the older technologies where, with high real labour costs, investment often has the employment-displacing bias which Giersch identified.

Figure 9.2 European implicit tax rates, 1980–96

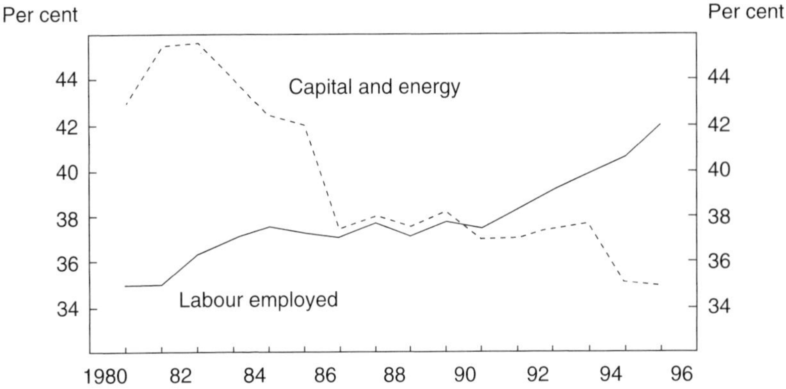

Source: European Commission.

In 1998, Romano Prodi, the former Italian Prime Minister who became President of the European Commission in 1999, and who is also a Professor of Economics, produced a fascinating insight into the comparative technical inertia of European industry in his Jean Monnet Lecture in the European University Institute in Florence. He pointed out that of the twenty-five largest US firms, nineteen did not exist or were 'virtually negligible' in 1960 when neither Microsoft nor Intel had come into being. In contrast in 1998, all twenty-five of Europe's largest companies had already been prominent in 1960, and Europe had created no large new new firms. According to Prodi: 'Europe can boast no leadership in the fundamental industries of microelectronics and information technology.' As for the fifty small European companies with the fastest growth rates, fifteen were British, nine were German, six were French and only four were Italian.[12]

Hence continental Europe has lacked the fast-growing companies, whether large or small, which have been so significant in job creation in the United States. The principal diagnosis of the European Commission is that European unemployment rises at economic growth rates of less than 2 per cent.[13] But overall unemployment in Euroland remained at 10.9 per cent between 1993 and 1998, when growth averaged 2.4 per cent. Faster growth was clearly accompanied by an accelerated level of labour-displacing investment.

European employment also suffers because of labour market rigidities. The IMF reports studies which indicate that real wage flexibility in Europe is only half that in the United States.[14] The IMF has also estimated that in 1997, of Europe's 11 per cent unemployment, between 8 and 9 per cent was structural, and this was especially associated with

> elaborate job and income protection arrangements that raise the cost of labour (including ... high taxes needed to finance social safety nets), discourage job creation and job search, and favor substitution of capital for labour.[15]

The European Commission produced two charts in 1996 to illustrate the adverse impact of labour market rigidities. The Employment and Social Affairs Directorate in Brussels objected to their publication, but the *Financial Times* none the less obtained copies and published the Commission's charts under the heading, 'The Charts they Tried to Suppress' (Figure 9.3). They illustrate how, across Europe, less flexible labour markets and higher costs of making workers redundant have been associated with higher unemployment. The countries with the highest unemployment have made no effort to address these rigidities.

In 1994 the OECD produced a table which showed which countries had the strictest employment protection legislation. The countries comprised the fifteen members of the EU other than Luxembourg with

Figure 9.3 The charts they tried to suppress

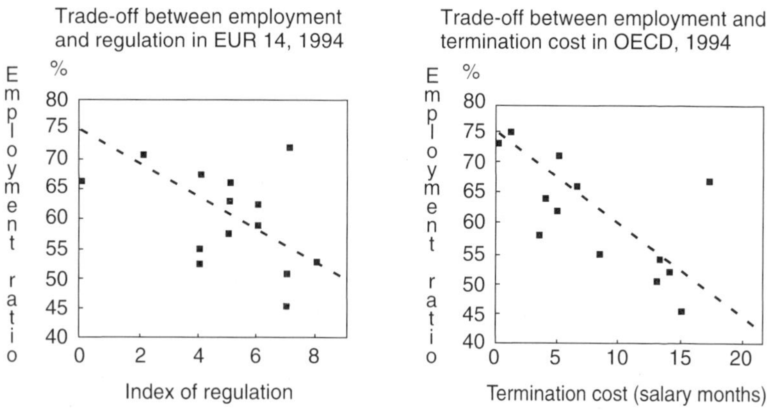

Source: European Commission.

Table 9.2 Indicators of the 'strictness' of employment protection legislation in the late 1980s (summary rankings by countries)[a]

	Regular procedural inconveniences	Notice and severance pay for no-fault dismissal	Difficulty of dismissal	Overall ranking for strictness of protection against dismissals
Austria	10.0	10.0	11.0	13.0
Belgium	4.5	13.0	3.0	5.0
Denmark	1.0	11.0	5.0	4.0
Finland	14.0	9.0	4.0	9.5
France	9.0	7.0	6.5	6.0
Germany	13.0	2.0	12.0	9.5
Greece	8.0	12.0	10.0	12.0
Ireland	6.5	3.0	6.5	3.0
Italy	3.0	16.0	15.0	14.0
Netherlands	16.0	1.0	8.0	7.0
Norway	6.5	6.0	14.0	8.0
Portugal	12.0	15.0	16.0	16.0
Spain	15.0	14.0	13.0	15.0
Sweden	11.0	8.0	9.0	11.0
Switzerland	2.0	4.0	2.0	1.0
United Kingdom	4.5	5.0	1.0	2.0

Note:
a All rankings increase with the strictness of employment protection.
Source: OECD *Jobs Study*: part II Paris: OECD (1994).

the addition of Norway and Switzerland (Table 9.2). Of these sixteen, employees were least protected against dismissal in Switzerland which had 4.7 per cent unemployment in 1994, while they were most strongly protected in Spain where unemployment was 23.7 per cent. Where employees are most protected, companies are apparently the least willing to take on additional staff with the extensive future social commitments they would thereby enter into.

Many of Europe's larger companies, especially in Germany, are restructuring in order to improve their global competitiveness. Typically this results in major job losses. A similar process occurred in the United States, but without negative effects on overall employment. The main explanation is that the United States has a vibrant and entreprenurial small business sector which created millions of new jobs in the 1980s and the 1990s. Continental Europe does not have this benefit, so insufficient new jobs are created to replace those which are lost through corporate restructuring.

The creation of new businesses is central to the achievement of growth in private sector employment, and this is especially inhibited by high taxation and the labour market rigidities which proliferate in continental Europe. Jobs are crowded out by uneconomic minimum wages, and especially those which must be paid to the young and inexperienced whom companies would be prepared to train on-the-job if they could employ them cheaply at the start of their careers. France is replete with firms which limit their employment to nine or forty-nine in order to escape the additional regulations which apply to firms with more than ten and more than fifty employees. Small service sector firms in France are registering to an increasing degree in the United Kingdom to reduce their tax liabilities. The total number of small firms rose by more than 1 million in the United Kingdom in the 1980s, and the self-employed increased by nearly $1^1/_2$ million between 1979 and 1996. France and Germany will require a similar development if the employment they lose through corporate restructuring is to be made good through additional job creation in small businesses.

The leading continental European economies are desperate to find solutions, but those they are actually implementing will add to unemployment. The former Communists on whom the French and Italian governments rely for their parliamentary majorities do not countenance fundamental labour market reforms, while the French and Italian trade unions cling to hard-won privileges which add to the rigidity of labour markets, and they have never been defeated in a significant conflict with government.

In Germany Gerhard Schröder's Red–Green coalition does not depend on the parliamentary support of former Communists, but the Greens are far on the European Left with a considerable Marxist background. The Socialists and the Greens are equally hostile to proposals from employers to reduce Germany's severe labour market rigidities. The German trade unions, which are politically close to leading members of the government, insist on national pay scales so that workers in areas of high unemployment cannot be priced into jobs. They also insist that the rights of those who already have jobs, the so-called 'insiders' in the labour market, cannot be diluted. Hence those in work prosper, while 'outsiders' without employment cannot be brought in. Employers have no desire to extend the insiders' privileges to additional workers. According to Table 9.2, there are nine European economies where it was easier to make workers redundant than in Germany. It is, moreover, in Germany that the relative cost of labour is highest and the bias towards labour-economising technologies is therefore greatest.

Europe's private sector employment would be assisted if overall taxation could be reduced, and the tax wedge diminished; but there is no possibility of any overall reduction in the ratio of public expenditure to GDP. The domestic policies of all the leading European countries have a tendency to raise public expenditure, and demographic trends, together with the manner in which the leading continental European economies have failed to fund their future pensions liabilities, will massively increase public expenditure and hence the need to raise taxation in the early decades of the next century. The OECD has estimated that over the next three decades, French taxes will need to rise by 6.6 per cent of GDP to finance growing pensions' liabilities, German taxes by 8.8 per cent and Italian taxes by 10.2 per cent.[16]

Faced by apparently intractable obstacles to orthodox economic solutions, several continental European governments have rediscovered the 'lump of labour' theory, based on the notion that the amount of employment which an economy provides is given, so that there will be jobs for more people if the hours during which each works is reduced. The IMF shows how such policies 'exacerbate structural problems':

> labour market policies have often sought to mask the underlying problems by promoting early retirement or work sharing. Such measures appear to be intended to reduce open unemployent not by increasing the demand for labor but by reducing labor supply. But with unreformed labor markets, such measures tend to improve the bargaining position of insiders and raise their real wages, with little benefit to outsiders who are likely to remain unemployed. (*Economic Outlook*, October 1997, p. 12)

The most striking example is the decision by the French and Italian governments (probably to be joined by Germany's Red–Green coalition) to reduce the working week from 39 to 35-hours with no reduction in pay. This will evidently raise the real cost of labour by 11 per cent and so destroy marginal employment (and thus reduce the economy's 'lump of labour') but higher pay per hour for insiders will price other workers out of jobs. There is some French recognition of the laws of economics, because the 35 hour week is to be implemented in full in the private but not the public sector: the government recognises that it cannot afford its inflationary consequences.

The 35-hour week is actually a reversion to the economics of *Das Kapital*, first published in 1867. The former Communists who became ministers in France in 1996 will know it extremely well; it shows how income distribution between profits and wages is determined by an economy's 'rate of exploitation' which Marx defined as the number of hours in which workers work for capitalists divided by the hours in which they work for themselves. Any reduction in the working week cuts the hours during which employees work for capitalists without reducing those in which they work to produce their own wages. There are numerous and extensive passages in *Das Kapital* which show how frequently the nineteenth-century class struggle took the form of efforts by workers to reduce the working week, and so diminish the rate of exploitation and the share of profits.[17] Industrial workers produce vastly more than their wages throughout Marx's writings so higher pay never prices them out of jobs. The marginal revolution entered economics only in the 1870s, a decade after the publication of *Das Kapital*.

That probably explains why former Communists and Germany's former Marxists attach such priority to the achievement of a shorter working week; but the acquiescence of the brilliant *énarques* who control the French Socialist party in this reversion to the economics of 1867 is more difficult to understand. It is doubtless a price they have had to pay for a parliamentary majority. Dominique Strauss-Kahn, France's Finance Minister until November 1999, has perceptively described the 35-hour week as 'economic madness'; but Lionel Jospin, France's Prime Minister, told a Socialist party meeting on 24 January 1998 that cutting the working week is 'a symbol of the workers' struggle which has been going on since the nineteenth century'.

It may be a symbol, but it underlines the irrelevance of the policies which are actually being addressed to Europe's unemployment crisis. The same is true of public sector 'make-work' schemes for the young in both France and Germany, consisting of work with no economic function. These may have a temporary cosmetic influence on the unemployment rate, but they will increase public expenditure and therefore overall taxation, raise the 'tax wedge' and render the creation of private sector jobs still more difficult. President Chirac understood this utterly when he said in 1998: 'It is the private sector which creates jobs and wealth: all the rest is nonsense.'

EMU's prospective instability

Faced by growing political discontent, Euroland's governments will be desperate to find solutions. Within EMU they will be able to do little or nothing to reduce unemployment. Fiscal expansion is apparently ruled out by the Stability Pact, which only permits budget deficits of up to 3 per cent of GDP. Most of 1999's eleven starters have entered EMU with deficits already at that level, so the rules permit no further fiscal expansion.

There is also no scope for general European reflation within the EU budget. Total EU budgetary expenditures are limited to 1.8 per cent of GDP, and this is already absorbed by previous commitments, including especially agricultural subsidies. Any increase in the EU budget has moreover, to be agreed unanimously.

It is likely that any possible attempts by Europe's governments to resurrect Keynesian policies will therefore be frustrated. Because most of the Euroland eleven already have 3 per cent deficits, net fiscal expansion will be achievable only through further manipulation of national accounts, the scope for which will be limited, or else attempts to renegotiate the stability-pact. France's Strauss-Kahn was entirely aware of how the large swing of the US economy into fiscal deficit in President Reagan's first years led to a massive escalation of US interest rates and an over-valued dollar, so France will be unsympathetic to any pressures for combined fiscal reflation. Euroland's high unemployment is, moroever, fundamentally structural, and even if significant Keynesian reflation could be negotiated, despite the Stability Pact, it would do little to arrest the growing unemployment associated with the inability of most of Europe's private sectors to create jobs.

With the EU's overall ratio of taxation in GDP at 50 per cent and its continuing tendency to rise, and the introduction of new 'flat-earth' rigidities in France and Italy, private sector job creation will not revive. New government attempts to create employment will raise taxation further and accentuate the labour-displacing tendency of investment in the private sector. European governments will therefore be powerless to prevent the next step jump in unemployment.

Even if Euroland's mainly Centre-Left governments agree to implement policies to reduce labour market rigidities, despite the uncompromising opposition of trade unions and unreformed Socialist ministers, the UK example suggests that it would take up to ten years for such reforms to significantly influence the overall level of structural unemployment. Britain's equilibrium unemployment rate came down only in the 1990s after more than a decade of market-freeing reforms which went far further than most Euroland governments would conceivably contemplate.

After the large further step rise in unemployment which is to be expected in the next recession, Europe's electorates and the politicians who represent them will become desperate. If they are unable to face the realities of labour market rigidities and rising taxation, they may thrash around for false solutions and insist on the adoption of monetary policies which undermine the authority of Europe's Central Bank and the stability of the euro.

In theory, the euro is controlled by some of Europe's most distinguished central bankers, but will governments actually be content to leave the principal monetary decisions to Wim Duesenberg and Otmar Issing and their fellow directors?

Europe's politicians have an immediate means to influence the monetary decisions of the European Central Bank because exchange rate policy remains with national governments. In theory these can seek exchange rates between the euro, the dollar and the yen which would oblige the European Central Bank to adopt inappropriate interest rates. In 1987, when Nigel Lawson decided that the pound would shadow the D-Mark, it followed that London interest rates had to be set at inappropriately low levels to hold sterling down. If EMU's eleven founder governments decide to initiate an exchange rate strategy, they could oblige the European Central Bank to set interest rates accordingly.

The machinery for inter-governmental agreement on such interventions already exists in the Euro-X Committee of Euroland's eleven finance ministers, which France insisted on as a political counterweight to the otherwise dominant and legally independent bankers. President Chirac has spoken of the desirability of target exchange rate zones between the euro, the dollar and the yen. The US government is entirely opposed to these, and sustainable target zones can be established only through agreement between the European, US and Japanese governments. The costs of foreign exchange market intervention to sustain target exchange rates which markets consider inappropriate could not be met by European governments alone, and there would be difficulty, even if the world's leading governments agreed, because *daily* foreign exchange market turnover approximately equals the combined reserves of all the world's governments. Hence, any Euroland ambitions for exchange rate targets are also likely to be frustrated. But if there is growing frustration in the Euro-X committee, there will be all kinds of efforts to influence the bankers who control the European Central Bank. Whether they will be allowed to run the euro free from political pressure remains an open question, which will be resolved only when it is entirely clear that Duesenberg's successor, who will owe his appointment to President Chirac (see Chapter 7 above), is equally determined to preside over an independent monetary policy.

With a continuing inability to reduce unemployment, politicians in countries where its rise appears most intractable may begin to question the constraints of EMU membership. This prevents individual governments from adjusting their relative interest and exchange rates, and if significant fiscal adjustment is also denied them because their deficits are already close to 3 per cent, no way will remain for them to satisfy the expectations of their electorates. The world's financial community will note any speeches by potential future ministers which regret the constraints of EMU membership. It will do so by avoiding bills and bonds issued by companies and governments in countries where there are speeches against EMU. This will create a significant interest rate differential against these countries' bonds. That would accentuate their financial difficulties in the manner which has been described. This is one scenario for an EMU break-up, close to the one which David Lascelles of the Centre for the Study of Financial Institutions has outlined,[18] and to George Soros' 1996 account of EMU's vulnerability.[19] There are many others.

There was no provision in the Maastricht Treaty for the European Central bank to fulfil the lender of last resort function which has been required of all central banks from time to time. The United States had to rescue the 'Thrifts and Loans' in the 1980s at a cost of approximately 9 per cent of GDP. Non-performing loans in the Japanese banking system totalled up to 30 per cent of GDP in 1998, and banks are now receiving massive government support. If it emerges that, for instance, Spain's banks are over-committed to Latin America, or Germany's to Eastern Europe, their rescue will require far more than 3 per cent of Spain's or Germany's GDP. No official provision has been made for such eventualities, and their inevitable monetary consequences. It goes without saying that huge issues of government bonds by any one government to finance bank rescues could create a considerable adverse interest rate differential against that government if there was any question that they would be serviced.

General Von Moltke, who presided over Germany's victory over France at Sedan in 1870, used to say that: 'the enemy has three alternatives, and of these he will choose the fourth.' The ways in which EMU may founder are equally various.

The United Kingdom should continue to keep clear of these developments. It is at last beginning to succeed in the independent management of its monetary policy. Even if EMU prospers, Britain will generally require higher or lower interest rates than those in continental Europe. Outside a successful EMU, The City of London will enjoy the advantages which have made Switzerland a great financial centre. If EMU fails, for whatever reason, it will prove to be greatly in Britain's interests if it has continued to keep its distance from arrangements which expensively fall apart.

Notes

1. HM Treasury (1997), p. 1.
2. Dresdner Kleinwort Benson Research (1998) p. 132.
3. Pennant-Rea Committee (1997), p. 17.
4. Roach (1996).
5. *Bank of England Quarterly Bulletin* (November 1998), p. 349.
6. *Ibid.*, p. 353.
7. Corporation of Lloyds.
8. 'Country shares in Selected International Markets', City Competitiveness Group, Bank of England.
9. Gedmin (1997) p. 40.
10. Resolution of the European Council of 7 July 1997, 'on the legal framework for the introduction of the Euro' (97/C 236/04).
11. Giersch (1991).
12. Prodi (1998), pp. 111–12.
13. European Commission (1997b), p. 6.
14. IMF (1997a), p. 64.
15. IMF (1997b), pp. 11–13.
16. Dresdner Kleinwort Benson Research (1998), p. 135.
17. The index of the first volume of *Das Kapital* ([1867] 1974) has references to 'workers' struggle for shorter working-day' on pp. 171–2, 219–20, 225, 241, 257–8, 265, 268–9, 274–7 and 385–6; and to 'the prolongation of working-day and magnitude of surplus-value' on pp. 486–96 and 513–14.
18. Lascelles (1996).
19. Soros (1996).

Part IV

Historical Lessons

10
John Locke and the Establishment of a Sound Currency*

We owe one of the first coherent statements of the relationship between the quantity of money and the price level to John Locke, who achieved distinction over a far wider range of professions than his philosophy, for which he is most honoured and remembered.

His *Essay Concerning Human Understanding* (Locke, 1689b) established his reputation as one of the greatest philosophers. In addition, he achieved significant cures as a doctor and surgeon. As a participant in English politics he was appointed to distinguished positions and had to flee the country for five years to save his life when his political friends were accused of treason. He was also an extremely effective and original economic writer who provided one of the first statements of the relationship between the quantity of money and the price level in *Some Considerations of the Consequences of the Lowering of Interest and Raising the Value of Money* (Locke, 1692).

How he acquired a detailed knowledge of the financial world that enabled him to achieve a major advance in monetary economics, which commanded the attention of William III and his Council and led to decisions which established sterling on a sound basis for more than 200 years, is a remarkable story.

Locke, the son of a Somerset lawyer who left him land worth £75 a year, was one of the most academically distinguished of his generation. In 1660 he was appointed a lecturer in Greek at Oxford University. Two years later he also became a lecturer in Rhetoric, and he was soon

* From 'John Locke, the Quantity Theory of Money and the Establishment of a Sound Currency', Chapter 1 in M. Blaug (ed.), *The Quantity Theory of Money from Locke to Keynes and Friedman* (Aldershot: Edward Elgar, 1995), pp. 4–26.

elected to a permanent Fellowship at Christ Church. His friends included the great chemist Robert Boyle, and he wished to move from Greek and Rhetoric to natural science and in particular medicine. He studied the subject, but Oxford University would not allow him to become a Doctor of Medicine.

An opportunity then came to Locke which transformed his life. Oxford tutors often meet the great and the children of the great. Locke taught the son of Anthony Ashley Cooper, the Protestant Whig statesman who later became the Earl of Shaftesbury and Lord Chancellor. Shaftesbury was ill, and his grandson, the third Earl, has written that 'he had this young physician [Locke] presented to him, who though he had never practised physic, yet appeared to my grandfather to be such a genius that he valued him above all his other physicians, the great men in practice of those times' (Cranston, 1957, p. 95). Locke was immediately invited to make Shaftesbury's family his own, and two years later he presided over a successful operation to remove a cyst from Shaftesbury's liver. Pepys the diarist has written that Shaftesbury is 'like to die, having some imposthume in his breast, that he hath been fain to be cut into his body' (*ibid.*, p. 113) Locke saved his life and from that point he left Oxford and embarked on a career in British public life in the personal entourage of a future Lord Chancellor.

The immediate product of Locke's residence in Exeter House, Shaftesbury's London home, was an economic paper on the lowering of interest, which provided the original draft of the first half of *Some Considerations of the Consequences of the Lowering of Interest*. He wrote four other brief economic papers in 1688–9 which were published for the first time in 1991 (Locke, 1991, pp. 485–500). Shaftesbury made Locke Secretary to the Lord Proprietors of Carolina, where he drew up the *Fundamental Constitution for the Government of Carolina*. Locke's draft had the Lord Proprietors running Carolina, but it was not long before democracy was preferred to oligarchy in North America, and Locke's constitution was never adopted.

In 1672 Shaftesbury became the leading minister and Locke was given one government appointment as Registrar of the Excise with a salary of £175 a year, another as Secretary of Presentations with a Salary of £300 a year (for which he had to handle the Lord Chancellor's right to make appointments in the Church of England), and a third a year later as Secretary to the Council of Trade and Plantations at an official salary of £600, which he had to wait until 1693 to receive. At this time his income at Christ Church would have been less than £50 a year. The Council of Trade and Plantations was concerned with all the involvements of government with trade and colonies.

Locke's period in government in his early forties was to last only two years, because in 1674 Shaftesbury was replaced by the Earl of Danby as chief minister, and Locke lost the official positions he had owed to Shaftesbury. He stayed in Oxford only briefly, and embarked almost immediately on a five-year visit to France. Locke's principal biographer, Maurice Cranston, has remarked that it is curious that Locke went to France just before Shaftesbury's negotiations with the French Court began, and returned to England immediately after their objective, the fall of Danby, was achieved. Shaftesbury's grandson, the third Earl, has remarked that Locke was entrusted with the most secret negotiations and that he now shared in Shaftesbury's danger as before he had shared in honours and advantages (Cranston, 1957, p. 159). It was probably while he was living in the Paris Embassy that he conducted negotiations between the French Court and the English opposition and the Ambassador is thought to have been a co-conspirator.

On Danby's fall in 1679 Locke returned immediately to London, where Shaftesbury was now again a minister, but was there for only six months and no government appointments came his way. Locke actually returned to Oxford where he arranged accommodation for Shaftesbury's entourage when Parliament met there is 1681. Later in 1681 Shaftesbury's fortunes fell further and he was imprisoned in the Tower of London and accused of high treason. In late seventeenth century English politics evidence was manufactured against political opponents accused of treason through adventurers prepared to give perjured evidence in Court, and those found guilty were executed. Shaftesbury was accused of having used such people, and while he himself was acquitted of treason and released, his associates began to be prosecuted and executed. One of Locke's colleagues at Christ Church had been making regular reports on him for two years and it was suggested that the Bishop of Oxford and the Dean of Christ Church should have his rooms searched for incriminating documents. He had in fact destroyed or passed on the papers which concerned his work with Shaftesbury to a close friend, but in 1683 he perceived that the net was closing and that prosecution was likely, so he went into exile in Amsterdam. Shaftesbury had in the meantime organised a further conspiracy that failed, and had already escaped to Holland in 1682, where he died shortly before Locke's arrival.

Locke was a strong believer in the political liberties associated with parliamentary government, and in his *Two Treatises of Government*

(Locke, 1689a) he argued that there was an implicit contract between the people of a country and the sovereign, and that the king might be removed and another substituted if he broke his part of the contract by failing to maintain the liberties and property rights of his subjects. He wrote these books in Holland and also his *Essay Concerning Human Understanding*, his principal contribution to philosophy, but they remained unpublished until his return to England. His *Two Treatises of Government* provided an intellectual foundation for the removal of the Roman Catholic James II from the throne of England and his replacement by William, the Protestant Prince of Orange who ruled in Holland and was married to James II's daughter, Mary.

By 1688, William was aware that he would receive much support if he crossed the Channel with an army. He sailed for England with 400 ships in 1688, much of James II's army went over to him and James fled the country. The Prince of Orange shortly afterwards became King William III of England and reigned jointly with his wife Mary. Locke was close to those who were advising the new King, especially Lord Mordaunt, a Christ Church man who became Earl of Peterborough and one of William's principal ministers. His *Two Treatises of Government* provided a philosophical justification for the 'Glorious Revolution', as Whig Historians were to describe the events of 1688, and Locke returned to England eleven days after William accepted the throne. Lord Mordaunt wrote to Locke to offer him the English Ambassadorship to Frederic III, Elector of Brandenburg. Locke declined the offer. He was then offered the Vienna embassy, which he also turned down. He accepted the post of Commissioner of Appeals with a salary of £200 a year, and minimal duties which allowed him to devote all his energies to philosophy and, from 1691, economics, and to the controversies his publications were soon to arouse. In 1689 he published the great books he had been writing in Holland and so established a reputation as one of the greatest living philosophers.

Locke lived the life of a scholar in his newly purchased country home 'Oates' in Essex, with frequent visits to London where his influential friends now included several Members of Parliament and, in particular, Sir John Somers, the Solicitor General, who had successfully defended seven Protestant bishops when they were prosecuted by James II. Somers went on to become Lord Chancellor; he has a statue in today's House of Commons. He persuaded Locke to elaborate and publish the study of the rate of interest that he had written for Shaftesbury in 1668. This had become highly topical. Locke's study had been written as a response to Sir Josiah Child, who had published an influential book, *Brief Observations concerning Trade, and Interest of Money*, in 1668. In it, he advocated a reduction in the maximum rate of interest anyone was allowed to charge from 6 to 4 per cent. This was republished in a revised version in 1690, together with several new pamphlets by others (Horsefield, 1960, pp. 283–4), and there were proposals in the House of Commons to cut the maximum legally chargeable interest rate. Locke believed that this would have highly damaging effects.

At the same time England's silver coinage was losing its value, because the practice of clipping silver from the edges of the coins was becoming widespread. The Mint was issuing new full-sized coins with milled edges to prevent clipping, and these were becoming the only English coins that foreign merchants would accept, so the new heavy coins quickly went abroad. The lighter and smaller clipped coins which had had some of their silver removed predominated in domestic circulation.

Some were beginning to propose that the new official coins should be minted smaller so that they would contain equivalent silver to the smaller clipped coins in circulation. It was suggested alternatively that newly minted full-sized coins should legally be worth more shillings and pence than before. Locke was strongly opposed to these proposals to reduce the amount of silver in the pound sterling because he regarded them as highly inflationary and because they would in effect defraud all those who were contractually entitled to receive fixed sums of money. In his own case he had the right to receive rents of approximately £75 a year. If the new proposals were implemented, these would either be paid in smaller silver coins, or else in coins of the same size but with a larger number of shillings stamped on them. In either case he would receive less silver for the £75 of rent to which he was legally entitled, so he and others in his situation would be deprived of some of their former income when this was measured in silver, for they would inevitably receive fewer ounces of silver.

Locke was also concerned that because light and heavy silver coins apparently worth the same number of shillings coexisted in English money, all who spent or received money were beginning to take time and trouble to discover which kind of coin they should receive. Foreigners insisted on receiving the heavy ones. The mercenary at home were beginning to do the same; where they received heavy coins, they had an incentive to keep them or melt them down rather than pass them on to someone who might accept a lighter coin that contained less silver. That meant that monetary transactions were becoming more time-consuming than before and English trade and commerce was being handicapped by an inadequate coinage. Locke regarded this as a transaction cost which would damage every family in England. Lady Masham wrote after his death:

> I am ... sure that what loss our nation suffered by the slowness with which men were made sensible of what must be the remedy to our disease in the debasing and clipping of our coin might, had he been hearkened to, have had a much earlier cure, for from the first year of his return into England [in 1688] (when nobody else appeared sensible of this matter) he was very much troubled concerning it; and in talking on the subject of our public affairs, has often said to me that we had one evil which nobody complained of that was more surely ominous than many others wherewith we were easily frightened, and that if that unminded leak in our vessel were not timely looked after, we should infallibly sink, though all the rest were ever so safe. And when at my lodgings in London, the company there finding him often afflicted about a matter which nobody else took any notice of, railed him upon this uneasiness as being a visionary trouble he has more than once replied [that] we might laugh at it, but it would not be long before we should want money to send our servants to market with for bread and meat, which was so true five or six years after that there was not a family in England which did not find this a difficulty. (Cranston, 1957, pp. 351–2)

It is not surprising, given these perceptions, that Locke decided to explain why those who were tampering with the English currency were doing serious damage. With this significant economic concern, in addition to his objections to a reduction in the maximum legally chargeable interest rate, Locke decided to write a major book on monetary economics, and he hardly needed Sir John Somers' encouragement to do so. His qualifications were his period of six years close to the centre of government from 1668 to 1674, when Shaftesbury held high office, and the many years he had since spent near to those at the heart of political and financial affairs.

The content of *Some Considerations of the Lowering of Interest*

The content of Locke's book of 1692 is most easily grasped by examining the principal economic propositions he took care to explain, which together make up a powerful policy position. He sought to establish:

1. That a market or 'natural' rate of interest would be established by the supply and demand for loans, and any attempt to fix a lower interest rate by law would cause some potential lenders to hoard their money, so that there would be less money in active circulation.
2. That there is a specific need for money to circulate the produce of the nation that varies with the level of total production and the price level. Any shortfall of money below this necessary amount would lead to lower production or to lower prices. Hence a ceiling to interest rates which reduced the money supply would force down production or prices.
3. That the money supply could only be raised by bringing in money from overseas through an excess of exports over imports. Hence free markets for borrowing and lending, and the establishment of a trade surplus are the means to acquire a money supply that is sufficient to allow the nation to achieve its productive potential.
4. That any attempt to tamper with the currency by reducing the amount of silver in the pound sterling would defraud creditors and the government (as a tax collector), and raise prices in line with any reduction in the silver content of the pound.

Locke's demonstration of these four key propositions will be explained in turn.

The economic damage from establishing a maximum legal interest rate below the market rate

Locke's 1668 essay for Shaftesbury and his 1692 book which he dedicated to Somers both open with very full statements of the proposition that maximum interest rates cannot be fixed by law without causing serious economic damage. Locke explains how the market rate of interest, which he calls the 'natural' rate, will be determined by market forces depending on the demand for loans and the supply of funds available for lending. But what will happen if a statutory maximum rate of interest is fixed below this 'natural' or market rate?

First, widows and orphans will lose because they will merely receive the legal maximum rate instead of the higher 'natural' market rate, while bankers and merchants will to a degree get round the prohibitions. They will freely swear untruths because this is common in commerce: Locke points out that captains of ships regularly swear to lies about the origins of their cargoes to the Customs and Excise. This is socially tolerated, but it has the effect of bringing oaths into general disrepute. There are also ways of making interest appear to be something else which Locke does not explain. Antoin Murphy, in his book on Richard Cantillon's financial transactions in the early seventeenth century (Murphy, 1986), explains how merchants and financiers can set out loan contracts so that interest is disguised in a transaction involving foreign exchange. If a merchant agrees to lend pounds sterling in 1691 and to receive back Dutch guilders in 1692, the number of guilders he will receive in a year's time will partly depend on the rate of interest and partly on the exchange rate between the pound and the guilder, so none will readily discover whether the merchant will receive more than the 6 per cent maximum legal rate that prevailed in 1692 or the 4 per cent that reformers were seeking to establish.

In so far as the proposed prohibition of interest rates in excess of 4 per cent was actually operative, the desired effect of assisting industry and commerce by cheapening commercial loans would not be achieved. Those who hold money are under no obligation to place it in the loans market. There are always risks in lending, and the rate of interest must be high enough to compensate for the possibility that a loan will not be repaid. Locke argued that, for some, a 4 per cent interest rate would be inadequate to cover those risks, and this money would not be put out on loan. It would either be held unproductively or else it would go abroad, while less foreign money would come to England for investment purposes if it earned lower interest rates in London. Reducing the legal maximum interest rate would therefore cut the amount of money in active circulation.

The influence of the money supply on prices and output

Locke explains that any commodity can act as money, and any quantity of it can finance any level of domestic output:

> That if in any Country they use for Money any lasting Material, whereof there is not any more to be got ... any quantity of that Money (if it were but so much that every body might have some) would serve to drive any proportion of Trade, whether more or less, there being Counters enough to reckon by. (Locke, 1692, pp. 75–6)

But the finance of international trade requires that these counters be recognised and accepted as money in other countries:

> Navigation and Commerce have brought all parts acquainted with one another, and introduced the use of Gold and Silver Money into all Trading parts of the World ...

> That therefore in any Country that hath Commerce with the rest of the World, it is almost impossible now to be without the use of Silver Coin; and having Money of that, and Accounts kept in such Money. (Locke, 1692, pp. 76–7)

With silver established as the monetary metal in a world where there is trade, it no longer follows that any quantity of money will suffice to finance any level of transactions:

> That in a Country that hath open Commerce with the rest of the World, and uses Money made of the same Materials with their Neighbours, any quantity of that Money will not serve to drive any quantity of Trade; but there must be a certain proportion between their *Money* and *Trade*. (Locke, 1692, p. 77)

Locke then set out his explanation of the relationship between the quantity of silver, the level of output and the price level. He did this by setting out the main kinds of economic transaction in 1692; the regular payments of rent and wages, and continual commercial dealing, and estimated how much money would be required for each. Workers were paid weekly, so Locke estimated that a money supply equal to one-fiftieth of annual wages would be needed to finance the transactions of workers. Rents were paid twice yearly, so further money equal to approximately half of annual rents would be necessary, and he estimated that merchants (Locke called them brokers) would need average money balances of one-twentieth of their annual incomes. 'Country Scholars of all sorts, Women, Gamesters and Great Mens menial Servants' (Locke 1692, p. 41) would also need money, but the demand for this stemmed primarily from the need to finance the transactions of workers, tenant farmers, landlords and merchants. He therefore derived a complete statement of the amount of money a country would need 'to carry on trade', by setting out the components of what would today be called a demand for money schedule. He went on to show the implications of a fall in the quantity of money in a country where each kind of economic transaction required a particular amount of money at the then ruling level of prices:

> Supposing then, that we had now in *England* but half as much Money, as we had seven Years ago, and yet had still as much yearly Product of Commodities, as many Hands to Work them, and as many Brokers to disperse them, as before; and that the rest of the

> World we Trade with, had as much Money, as they had before, (for 'tis likely they should have more by our Moiety shared amongst them) 'tis certain, that either half our *Rents* should not be paid, half our *Commodities* not vented, and half our *Labourers* not imployed, and so half the *Trade* be clearly lost; or else, that every one of these must receive but half the Money, for their Commodities and Labour, they did before, and but half so much as our Neighbours do receive the same Labour and the same natural Product, at the same time. (Locke, 1692, pp. 77–8)

So, given Locke's demand for money schedule, halving the money supply in England would lead either to a halving of output and employment or to a halving of wages, prices and rents. Locke explains carefully how the value of money, like the value of everything else, will depend on a comparison of the quantity of that thing and its vent, that is the market demand for it. In the case of money, there is a quantity of money in circulation and a demand for money which depends on what is needed to finance transactions, and the value of money will depend on their interaction.

Laws which set an upper limit to the rate of interest would cut the quantity of money in circulation for:

> we may see what Injury the Lowering of *Interest* is like to do to us by hindering Trade, when it shall either make the Foreigner call home his Money, or your own People backward to lend, the Reward not being judged proportionable to the risque. (Locke, 1692, p. 44)

This will go on to force down output or the price level which depends on the quantity of money in active circulation.

The relationship between the trade balance and the money supply

Since money is indispensable for the financing of all the financial transactions that make trade possible, it is important to discover how a country can actually get more money into circulation so that it can raise the demand for its produce. Here Locke was utterly aware of what Thomas Mun had demonstrated in 1664: that changes in the domestic money supply will depend on whether trade is in surplus, in which case silver or gold will flow into England, or in deficit, when silver or gold must flow out to pay for such English imports as are not being paid for with exports. Locke writes similarly that 'Money is brought into *England* by nothing but spending here less of Foreign Commodities, than what we carry to Market can pay for' (Locke, 1692, p. 29) and:

> if your Exportation will not Ballance your Importation ... away must your Silver go again, whether Monied or not Monied. For where Goods do not, Silver must pay for the Commodities you spend. (Locke, 1692, p. 149)

Locke explains carefully how a farmer will gradually lose his silver and gold if his expenditure exceeds his income, and gain silver and gold to the extent that he saves some of his income. He goes on to say that 'A Kingdom grows Rich, or Poor just as a Farmer doth, and no otherwise'. (Locke, 1692, p. 26).In both cases money can be brought in if sales are adequate (in the case of the kingdom, sales overseas) but it is also necessary that less than the full income be spent: 'We may Trade, and be busie, and grow Poor by it, unless we regulate our Expences' (Locke, 1692, p. 28).

Whether the English money supply rises or falls will therefore depend fundamentally on the balance of trade, which in turn will depend mainly on the level of exports, and whether domestic extravagance or foreign wars are producing a still higher level of imports or other expenditures overseas. If they are, the English money supply must fall, but it will grow if there is sufficient moderation in domestic expenditure to allow some export revenues to bring in money instead of imported commodities.

Prosperity will then depend on an adequate supply of money to keep up employment and prices, and this in turn will depend upon sufficient economies in domestic expenditure to prevent export revenues from being overbalanced by imports. With an export surplus, money must come in and bid up employment or prices. These are the fundamentals, and any expedient such as fixing a maximum interest rate by law will make money more scarce instead of more plentiful because it will cause some of the potential money supply to be withdrawn from circulation. These are the main propositions in the first part of Locke's book, and they are an elaboration of his essay of 1668.

The damage from a reduction in the silver content of the pound sterling

In 1692 Locke added a second section to his argument to set out the dangers inherent in the proposal to devalue England's silver currency. The actual proposal he addressed was one to change the face value of silver coins so that a 5 shilling crown piece would become a coin worth 5 shillings and 3 pence; so, with 12 English pence in the shilling, this silver coin that was worth 60 pence would now become worth 63 pence, a devaluation of just 3/60 or 5 per cent. Locke severely criticised this 5 per cent devaluation proposal which implied that 19 ounces of silver could perform the monetary function for which 20 ounces were previously required:

> from henceforth our Crown Pieces [must be] Coin'd one Twentieth lighter; which is nothing but changing the Denomination, calling that a Crown now, which yesterday was but a part, viz. Nineteen twentieths of a Crown; whereby you have only raised 19 parts to the Denomination formerly given to 20. For I think no body can be so senseless, as to imagine, that 19 Grains or Ounces of Silver can be raised to the Value of 20; or that 19 Grains or Ounces of Silver shall at the same time exchange for, or buy as much Corn, Oyl, or Wine, as 20; which is to raise it to the *Value* of 20. For if 19 Ounces of Silver can be worth 20 Ounces of Silver, or pay for as much of any other Commodity, then 18, 10, or 1 Ounce may do the same. For if the abating One twentieth of the quantity of the Silver of any Coin, does not lessen its Value, the abating Nineteen twentieths of the quantity of the Silver of any Coin, will not abate its Value. And so a single Threepence, or a single Penny, being call'd a Crown, will buy as much Spice, or Silk, or any other Commodity, as a Crown-piece, which contains 20 or 60 times as much Silver; which is an Absurdity so great, That I think no body will want Eyes to see, and Sense to disown (Locke, 1692, pp. 137–8)

There is also the breach of contract involved in repaying debts with less silver than the amount originally contracted for, and this will deprive all creditors of 5 per cent of what they were entitled to expect to receive:

> For Money having been Lent, and Leases and other Bargains made, when Money was of the same Weight and Fineness that it is now, upon Confidence that under the same names of *Pounds, Shillings and Pence*, they should receive the same *value*, (*i.e.* the same *quantity* of Silver) by giving the denomination now to less quantities of Silver by One twentieth, you take from them 5 *per Cent.* of their due. (Locke 1692, p. 143)

> It will rob all *Creditors* of One twentieth (or 5 *per Cent.*) of their Debts, and all Landlords One twentieth of their quit Rents for ever; and in all other Rents as far as their former Contracts reach, of 5 *per Cent.* of their yearly Income. (Locke, 1692, p. 142)

This breach of contract will also damage the finances of government:

> It diminishes all the King's Revenue 5 *per Cent.* For though the same number of Pounds, Shillings, and Pence are paid into the Exchequer as were wont, yet these Names [will be] given to Coin that have each of them One twentieth less of Silver in them. (Locke, 1692, p. 147)

The reduction of the silver content of the English coinage would go on to lead to a 5 per cent rise in the prices of commodities because these tend to be stable in relation to silver:

> When Men go to Market to buy any other Commodities with their new, but lighter Money, they will find 20s. Of their new Money will buy no more of any Commodity than 19 would before. For it not being the denomination but the *quantity* of Silver, that gives the value to any Coin. (Locke, 1692, p. 143)

Locke regarded the proposal as entirely misconceived, and he was convinced that it could have no helpful and many damaging consequences. He exposed the weaknesses especially by pushing to its limits the proposal that the number of shillings and pence that a silver coin of unchanged weight represented should be raised:

> If it be good to *raise* the Crown Piece this way One twentieth this Week, I suppose it will be as good and profitable to raise it as much again the next Week. For there is no reason, why it will not be as good to *raise* it again another One twentieth the next Week, and so on; wherein, if you proceed but 10 weeks successively, you will be New-Years-Day next have every half-Crown raised to a Crown, to the loss of one half of Peoples Debts and Rents, and the King's Revenue, besides the Confusion of all your affairs: And if you please to go on in this beneficial way of *raising* your Money, you may by the same Art bring a Penny-weight of Silver to be a Crown. (Locke, 1692, pp. 144–5)

He did not realise when he wrote these pages that within three years these proposals would reappear with the Chancellor of the Exchequer and the Secretary to the Treasury as sponsors. In 1691 he must have hoped that his book would kill the plans to reduce the maximum legal interest rate to 4 per cent, and to alter the face value of an English crown coin of unchanged size and weight from 5 shillings to 5 shillings and 3 pence.

The publication of *Further Considerations Concerning Raising the Value of Money*, and the historical relevance of Locke's monetary economics

The publication of *Some Considerations of the Consequences of the Lowering of Interest and Raising the Value of Money* failed in its immediate purpose because in 1692 Parliament passed a Bill to cut the maximum legal interest rate from 6 to 5 per cent, where it remained until the nineteenth century. Edward Clarke, a Member of Parliament who was a close friend of Locke, wrote to him:

> This day the Byll for Reduceing the Interest of money to 5 per Cent. Passed the House of Commons; severall Attempts wee had upon the first, second and third Reading of the Byll, to have thrown it out, wherein all imaginable Reasons were used to that End, In which Debates, I was not a little pleas'd, to heare all the Arguments used, that are contain'd in the Considerations upon Lowering the Interest of money, whereby 'twas manifest to mee that the Greatest and best men in our House were obleiged to that Treatise for all the Arguments they used in those Debates, But I am satisfied if an Angell from Heaven had mannaged the Debate, the Votes would have been the same as now, For 'tis not Reason but a supposed Benifit to the Borrower that hath Passed the Byll, and I beleive 'tis that will carry it through the House of Lords likewise; I wish wee may have better successe upon the Byll of Coynage, and soe I Rest. (Locke, 1976–89, IV, p. 373)

The clear implication of Clarke's letter is that Members of Parliament were predominantly borrowers, with inducements to vote to reduce the interest rates they had to pay.

Most of Locke's correspondence in 1691, 1692, 1693 and 1694 reflects his main activities and concerns philosophy and education, but in 1695 an economic crisis developed. The English silver coinage deteriorated further, and the cost of maintaining William III's armies on the continent grew in the continuing war by England and Holland against France. Because of the need to maintain the armies, English imports and expenditure overseas exceeded exports by growing amounts, and Locke had demonstrated very clearly how this must produce a drain of silver or gold. In 1693 the loss of silver was more than £350 000; in 1694 it was more than £700 000, and there was a further loss of almost £400 000 in 1695. The total English silver coinage at this time amounted to around £20 million so the monetary loss was almost 2 per cent of the coinage in 1693, $3^1/_2$ per cent in 1694, and a further 2 per cent in 1695 (Kelly, 1991, I, pp. 112–15).

Recent scholarship has suggested that the clipping of the coins, which was all the time becoming more extensive, may well have provided the silver that financed a considerable fraction of these deficits (Jones, 1988, Chapter 7). But the continual attrition of the English coinage was making the coins smaller from year to year, so the discrepancy between full-sized newly minted coins and those in general circulation was growing. Moreover, with a fall in the silver content of the typical English coin, the shilling collapsed and the gold guinea coin, which was originally worth £1 sterling, or 20 silver shillings, rose to 30 shillings in 1695. Because the English silver shilling was collapsing, prices measured in silver were rising sharply. At the same time transaction costs grew as the quality of the coinage deteriorated. Something had to be done, but what?

The Treasury solution was set out in print in September 1695 by William Lowndes, the Secretary to the Treasury. He accepted that all economic activity was being severely damaged by the condition of the coinage:

> In Consequence of the Vitiating, Diminishing and Counterfeiting of the Currant Moneys, it is come to pass, That great Contentions do daily arise amongst the King's Subjects, in Fairs, Markets, Shops, and other Places throughout the Kingdom, about the Passing or Refusing of the same, to the disturbance of the Publick Peace; many Bargains, Doings and Dealings are totally prevented and laid aside, which lessens Trade in general; Persons before they conclude in any Bargains, are necessitated first to settle the Price or Value of the the very Money they are to Receive for their Goods; and if it be in Guineas at a High Rate, or in Clipt or Bad Moneys, they set the Price of their Goods accordingly, which I think has been One great Cause of Raising the Price not only of Merchandizes, but even of Edibles, and other Necessaries for the sustenance of the Common People, to

> their great Grievance ... In fine, the Mischiefs of the Bad Money (too many to enumerate) are so sensibly Felt, that (I humbly conceive) they are sufficient to Confute all the Arguments against the Recoining the same. (Lowndes, 1695, pp. 115–16)

Lowndes saw the state of the coinage and the damage it was causing to the real economy exactly as Locke had predicted some years previously, but he went on to propose a very different remedy. He proposed, first, that the existing five shilling pieces or Crowns which were still at their proper silver weight should have their face value raised from 5 shillings to 6 shillings and 3 pence, that full weight half crowns should be revalued from 2 shillings and 6 pence to 3 shillings and $1^1/_2$ pence, full-weight shillings from 12 pence to 15 pence, and half-shillings or sixpences to $7^1/_2$ pence. He suggested later that the new 15 pence shilling should be given a new name, a 'Testoon':

> That all such Silver Moneys as are after Enumerated of the Lawful Coins of this Realm of *England*, which are now in being, and are not at all diminished by Clipping, Rounding, Filing, Washing, or any other Artifice, be Rais'd by Publick Authority to the foot of Six shillings and Three pence for the Crown, and proportionably for the other Species, namely, the Crown to go for Seventy five pence, the Half Crown to go for Thirty seven pence and an half peny, the Shilling for Fifteen pence, and the half-shilling for Seven pence half-peny. (Lowndes, 1695, pp. 61–2)

Lowndes' second proposal was that the silver from all damaged coins should be reminted into new full-sized coins, those the size of the former Crowns to be renamed 'Sceptres' and to have a face value of 6 shillings and 3 pence:

> And that the New Coins to be made, either of the Clipt Money, as it shall be brought in, or of any other *Sterling Silver*, be made in their respective Weights or Bignes by the present *Indenture of the Mint*, that is to say, One Piece which may be called the *Sceptre*, or the *Silver-Unite*, or by such other name as His Majesty shall Appoint, and to be exactly of the Weight and Fineness of the present Unclipt Crown Piece, but to run for Seventy five pence *Sterling*. (Lowndes, 1695, p. 62)

Lowndes' third proposal was that in all accounts the pound sterling would continue at its historical value of 20 shillings, or 240 pence, so a debt of £1 sterling would be discharged with three Sceptres, each worth 6 shillings and 3 pence, which would produce 18 shillings and 9 pence, and the pound would be made up by adding a new Testoon worth 1 shilling and 3 pence:

> and Three of the said Pieces called *Sceptres* or *Unites*, or by such other Name, as aforesaid, together with a Fifteen peny Piece, after mentioned, shall make by Tale One Pound *Sterling*, or One Pound of Lawful Money of England, in all Accounts and Lawful Payments whatsoever. (Lowndes, 1695, pp. 62–3)

When Napoleon reformed the French currency, he decimalised it to simplify calculations and reduce transactions costs. In 1695 the English Treasury's approach to monetary reform was to establish a pound sterling which was to be worth three 6 shilling and 3 pence Crowns (or Sceptres) plus a 1 shilling and 3 pence Shilling (or Testoon). There have been occasions since when HM Treasury has been equally out of touch with the needs of a productive and commercial economy.

But one of the principal economic effects of Lowndes's reforms would be a devaluation of the pound sterling by 20 per cent in relation to silver. Instead of requiring four Crowns of the former weight to discharge a debt of £1 sterling, this would now be legally met by paying three former Crowns (relabelled Sceptres) and one former Shilling (relabelled a Testoon), so the silver contained in 16 former shillings would suffice to settle a debt of £1 sterling. When Locke criticised the similar proposal in 1692, it had merely been suggested that the pound sterling should be devalued by 5 per cent. Lowndes was now proposing that it should be devalued by 20 per cent. This was intended to bring the official value of newly-minted coins more closely into line with the former clipped coins in general circulation.

When British governments seek economic advice today they generally turn to economists in Britain's 100 universities, but in 1695 there was no academic economics. The Council, the Cabinet that advised William III, guided by Somers, in addition to seeking the opinion of Locke, England's leading philosopher, also invited Isaac Newton, the leading natural scientist, Christopher Wren, the leading architect, and five others to submit memoranda. Newton accepted the Treasury's argument that there should be a reduction in the silver content of the pound sterling to match the inflation that had already occurred. If the silver in the pound was restored to its previous official level, the shilling would have to contain 20 or 30 per cent more silver than in the coins currently circulating, so the number of shillings in circulation would fall 20 or 30 per cent. That would force prices down 20 or 30 per cent, or else cut production and so severely depress the economy. Newton argued that it was better to acquiesce in the inflation that had already occurred by reducing the silver in the official coinage than to attempt to restore prices to their previous level by going back to the original value of sterling. Otherwise it would be too difficult for British producers to compete internationally (Kelly, 1991, I, p. 29).

Most of the other submission, including Wren's, were brief, but Locke responded with a distinguished and detailed pamphlet, *Further Considerations Concerning Raising the Value of Money* which he published in December 1695. This updated his 1692 book and dealt in detail with the arguments of Lowndes and his supporters. He opened with a passage which reflects his contributions to philosophy:

> I have a long time foreseen the Mischief and Ruine coming upon us by clipp'd Money, if it were not timely stopp'd: And had Concern enough for the Publick, to make me print some Thoughts touching our Coin some Years since. The Principles I there went on, I see no reason to alter: They have, if I mistake not, their Foundation in Nature, and will stand: They have their foundation in Nature, and are clear; and will be so, in all the Train of their Consequences throughout this whole (as it is thought) mysterious Business of Money, to all those, who will but be at the easie Trouble of stripping this Subject of hard, obscure and doubtful Words, wherewith Men are often misled and mislead others. And now the disorder is come to Extremity, and can no longer be plaid with, I wish it may find a suddain and effectual Cure; not a Remedy in Sound and Appearance, which may flatter us on to Ruine in the Continuation of a growing Mischief, that calls for present Help. (Locke, 1695, Dedication to Sir John Sommers Kt)

Locke reiterated that a 20 per cent devaluation of sterling in relation to silver would involve a breach of all financial agreements because all who were contracted to receive money would be paid 20 per cent less:

> all People who are to receive money upon Contracts already made, will be defrauded of 20 *per Cent.* of their due: And thus all Men will lose one fifth of their settled Revenues; and all men that have lent Money one fifth of their Principal and Use ... the Publick Authority

> was Guarantee that the same Summ should have the same quantity of Silver under the same Denomination (Locke, 1695, p. 43)

Locke reiterated, and this was crucial to his argument, that the prices of imported commodities, measured in silver, would remain unchanged:

> The Salt, Wine, Oyl, Silk, Naval-Stores, and all Foreign Commodities, will none of them be sold us by Foreigners for a less Quantity of Silver than before, because we have given the name of more Pence to it, is I think Demonstration. All our Names (if they are any more to us) are to them but bare Sounds: and our Coin, as theirs to us, but meer Bullion, valued only by its Weight. (Locke, 1695, pp. 51–2)

Locke went on to produce a statement which would be easily recognised by those who produced 'corn models' over the next century and a half. The silver price of corn, like that of oil, silk and naval stores, would remain unchanged, so the new devalued sterling would buy one-fifth less corn, and because the cost of labour was fixed in corn, the new devalued sterling would buy one-fifth less labour. Hence the sterling price of labour would rise in line with the devaluation:

> we must certainly make account that since the Money is One fifth lighter, it will buy One fifth less Corn *Communibus annis*. And this being the great Expence of the Poor, that takes up almost all their Earnings; if Corn be *Communibus annis* sold for One fifth more Money in Tale, than before the change of our Money, they too must have One fifth more in Tale of the new Money for their Wages, than they have now; and the Day-Labourer must have, not only twelve, but fifteen Pence of the new Money a day, which is the present Shilling, that he has now, or else he cannot live. (Locke, 1695, pp. 52–3)

Locke concludes that all prices will rise in line with the devaluation of sterling:

> 'Twould be easie to shew the same thing concerning our other native Commodities, and make it clear, that we have no reason to expect they should abate of their present price [in silver], any more than Corn and Labour. But this is enough, and any one, who has a mind to it, may trace the rest at his leisure. (Locke, 1695, p. 53)

Locke went on to ridicule Lowndes' insistence that increasing the number of pence a silver Crown and a silver Shilling represented by one-quarter would relieve the shortage of money in England:

> Just as the Boy cut his Leather into five Quarters (as he called them) to cover his Ball, when cut into four Quarters it fell short: But after all his pains, as much of his Ball lay bare as before. If the quantity of Coin'd Silver employ'd in *England* falls short, the arbitrary denomination of a greater number of Pence given to it, or which is all one, to the several Coin'd pieces of it, will not make it commensurate to the size of our trade, or the greatness of our occasions. This is as certain, as that if the quantity of a Board which is to stop a Leak of a Ship fifteen Inches square, be but twelve Inches square, it will not be made to do it, by being measured by a Foot that is divided into fifteen Inches instead of twelve, and so having a larger *Tale* or number of Inches in denomination given to it. (Locke, 1695, pp. 64–5)

One of Locke's most striking statements is an assertion of the neutrality of money which is as much ahead of its time as David Hume's monetary essays of 1752:

> The having the Species of our Coin One fifth bigger, or One fifth less than they are at present, would be neither good nor harm to *England*, if they had always been so. Our Standard has continued in weight and fineness just as it is now, for very near this hundred Years last past: And those who think the Denomination and Size of our Money have any Influence on the State of our Wealth, have no reason to change the present Standard of our Coin; since under that we have had a greater Increase, and longer Continuance of Plenty of Money, than perhaps any other Country can shew; I see no reason to think, that a little bigger or less Size of the pieces Coin'd, is of any moment one way or t'other. The Species of Money in any Country, of whatsoever Sizes, fit for Coining, if their Proportions to one another be suited to Arithmetick and Calculations, in whole Numbers, and the Ways of Account in that Country; if they are adapted to small Payments, and carefully kept to their just Weight and Fineness, can have no Harm in them. The Harm comes by the change, which unreasonably and unjustly gives away and transfers Mens properties, disorders Trade, Puzzels Accounts, and needs a new Arithmetick to cast up Reckonings, and keep Accounts in; besides a thousand other Inconveniences. (Locke, 1695, pp. 84–5)

Locke condemned Lowndes' proposed coinage where a pound sterling would be made up of three 6 shilling and 3 pence Sceptres and a 1 shilling and 3 pence Testoon because of its total unsuitability for 'Arithmetick and Calculations, in whole Numbers':

> And I fear it will puzzle a better Arithmetician, than most Country-men are, to tell, without Pen and Ink, how many of the lesser pieces (except the Shillings) however combined, will make just sixteen or seventeen Shillings. And I imagine there is not one Country-man of three, but may have it for his Pains, if he can tell an Hundred Pounds made up of a promiscuous Mixture of the Species of this new raised Money (excluding the Shillings) in a days time. And that which will help to confound him, and every body else, will be the *old Crowns, Half-crowns, Shillings,* and *Six-pences* current for new numbers of *Pence*. (Locke, 1695, pp. 87–8)

Locke's own proposal for the re-establishment of a usable currency was direct and clear:

> To conclude, I confess my self not to see the least Reason why our present mil'd Money should be at all altered in Fineness, Weight, or Value. I look upon it to be the best and safest from counterfeiting, adulterating, or any ways being fraudulently diminished, of any that ever was coined. It is adjusted to our legal Payments, Reckonings, and Accounts, to which our Money must be reduced. The raising its Denomination will neither add to its Worth, nor make the Stock we have, more proportionate to our Occasions, not bring one Grain of Silver the more into *England*, or one Farthing Advantage to the publick: It will only serve to defraud the King, and a great number of his Subjects, and Perplex all, and put the Kingdom to a needless Charge of recoining all, both mill'd as well as clip'd Money. (Locke, 1695, p. 109)

The clipped money would of course need to be recoined into milled money so that the entire currency had milled edges, which would make it unclippable in future.

The Council advised the Sovereign, and William III decided to take Locke's advice. It was proposed that the official silver content of the pound sterling should remain unchanged and that the currency should be renewed with heavy silver coins with milled edges which no one could chip away at. The lighter coins then current would cease to be legal tender and have to be exchanged into new ones on the basis of their weight, so those who thought they had a pound with four light five shilling crowns might only get back two heavy ones worth just ten shillings.

But William III and his ministers could only make proposals to Parliament. The actual decisions were taken there and in January 1696 Parliament insisted that some of those who would lose because their light silver coins would no longer be legal tender should be compensated. The House of Commons decided to allow silver coins, however light, to be accepted at their full face value in payments made to government until 4 May. Everyone therefore sought to make the silver coins which the Exchequer had to accept as small as possible. Coins were first hammered thin and the outside silver was then cut away and what was left was rushed to the Treasury to meet the deadline. The thin hammered coins, just before the clippers got at them, were described as 'broad money', a term with an entirely different meaning today. The hyperactivity to exploit the Treasury's open back door by clipping, melting, recoining and reclipping is vividly described by Locke:

> Methinks the silver does wisely not to come into England at this time where it is like to run a perpetuall circle of torment if it stay here. Into the fire it goes at the Exchequer and is noe sooner out but it is committd to the mint there to goe into the furnace again to be brought to Standard and then to size and then be pressed in the mill. As soon as it get free out of the mint it is either lockd up in some Jaylors chest from comeing abroad or if it peeps out tis ten to one but the thriveing company of Coiners and clippers put it again into the fire to be joynd with bad company. and then to be hammerd and cut and so conveyd to the Exchequer to run the same Gantlet again. (Locke, 1976–89, V, p. 540)

The avalanche of light and 'narrow' money to the Exchequer represented a large loss to government and the creation of the new coinage was also expensive. The establishment of the Bank of England in 1694 inserted a little paper into the equation, but there was a severe economic depression as prices were forced downwards in line with the new heavy coinage. When the sound money policy went on to produce the depressed business conditions Newton had predicted, William III is said to have regretted that he had taken Locke's advice to restore the integrity of the currency (Kelly, 1991, I, pp. 64–5).

The Council's two principal economic advisers were both rewarded later in 1696. On 19 March Charles Montague, the Chancellor of the Exchequer, appointed Newton to be Warden of the Mint; on 15 May Somers, now Lord Chancellor, appointed Locke a Member of the Board of Trade at a salary of £1000 a year, and Locke remained there until 1700, when he retired from public life at the age of 68. He died four years after his retirement from the Board of Trade.

While Locke was strongly opposed to government policies to tamper with the currency, he ran a very interventionist industrial policy at the Board of Trade. He protected the British wollen industry from Irish competition, but sought none the less to give Ireland something by subsidising the start-up of an Irish linen industry. A proposal for legislation to take vagabonds off the streets and set them to work (with three years' enlistment in the Navy if they declined all other employment) rounded off a policy mix that is quite familiar in Conservative politics in several countries in the twentieth century.

Newton went on to become Master of the Mint and played a part in the gradual switch of the money used in most English transactions from silver to gold. In 1711 he fixed the value of the pound at £3 17*s* 9*d* to an ounce of gold and it remained at that value with two wartime departures until Britain finally left the gold standard in 1931.

A price index that Sir Henry Phelps Brown has constructed, based on six commodities, rose by just 29 per cent in the 220 years from 1711 to 1931, so the average inflation rate in these two centuries on the gold standard averaged just 0.1 per cent per annum. West Germany, the most successful European Community economy at controlling inflation, achieved an average annual inflation rate of 2.9 per cent in the 1980s and in 220 years that would have raised prices more than 50 000 per cent against the 29 per cent increase under Newton's gold standard. Locke, the great philosopher–economist, and Newton, the great mathematician–natural scientist, who both saw merit in a stable currency and re-established the integrity of sterling in 1696 and in 1711, therefore set in train a series of monetary developments which served Britain well for two centuries.

Locke also made significant contributions to the future of economics. He is best known and most respected today for his analysis of the demand for money and his embryonic outline of the Quantity Theory (Vaughn, 1980, Chapter 2). In the essay by Mark Blaug on, 'Why is the Quantity Theory of Money the Oldest Surviving Theory in Economics?', he suggests that a coherent statement of the quantity theory should include three crucial propositions (Blaug, 1995, pp. 29–30).

First, a larger money supply must produce a higher price level: causation must run from money to prices, and not the other way round. Locke certainly passes that test. He reiterates that increasing the number of shillings the UK's silver coins represent will raise prices correspondingly. More shillings to a pound of silver and therefore more shillings in UK circulation will raise prices proportionately. The amount of silver in the coinage will be influenced to a degree by international movements of silver, both as money and as bullion, which will be influenced by the balance of payments and by interest rates; but broadly speaking the amount of silver in the English coinage is given and the monetary sums it represents determine the price level.

Blaug's second proposition is that there must be a stable and predictable demand for money in relation to the national income. Locke's contribution is especially strong here, for he set out the first detailed account of the demand to hold money of the various groups in the community.

Blaug's third proposition is that the equilibrium level of the real national income should be given independently of the money supply and the price level. Locke does not specifically say this, but his several statements that increases in the monetary units represented by silver coins merely raise prices implies that there is not a sustained impact on the level of output.

David Hume produced a far fuller account of the quantity theory in 1752, but with none of Locke's detailed analysis of the determination of the transactions demand for money. The French Physiocrats, Adam Smith, Robert Malthus and David Ricardo all similarly failed to go as far as Locke in setting out a detailed account of the transactions demand for money, and in this he was almost two centuries ahead of what later became generally known and understood.

Two aspects of Locke's contribution have been criticised (Appleby, 1980, Chapter 8; Horsefield, 1960, Chapter 6; and Vickers, 1959, Chapter 4). He believed that it was impossible for any society to acquire token money, made for instance of copper or nickel or paper, which could command a purchasing power that exceeded the value of what went into the coins or notes. In 1692 such money did not exist in any country, but only 105 years later England used a paper currency for 24 years (from 1797 to 1821) that was not convertible into silver or gold. In the late twentieth century the whole world has such money, a development which Locke failed to envisage. Defenders of his analysis could none the less point out that the price stability that followed for 220 years from the stable metallic money that Locke and Newton established has not been matched by any of the paper money regimes of the twentieth century.

Locke's British critics have also argued that he was wrong in his advice to William III because this led to a severe deflation when the pound sterling was restored to its previous value. That criticism and Locke's defence of stable money and an unchanging value of sterling was echoed in subsequent debates when sterling was temporarily devalued and then restored to its original parity. In the Napoleonic wars, sterling fell 30 per cent after the gold anchor was lost in 1797 and David Ricardo argued strongly for a return to the prewar gold parity which was achieved in 1821. The need to restore the gold value of sterling led to a severe deflation after 1815, with agricultural distress and riots which were only put down by shooting and hanging rioters or, more humanely, transporting them to the Australian wilderness.

When war was declared in 1914 sterling again lost its gold anchor, and Winston Churchill as Chancellor of the Exchequer restored the prewar gold parity in 1925, which forced British prices down as in 1696 and 1821. The deflation on this occasion led to a coalminers' strike that lasted nine months, to a general strike by all trade unionists, and to a pamphlet by John Maynard Keynes, *The Economic Consequences of Mr Churchill* (Keynes, 1925), which strongly condemned the policy of forcing prices downwards to restore the gold value of the pound. In the restoration of the currency after the Napoleonic Wars and the First World War the same decisions were taken as in William III's wars: to accept whatever deflationary steps were necessary in order to maintain the value of sterling. That was Locke's advice in 1695 and the arguments which were deployed in favour of price stability in 1821 and in 1925 were similar to those that he so effectively set out in 1692 and in 1695.

After 1931, when Britain finally departed from Newton's gold standard, the argument that the real value of sterling should be maintained was superseded by the over-riding argument that governments should at all times seek to avoid any adverse, short-term impact on output and employment. Under pressures similar to those that Locke so strongly advised William III to resist, sterling was devalued in 1931, in 1949, in 1967 and still more sharply in the 1970s. The ounce of gold which Newton had fixed at £3 17*s.* 9*d.* in 1711 became worth more than £220 by the 1980s. Hence it took just 50 years to fulfil Locke's prediction that if sterling was once allowed to fall, there would be nothing to prevent it from falling so far that the value of a crown would be reduced to a penny.

11
Debt, Deficits and Default*

The economic analysis of public debt mainly describes a world where governments honour their obligations and are expected to do so. But there is also a darker history. What if governments repudiate or demand rescheduling which is tantamount to repudiation?

In the 1760s David Hume welcomed the possibility of a British repudiation of a National Debt that then exceeded 100 per cent of the national income (Winch, 1998). The Bourbons repudiated debt in 1598, in 1648 and in 1661 (Brewer, 1989, p. 24) and before the Revolution the French state had to pay higher interest rates than most French private sector borrowers because another royal default was rightly seen as a possibility (Bosher, 1965). Today, the possibility of repudiation enters financial calculation in the most mature and apparently well governed countries. In 1994 the interest rates Canadian provincial governments paid on their debt varied by up to 0.6 percentage points. Newfoundland with a debt to locally generated national income ratio of 50 per cent paid 0.6 percentage points more than Alberta and British Columbia which had provincial debt ratios of beween 10 and 20 per cent (Hoeller, Louppe and Vergiete, 1996, p. 56). This is explicable if markets were marginally less convinced that the Newfoundland provincial government would necessarily honour its debts, and required some additional interest to compensate for this risk. The quality of US municipal bonds varies similarly and the credit

* This is a revised version of the article 'Debt, Deficits and Default', chapter 6 in J. Malony (ed.), *Debt and Deficits: A Historical Perspective* (Aldershot: Edward Elgar, 1998).

ratings of states and cities are all the time assessed with a corresponding impact on the interest rates they have to pay.

None of the governments of the developed economy members of OECD have defaulted since the Second World War, but many developing countries have rescheduled their debt, some more than once. Even though no developed economy has defaulted, the possibility that this could occur has been taken into account by markets, with the consequence that some have had to pay higher real interest rates than others.

Debt and default in the eighteenth and nineteenth centuries

In the eighteenth century, default was widely seen as a possibility and taken into account in the determination of interest rates. Hume was pessimistic about Britain's ability to sustain interest payments on its growing debt:

> Suppose the public once fairly brought to that condition, to which it is hastening with such amazing rapidity; suppose the land to be taxed eighteen or nineteen shillings in the pound; for it can never bear the whole twenty; suppose all the excises and customs to be screwed up to the utmost which the nation can bear, without entirely losing its commerce and industry; and suppose that all those funds are mortgaged to perpetuity, and that the invention and wit of all our projectors can find no new imposition, which may serve as the foundation of a new loan; and let us consider the necessary consequences of this situation ... the seeds of ruin are here scattered with such profusion as not to escape the eye of the most careless observer ...
>
> any great blow given to trade, whether by injudicious taxes, or by other accidents, throws the whole system of government into confusion. (Hume [1752] 1985, pp. 357–8)

Inability to find the taxation required to finance Britain's ever-growing debt could lead to default for:

> when the nation becomes heartily sick of their debts, and is cruelly oppressed by them, some daring projector may arise with visionary schemes for their discharge'. [Hume clearly had John Law in mind]. And as the public credit will begin, by that time, to be a little frail,

> the least touch will destroy it, as happened in FRANCE during the regency'. (Hume, [1752] 1985, pp. 361)

He asked when the point would be reached where industry and commerce could no longer finance growing debt, and concluded:

> One would incline to assign to this event a very near period, such as half a century, had not our fathers' prophecies of this kind been already found fallacious ... We shall, therefore, be more cautious than to assign any precise date; and content ourselves with pointing out the event in general. (Hume, [1752] 1985, pp. 364–5)

He believed that credit would recover rapidly when repudiation in the end occurred:

> So great dupes are the generality of mankind, that, notwithstanding such a violent shock to public credit, as a voluntary bankruptcy in ENGLAND would occasion, it would not probably be long ere credit would again revive in as flourishing a condition as before ... Mankind are, in all ages, caught by the same baits: The same tricks, played over and over again, still trepan them. (Hume, [1752] 1985, p. 363)

Hume's account of the possibility and consequences of repudiation was echoed by Sir James Steuart who asked in 1767, 'If the interest paid upon the national debt of England, for example, be found constantly to increase upon every new war ... How far may debts extend? ... How far may taxes be carried?' (Steuart [1767] 1998, IV, p. 105). He speculated that the land tax, for instance, where Hume had referred to a rate of eighteen or nineteen shillings in the pound, 'may be carried to the full value of all the real estates in England' (Steuart [1767] 1988, IV, p. 106). He concluded:

> If no check be put to the augmentation of public debts, if they be allowed constantly to accumulate, and if the spirit of a nation can patiently submit to the natural consequences of such a plan, it must end in this, that all property, that is income, will be swallowed up by taxes. (Steuart [1767] 1988, IV, p. 287)

After the landowners had been taxed to destruction to provide interest on equivalent government bonds, Steuart inquired, could not the holders of these bonds be taxed in their turn to provide interest on new bonds to finance still further borrowing?

> The state ... will always consider those who enjoy the national income as the body of proprietors. This income will continue the same, and the real proprietors of it, namely the creditors, will pay the taxes imposed; which taxes may be mortgaged again to a new set of men, who will retain the denomination of creditors; until by swallowing up the former set of creditors they will slip into their places, and become the body of proprietors in their turn, and thus perpetuate the circle. (Steuart [1767] 1988, IV, p. 287)

Will there be a reluctance to lend to governments which repeatedly destroy the incomes of those who lend to them? Steuart's response follows Hume's and anticipates the twentieth-century facility of certain countries to continue to obtain finance after repeated defaults:

> The prospect of a second revolution of the same kind with the first would be very distant; and in matters of credit, which are constantly exposed to risk, such events being beyond the reach of calculation, are never taken into any man's account who has money to lend. (Steuart [1767] 1988, IV, 107)

In the twentieth century, a succession of Mexican governments have defaulted and there have been continuing markets for their bonds, with higher interest rates which reflect the imminence of default. Bankers who enjoy the extra interest and avoid the bonds immediately prior to default profit, while those who still hold them are caught short.

There were eight bond issues by the Egyptian government between 1862 and 1874, and it defaulted on all of them in 1876. They raised a total of £65 million in London, 8 per cent of the outstanding level of British government debt. There had been previous defaults in the 1870s by the governments of Honduras, Costa Rica, Santa Domingo, Paraguay, Spain and Turkey. It has been estimated econometrically that the *ex ante* probability of eventual default on the Egyptian bond issues of 1867, 1868, 1870, 1873 and 1874 exceeded 50 per cent, but they were none the less fully subscribed (Gershon and Just, 1984). The explanation is that lenders in London who were caught short believed that:

> Egypt would be able to continue to roll over its foreign debt – a procedure that Egypt, as well as many other countries, has followed over the

> years. While the lenders were perhaps aware that a roll-over strategy could not continue indefinitely, their attitude in this case may be explained, by an analogy with a chain letter – participants know that it is almost certain to collapse eventually but, at the same time, they hope to be among the lucky ones who manage to get out with a handsome profit before the collapse. (Gershon and Just, 1984, pp. 352–3)

Gershon and Just, writing about the Egyptian default in the midst of twentieth-century defaults quote from *Ecclesiastes* to describe the eternality of investors' myopia:

> The thing that hath been, it is *that* which shall be; and that which is done is that which shall be done; and *there* is no new *thing* under the sun. (1.ix)

There had been a similar willingness to subscribe to bond issues which subsequently failed in the eighteenth century, and Hume was proved correct in his suspicion of French government finances.

In contrast, the British House of Commons, in which both landowners and the holders of government bonds were strongly represented, avoided repudiation or rescheduling despite a rise in the ratio of public debt to the national income to a peak of more than 275 per cent in 1821. The evidence is summarised in Table 11.1.

Donald Winch (1998) shows how the ratio of public debt to the national income rose from virtually zero at the time of the 'Glorious Revolution' of 1688 to almost 200 per cent after the War of American Independence and more than 275 per cent after the Napoleonic Wars. But by the beginning of the twentieth century the ratio of government debt to the national income had been reduced to less than 40 per cent.

The sound Gladstonian finance of Gladstone himself which John Maloney (1998) describes, and of his predecessors and successors, reduced the debt from £805 million in 1821 to £629 million by the end of the century, so budget surpluses predominated sufficiently over deficits during these eighty years to reduce the debt by £176 million. At the same time the national income rose more than five-fold from £291 million in 1821 to £1621 million in 1901 with the result that the ratio of public debt to the national income was reduced from 276 per cent in 1821 to 38 per cent in 1901. Total debt interest was reduced from 11.0 per cent of the national income in 1821 to 1.3 per cent in 1901, a huge reduction in this principal item of public expenditure. That was the outcome of the policies Maloney describes.

Table 11.1 Great Britain's public finances, 1700–1901 (in contemporary prices)

Year	Public debt (£ million)	National income (£ million)	Public debt/ national income (per cent)	Interest/ debt (per cent)	Consols yield (per cent)
1700	14.2	50	28.4	8.81	
1720	54.0	53.9	100.2	5.13	
1740	47.4	64.5	73.5	4.43	
1760	101.7	74.0	137.4	3.28	3.8
1780	167.2	100.2	166.9	3.31	4.9
1801	456.1	232.0	196.6	3.67	4.9
1821	804.9	291.0	276.6	3.98	4.1
1861	805.7	668.0	120.6	3.26	3.3
1901	629.3	1642.9	38.3	3.15	2.9

Sources: Mitchell (1988), p. 822 for the national income from 1801, (1988) pp. 600–12 for public debt, (1988), pp. 578–80, 587–90 for debt interest and (1988), p. 678 for the interest yield on consols: irredeemable fixed interest securities; and O'Brien (1988, p. 3) for estimates of the national income before 1801.

In twentieth-century language, Britain ran a primary budget surplus (the surplus net of debt interest) of 11 per cent of the national income in 1821; for the overall budget was balanced and debt interest totalled 11 per cent of the national income. In the course of the nineteenth century the budget remained balanced (or in surplus) and the primary surplus required to stabilise the absolute level of public debt gradually fell from 11 per cent of the national income in 1821 to 1.3 per cent in 1901.

The principal pressures from growing public debt arose during the Napoleonic wars and their immediate aftermath when the ratio of public debt to the national income reached twice the levels of current Italian and Belgian debt which are themselves more than twice the limit of 60 per cent of GDP established in the Maastricht Treaty as a condition for membership of European Economic and Monetary Union (EMU). The Britain that emerged from the Napoleonic Wars as the dominant world economy owed more than four times as much as the Maastricht Treaty now permits, and the primary budget surplus it then established was twice what any twentieth-century European economy has achieved in its efforts to meet the Maastricht criteria.

British government debt was financed at an average interest cost of less than 5 per cent throughout most of its growth in the eighteenth century and decline in the nineteenth. In 1720, a mere twenty-six years after the foundation of the Bank of England which had the predominant role in the financing and funding of the debt, the average interest cost of the then quite modest debt was almost 9 per cent. In these initial years of borrowing, governments and the Bank of England had to learn how to borrow economically. Before the credit of London was fully established they resorted to a variety of expedients including the sale of expensive annuities (Dickson, 1967). During the Napoleonic wars, when borrowing reached its peak and the debt rose from 200 to more than 275 per cent of the national income, the yield of consols exceeded 5 per cent only from 1797 to 1799 (when it peaked at 5.9 per cent) and in 1804 (when it reached 5.3 per cent), but apart from these years the debt was financed at 5 per cent or less, and at an average interest cost of less than 4 per cent.

Despite the growing public debt ratio during the Napoleonic wars no one spoke of default as any kind of possibility. This may have been because the members of the unreformed House of Commons of 1793 to 1815, elected and in some cases appointed by the wealthiest 1 per cent of the population, represented the holders of government bonds to a degree which made default inconceivable. Some of the more representative electorates of the twentieth century might discourage their parliaments or senates from levying taxation of 11 per cent of the national income to pay debt interest to the comparatively wealthy minority with large holdings of government bonds. The prospect of default (or else inflationary finance) has therefore become a real threat at debt levels far lower than Britain's in the eighteenth and nineteenth centuries.

David Ricardo and Robert Barro on Ricardian equivalence

When David Ricardo first published his equivalence theorem in 1817, he was addressing the early nineteenth century élite of wealth and influence which would never contemplate default. The credit of US governments was almost as strong in 1974 when Robert Barro independently discovered his own equivalence theorem, which he describes so lucidly together with Ricardo's in Barro (1998).

Barro and Ricardo can therefore say that when individuals are faced with a choice between paying to government interest of £100 a year in perpetuity or a capital sum of £2000 (Ricardo's example) these are by definition equivalents when the long-term rate of interest is 5 per cent (Ricardo [1817] 1953, pp. 247–8): in 1816 when Ricardo drafted this example for the first edition of *The Principles of Political Economy and Taxation*, the interest rate on consols was actually 5.0 per cent.

Since these are equivalents for each individual, it follows that when the taxpayers of a society are faced with a choice of collectively paying £20 million extra in taxes to finance £20 million of additional public expenditure or £1 million extra a year in perpetuity in debt interest because the government has issued £20 million of additional consols, these will also be equivalents. Can they therefore always be expected to have an equivalent impact on the individuals who incur these extra obligations? Ricardo himself believed that the impact on his contemporaries would be different: it makes us 'less thrifty' if 'a system of borrowing' is used to defray 'the extraordinary expenses of the State' because this must 'blind us to our true situation' (Ricardo [1817] 1953, p. 247) He therefore denied equivalence in practice.

The universal relevance of the equivalence theorem is moreover weakened because Barro and Ricardo both ignore the possibility of default. They each wrote in environments where the possibility that governments might fail to honour their long-term obligations could be regarded as minimal. What if the choice is between paying immediate taxes in Egypt or Mexico, or subscribing to their government bonds which yield 9 per cent because there is a significant possibility that they will not pay the full promised interest after a number of years which is itself uncertain?

Markets will equate \$100 million in cash and \$100 million of Mexican government bonds which yield 9 per cent when they are first issued, but the Mexican taxpayer will pay a clear \$100 million if his government's expenditure is tax-financed, and \$9 million a year until the next default if his government sells bonds through mainly overseas banks. The bankers will by definition regard the bonds they receive as the equivalent of the \$100 million they pay for them, but will some of the US bank executives who take the decision to buy Mexican government bonds be doing so to boost the apparent profits of their banks and believe that this will signal the excellence of their professional skills, with consequent prestige and promotion? After the next Mexican default (or rescheduling), the bonds will fall in value, but not in the books of all US banks, and by then the executives who bought them may have been promoted or moved on.

In the 1990s the loan books of the banks of the world's developed economies are replete with non-performing or under-performing Third World debt. Much was incurred in efforts to re-cycle oil revenues in the 1970s and the 1980s to countries with greater opportunities for development. It was even said then by some who knew no history that governments could not go bankrupt. Others welcomed the expansion in portfolios and deposits and banks' apparent extra profitability which recycling had achieved. Several will have believed that they were acting wholly on behalf of their shareholders, recognised entirely that additional risks counter-balanced the higher interest receipts from Third World lending, and believed they could get out of the 'chain-letter' in time.

Ricardo and Barro only needed to assume that taxpayers and government bond holders paid full regard to the interests of their heirs in their reactions to extra taxation or additional obligations to pay debt interest which were apparently equivalent. But would either regard additional taxation and additional obligations to pay debt interest which might be interrupted by default as equivalents? Parents may indeed see the finances of their children and grandchildren as equivalent to their own, but there are a variety of ways in which there can be divergeneces between the interests of the agents who manage the loan and share portfolios of financial institutions and the owners of the capital that employs them. In the world's most advanced financial centres where the shareholders of banks arguably receive the greatest protection, managers' reputations are frequently based on statements of current profits which fail to take account of default risks. In the United States and Japan (where non-performing bank loans totalled perhaps 30 per cent of GDP in 1998) accounts are allowed to be published which fail to reflect the under-performance of many of the assets which insolvent creditors can no longer service. With perfect knowledge by the owners of financial capital of the actions of the agents they employ and the risks inherent in the assets they manage, these divergencies would be greatly diminished, or even removed. The situation which actually prevails is one where the attitude to risk (and the knowledge of the risks involved) of those who buy the bonds of potentially defaulting governments and the shareholders who come to own those bonds can patently diverge.

There are therefore difficulties in transferring the Ricardian equivalence theorem which was conceived in economies where the financial reputation of governments was absolute, to conditions where there are substantial default risks.

British public debt in the twentieth century

There was no question of debt default in Britain's public finances in the twentieth century and there was never doubt that governments would honour their legal obligations. During the First World War and its immediate aftermath, British government debt rose from 26.3 per cent of the national income in 1914 to 138.5 per cent in 1920 (Mitchell, 1988, pp. 602, 829). By 1939 at the outbreak of the Second World War, the ratio of the national debt to the national income was slightly higher at 154 per cent. From 1920 to 1939 the total of funded and unfunded debt rose by £340 million, or by an average of £19 million a year, around $^1/_2$ per cent of the national income which averaged about £4000 million during these decades. (Mitchell, 1988, p. 829) Peter Clarke (1998) offers many insights into budgetary policy and the definition of the budget deficit in this period. Measured as the annual increase in the national debt, it was close to $^1/_2$ per cent of the national income from 1920 to 1939, so the budget was virtually balanced. Debt charges on the nearly constant debt were reduced from a peak of 8.5 per cent of the national income in 1923 to 4.1 per cent in 1939 (Mitchell, 1988, pp. 590–2, 829), so the 'burden of debt' was about three-quarters as great after the First World War as in the decades which immediately followed the Napoleonic Wars. With interest payments falling from $8^1/_2$ to $4^1/_4$ per cent of the national income, and overall net borrowing of no more than $^1/_2$ per cent of the national income, the primary budget surplus fell from about 8 to about 4 per cent of the national income. Until the achievement of low interest rates in the later 1930s when bank rate was held at 2 per cent for several years, the primary budget surplus was far larger than in any European economy since the Second World War.

It is no wonder that Keynes wrote so extensively about the desirability of lower interest rates, not just during the great slump but until the publication of *The General Theory* in 1936, and of the dead-weight burden of debt and the social and economic benefits which would follow the euthanasia of the rentier. But Keynes gave no countenance to the use of inflation to reduce the real burden of the National Debt. He was concerned by the acceleration of inflation to 5 per cent in 1936–7 when unemployment was still 12 per cent (Keynes, 1937; Skidelsky, 1992, pp. 629–30).

During the Second World War UK public debt trebled between 1939 and 1945 while the money national income rose by two-thirds (Mitchell, 1988, pp. 602–3, 829–30) and the ratio of public debt to the national income rose from the 154 per cent of 1939 to 267 per cent in 1946. Britain therefore ended the Second World War with a National Debt which was similar as a ratio of the national income to the 276 per cent which followed the Napoleonic Wars, and far greater than the 138 per cent which followed the First World War. But the post-

Keynesian generation of economists who dominated economic analysis and policy after the Second World War had an entirely new approach to the reduction of the debt burden.

The 276 per cent debt/national income ratio which followed the Napoleonic Wars was reduced to less than 30 per cent by 1914 through balanced budgets and sound finance, and there was no toleration of inflationary finance after the First World War, but already in 1943 the UK Treasury was contemplating an inflationary solution to the anticipated burden of debt when the war ended. A Treasury Steering Group, contemplating postwar policy, argued the advantages of moderate inflation:

> A rise in prices and incomes sufficiently slow to avoid a violent disturbance of the expectations of the recipients of fixed incomes, yet sufficiently perceptible gradually to unloose the dead hand of debt, has much to be said in its favour. (Booth, 1983, p. 113)

The members of this Steering Group evidently believed that the inflation rate could be increased without a corresponding need to raise interest rates. That judgement proved correct for a time and real interest rates were negative in most years between 1945 and 1979, while inflation reduced the debt to national income ratio from the 267 per cent of 1945 to about 48 per cent in 1980 (Mitchell, 1988, pp. 603, 830). Thirty-five years of inflation therefore reduced the burden of debt to about the same degree as a century of sound 'Gladstonian' finance.

The holders of government debt became aware of what was happening, despite the hopes of the wartime Treasury that their expectations would not be violently disturbed. Portfolios were gradually switched towards equity shares and real estate as holders of government bonds came to realise that the interest they received on these rarely covered inflation which was steadily destroying capital values. In 1955, Sir Dennis Robertson remarked when the Church of England announced that it was selling some of its government bonds to buy equity shares, 'if you can't fool the Church of England there is no one left you can fool any more'. The impact of the continuing inflation on the real value of the National Debt gradually came to be understood, but its holders none the less lost most of the real values they had invested.

The effect of the continuing inflation on the wealth of those who had lent to the British government was not dissimilar to the impact of the nineteenth-century Latin American, Egyptian, Spanish and Turkish defaults, but the British government did not default. It honoured its legal obligations to pay interest in sterling. That the sterling it honoured its obligations in was so dramatically devalued will have disappointed some of its creditors, but there was no breach of contract.

The inflation which played so large a large part in the more than four-fifths reduction in Britain's debt/national income ratio has had many damaging consequences, and while it may have been initially welcomed by the Treasury as a means to 'unloose the dead hand of debt', this soon returned to its traditional role of guardian of sound finance: after the 1950s nothing more was heard of the argument that inflation reduced the real value of debt. A retired Ambassador welcomed this feature of inflation in the presence of a high Treasury official during the 1980s, and the latter responded that after you have used inflation to get rid of your debt, 'your economy will be in such a mess that you will have to borrow it all over again'. Britain's national debt was £21 billion in 1945 and more than £320 billion in 1998, so the original debt was added to with further borrowing fifteen times as great in the repeated crises which accompanied the inflationary finance of the post-war years. Tim Congdon (1998) shows that the Treasury has not been especially Keynesian in its counter-cyclical policy since the Second World War, but there was something Keynesian in the greater tolerance of inflation. Keynes himself abhorred it, but his analysis focused on the economy's margin of unused resources in a manner that kept the eye of the authorities away from the inflationary ball until the damage caused by runaway inflation, which reached more than 25 per cent in the 1970s, became evident to all.

The experience of the other leading European economies has been similar. Apart from Switzerland, all governments have presided over substantial inflation, either during the war or in the decades that followed, and all long-term holders of government bonds have lost a considerable fraction of their real value. But there have been no defaults in Western Europe since the war while, as in the nineteenth century, the governments of many developing countries failed to honour their interest obligations.

They mainly borrow in US dollars, so they cannot reduce the real value of their debt by devaluing their currencies. Largely through inflation, Britain has been able to reduce its debt to national income ratio by five-sixths, while Mexico, which mainly borrows in dollars, lacks this option.

But following the Keynesian revolution, the world's developing countries have been drawn towards unfinanceable borrowing by a powerful new theorem which became a dangerous trap in the 1980s and the 1990s.

Domar's demonstration that economic growth will generally finance public debt

In 1939, Roy Harrod examined the long-term consequences of continual investment of *S* per cent of the national income and showed that in long-term equilibrium:

$$\frac{\text{Total capital}}{\text{National income}} \quad \text{will become} \quad \frac{\text{The savings ratio } (S)}{\text{Rate of growth } (g)}$$

In 1944 Evsey Domar showed, reasoning analogously, that if a government continuously borrows *B* per cent of its national income:

$$\frac{\text{Total debt}}{\text{National income}} \quad (D) \quad \text{will become} \quad \frac{\text{The borrowing ratio } (B)}{\text{Rate of growth } (g)}$$

In this Domar formula, *g* is the rate of growth of the money national income – that is, the real rate of growth *plus* the rate of inflation. Domar used this development of the Harrod–Domar equation which showed that the ratio of public debt to the national income (*D*) converged upon *B/g* to address the question of what 'burden of debt' a country could afford:

> The theory of the multiplier and our actual experience during this war have demonstrated, I believe, that money income can be raised to any desired level if the volume of public expenditure is sufficiently high. This view will be accepted also by the opponents of deficit financing. Their objections to such a policy are based on several grounds, the most important being the belief that continuous borrowing results in an ever-rising public debt, the servicing of which will require higher and higher taxes; and that the latter will eventually destroy our economy, or cause an outright repudiation of debt. (Domar, [1944] 1957, pp. 36–7)

The formula that the ratio of government debt to the national income will converge upon *B/g* allows the eventual level of its interest burden to be expressed. This will be the average nominal rate of interest the government pays on its debt, *i*, times the ratio of government debt to the national income, B/g, or $B(i/g)$. Thus the eventual 'interest burden' will become the budget deficit B times i/g, the ratio of the nominal rate of interest to the nominal rate of growth.

In estimating the implications of his analysis for the United States after the Second World War, Domar went on to assume that 'the interest rate is a given constant' (Domar, [1944] 1957, pp. 38–9) and in his numerical examples he assumes a real rate of interest of 2 per cent. In his numerical examples he assumes growth rates of 2 or 3 per cent. He believed that over the very long run, 'a 3 per cent rate of growth of real income may be too much to hope for, but a 2 per cent rate for the next 50 or even 100 years can probably be well defended' (Domar, [1944] 1957, p. 60)

When he assumes a real rate of interest that is less than the real rate of growth, the nominal rate of interest will also be less than the nominal rate of growth. By assuming a 2 per cent real rate of interest, Domar assumed a value for i/g of less than 1 when the long-term rate of growth is 3 per cent and of 1 when it is 2 per cent. Hence the eventual interest burden of the national debt which is the borrowing ratio times i/g could never become as high as the borrowing ratio in an economy which managed to grow at 3 per cent: while it would eventually rise to equal the borrowing ratio if it achieved only 2 per cent growth. The burden of interest would never exceed the borrowing ratio.

If a government that is initially without debt embarks on a policy of borrowing 6 per cent of the national income so that B is 6 per cent to further its social and military purposes, and it maintains its B at 6 per cent, its interest burden will gradually build up to 5 per cent of the national income if i/g equals 5/6, while the interest burden will rise to 6 per cent of the national income if growth proves no greater than the rate of interest.

Where i/g equals 5/6 the government begins by being able to deploy its full 6 per cent deficit for social and military purposes, but as its debt builds up its interest bill gradually rises to 5 per cent of the national income, leaving it with just 1 per cent extra to further its political and economic objectives. The fraction of the deficit which a government is free to use for these purposes is the deficit net of debt interest – that is, the primary deficit. The country with an i/g of 5/6 opens its debt-financing strategy with a primary deficit of 6 per cent of the national income and this gradually falls to 1 per cent, but even when the interest burden has accumulated to its full long-term level, it can still sustain a primary deficit of 1 per cent, and spend 1 per cent more of the national income for social and military purposes than it could if it had never borrowed, and it never needs to tax to obtain this additional 1 per cent.

The government in the economy with an *i/g* of 1 begins by having an extra 6 per cent of the national income to spend as it wishes, but debt interest gradually builds up to 6 per cent and absorbs all its borrowing, so its primary deficit gradually falls from 6 per cent of the national income to zero when debt interest will entirely absorb its borrowing. For a generation, the borrowing government commands extra real resources which it does not need to pay for through taxation, and after that its taxes become no higher than they would have been if it had never borrowed.

Neither government will experience an interest burden which threatens to undermine its social and military objectives. Both of Domar's hypothetical growing economies emerge with an interest burden which is no larger than its continual annual borrowing. Domar was therefore able to conclude:

> It is hoped that this paper has shown that the problem of the debt burden is essentially a problem of achieving a growing national income. A rising income is of course desired on general grounds, but in addition to its many other advantages it also solves the most important aspects of the problem of the debt. (Domar, [1944] 1957, p. 64)

Domar actually recommended that those who 'spend sleepness nights ... for fear of the debt' should 'forget about it for a while' and think instead about finding 'ways to achieve a growing national income'. He said that this would contribute to 'the benefit and welfare of humanity' (Domar, [1994] 1957, p. 64). Therefore in the final years of the Second World War, some of Britain's most distinguished public servants were contemplating an acquiescence in inflation to 'unloose the dead hand of debt' while one of America's most notable economists was recommending that his fellow-countrymen should forget about government debt and focus entirely on growth.

The debt traps of the 1980s and the 1990s

Domar's call to forget about debt succeeded all too well. His article was read by only a few, but the propositions he established none the less entered the conventional wisdom, and there was little concern about international borrowing until the oil shocks of the 1970s. Until then, Domar's assumption that growth rates can be expected to exceed or at worst equal interest rates proved correct. Developed economies achieved sustained growth of 3 per cent or more, while throughout the world real interest rates were barely positive, and rarely exceeded 2 per cent. Developing countries paid slightly higher interest rates but it was not difficult to achieve growing export revenues in a world where growth was uninterrupted.

The oil shocks slowed the growth of developed economies to little more than 2 per cent, and most maintained their rates of expansion of public expenditure despite a slow-down in their tax revenues. They responded to the deterioration in their public finances by allowing their budgets to drift into deficit and several and (especially the Europeans) also raised taxation. Developing countries were encouraged to expand their borrowing by banks replete with the accumulating revenues of the oil producers, and their lending policies were widely endorsed by those who believed that oil revenues could be beneficially re-cycled from the OPEC countries which would not spend them all to the mainly poorer countries which had a desperate need for investment. The gross public debt of OECD countries rose from 40 per cent of their combined national incomes in 1979 to 50 per cent in 1983, 60 per cent in 1991, and more than 70 per cent in 1997 (*OECD Economic Outlook*, Annex Table 34). In these eighteen years in which OECD debt rose by three-quarters as a ratio of national income, the rate of growth of real GDP fell to 2.5 per cent from 3.7 per cent in 1970–9, (*ibid.*, Annex Table 1), while real interest rates rose in OECD economies to a peak of more than 4 per cent.

Real interest rates rose so markedly because the great increases in government borrowing, especially in the United States, reduced the aggregate OECD savings ratio, and partly because the universal trend towards deregulation of financial markets increased the extent to which investable resources were allocated by price rather than through administrative decisions. With the fall in growth rates and the rise in real interest rates, i/g came to exceed 1 throughout most of the world in the 1980s and the 1990s.

Table 11.2 illustrates the extent to which nominal interest rates exceeded nominal growth rates in the G7 countries in the 1980s and the 1990s. The table shows that the proportional excess of interest rates over growth rates, and therefore the adverse budgetary pressures from debt-financing policies, became greater in the 1990s than the 1980s. In the 1980s average inflation was high in economies such as

Table 11.2 Nominal growth rates (*g*) and interest rates (*i*), 1980–97, per cent

	1980–9			1990–97		
	g	*i*(short)	*i*(long)	*g*	*i*(short)	*i* (long)
Canada	9.0	11.6	11.7	3.4	6.7	8.5
France	9.6	10.9	12.3	3.6	7.3	7.9
Germany	4.8	6.8	7.6	5.4	6.4	7.1
Italy	14.6	15.5	14.8	6.4	10.4	11.2
Japan	6.1	6.4	6.7	3.0	3.3	4.5
United Kingdom	10.1	12.0	11.5	5.4	8.3	8.7
United States	7.8	8.8	10.6	5.1	4.9	7.0

Source: OECD, *Economic Outlook*, Annex Table 2 for the rate of growth of nominal GDP and Annex Table 34 in 1994 and Annex Tables 36 and 37 in June 1998 for interest rates. Short-term rates are 3-month Treasury bill or 3-month interbank rates while long-term rates are for 10-year government bonds.

France, Italy and the United Kingdom and this boosted both nominal interest rates and nominal growth rates so that *i/g* was only slightly above 1. In the 1990s inflation came down sharply and *i/g* rose to more than 2 in Canada and France, to $1^3/_4$ in Italy and to 1.6 in the United Kingdom: while in Germany, Japan and the United States, *i/g* continued to be only a little above 1.

With the sharp fall in growth rates and the rise in real interest rates Domar's formula went horribly wrong. With interest rates at twice or close to twice growth rates in a good deal of the world, debt interest began to increase towards twice the level of government deficits. Many heavy borrowers in developing countries have less financial credibility than Canada, France, Italy and the United Kingdom, and therefore have to pay still higher interest rates. Some of the implications of such developments were set out in 1981 in the influential article, 'Some Unpleasant Monetarist Arithmetic' by Thomas Sargent and Neil Wallace. Faced by interest rates in excess of their growth rates, countries can seek to add their growing interest obligations to their borrowing, but in that case their debt and interest bill will escalate without limit. If their borrowing is international then at some point the world will decline to lend more to them, as with Egypt in the 1870s, and they will then have no alternative but to seek to reschedule – and, if they still fail to control their escalating deficits, to default. Countries with mainly domestic debt might monetise their borrowing and drift towards hyper-inflation. In 1988 Congdon set out many of the implications in *The Debt Threat*.

Since 1990, countries which have sought to avoid default or hyper-inflation have had no alternative but to correct their budgets to prevent their debt from escalating uncontrollably. That has been the solution which all OECD governments have adopted, and the effect on their debt arithmetic has been devastating. In Domar's world a continual deficit of 6 per cent of the national income could remain a primary deficit of 1 per cent in an economy with 3 per cent growth, and a primary balanced budget in an economy with 2 per cent growth. With interest rates that have become twice growth rates, continual borrowing of 6 per cent of the national income will eventually produce debt interest of 12 per cent of the national income, and a government which only begins to control its budget when that point is reached will require a primary surplus of 12 per cent of its national income merely to pay debt interest. It will then have 12 per cent less of its national income to spend on social welfare and defence than if it had never embarked on a borrowing strategy, or else it will require taxes that are higher by 12 per cent of the national income.

The heaviest borrowers among members of the OECD – Belgium, Canada, Italy and Ireland – all pulled back well before their interest payments became twice their deficits, the Europeans in part to move closer to fulfilment of the Maastricht criteria, and these four countries are now each running large primary surpluses (Belgium of 5.5 per cent of GDP, Canada of 5.6 per cent, Ireland of 4.2 per cent and Italy of 5.1 per cent). That is the extent to which these countries are spending less or taxing more than if they had never adopted a borrowing strategy. Winch (1998), Maloney (1998), Barro (1998) Clarke (1998) and Congdon (1998) show how, without exception, initial heavy borrowing is followed by a need to finance the consequent growth of debt through higher taxation, and this has certainly been the experience of these countries.

Many of the developing countries which have allowed their debt to grow, and were caught off-balance by the subsequent rise in interest rates to levels far above their export growth rates, have defaulted like their predecessors in the nineteenth century, and the fall in the world oil price was a significant factor in the Russian default of 1998. These defaults apparently preclude such economies from entering the world's capital markets as net borrowers for new investment until they are forgotten, as they will be if the eighteenth-century judgements of Steuart and Hume on this question prove correct. The underlying force of their far-sighted analysis is reinforced by the repeated examples of bankers returning to countries which defaulted under a previous President or Finance Minister, where a mere change of personalities sometimes suffices to bring back banks anxious to expand their loan portfolios.

Some economies and cities and provinces in Europe and North America which have not defaulted have had to pay interest rate premia over the rates paid by unquestionably sound borrowers because markets have seen a possibility of default. Obvious examples are Italy, Quebec and Orange County. The need to pay interest rate premia is a powerful inducement to convert primary deficits into surpluses.

It emerges that default or market judgements of the possibility of default have had a significant bearing on the finances of those who allowed their debt to drift upwards after the Second World War, for which they paid a heavy price in the 1980s and the 1990s. It has therefore been an integral element in the explanation of debt and deficits in the post-Domar world.

Some may regard the conditions of the 1980s and the 1990s as a financial aberration and hope for a return of the former conditions where growth could costlessly solve most debt problems, and finance ministers could be advised to 'forget' debt.

The evidence suggests that it is Domar's world that has been aberrant. In the eighteenth and the early nineteenth centuries Britain incurred public debt of 276 per cent of its national income at 3–5 per cent interest rates when growth was no more than 1–2 per cent per annum. US growth in the nineteenth century was little more than 2 per cent while interest rates were far higher. In the inter-war years, interest rates were far above growth rates throughout the world. It has only been in capitalism's so-called 'Golden Age' from 1945 to 1973 that growth in much of the world has been strong enough to over-ride debt, and the description of those decades as 'Golden' signifies that few anticipate their return.

12
France's Free Market Reforms in 1774–6 and Russia's in the 1990s: The Immediate Relevance of the Abbé de Condillac's Analysis*

The great reforming minister whose appointment had been greeted with acclamation did what leading contemporary economists had been advocating for over a decade. Markets were freed, and above all the market for food. Farmers were allowed to sell for the best prices they could find. The cost of food rose sharply and riots followed. A so-called 'Parlement' met and passed a resolution that it was the state's responsibility to provide food at prices the people could afford. The minister found this subversive, had the posters announcing the resolution placarded over, and imprisoned rioters with the full support of the Head of State. The minister then issued further edicts which removed the obligation on workers to provide forced labour, and threatened the privileges of those who were making personal fortunes from financing the state. By this point he had alienated those in the cities who had to pay more for food, those who relied upon forced labour, those who had been most prosperous under the previous régime and those who preferred orderly government to radical reforms which produced riots. After just twenty months the Head of State removed the reforming minister, and replaced him with another who reversed his policies. The reestablishment of the previous régime proved unviable and it was

* This is a revised version of the article 'France's Free Market Reforms in 1774–6 and Russia's in 1991–3: The Immediate Relevance of l'Abbé de Condillac's Analysis', *European Journal for the History of European Thought*, 1(i) (autumn 1993), pp. 5–19.

swept away a little over a decade later, and the Head of State who had been prepared to support his reforming minister for only 20 months was executed.

This did not occur in Eastern Europe in the 1990s although it has evident echoes in contemporary events, but happily it is now rare for those who fail politically to face execution. The events described occurred in France more than two centuries ago.

The failure of Turgot's reforms in France in 1774–6

One of Louis XVI's first acts on his accession in 1774 was to appoint Anne Robert Jacques Turgot Minister for the Navy and shortly afterwards Controller-General of Finances, one of the two leading positions in government. Since 1761 Turgot had been a reforming Intendant in Limoges, in effect head of local government there. In 1769 he had published one of the great classical economic texts, *Réflexions sur la Formation et la Distribution des Richesses*, and his numerous publications commanded high respect. He corresponded regularly with de Condorcet and Du Pont de Nemours, the father of the founders of the United States chemical empire and the original editor of *Les Éphémérides du Citoyen*, one of the two physiocratic economic journals. Turgot had always been close to the philosophes and encylopédistes and he was elected President of the Académie des Belles Lettres in 1778. He was well known to Benjamin Franklin, Edward Gibbon and Adam Smith.

His economics is best described as enlightened and practical physiocracy. Agriculture provided the economy's sole taxable surplus, with the result that the prosperity of the State and economic growth depended predominantly upon it. However industry and commerce contributed to employment profits and wealth, so Turgot did not follow the physiocrats in regarding these as 'sterile'. He avoided the use of that pejorative word to describe the activities of industry and commerce; but because the profits from commerce would go overseas if they were taxed in France, while manufacturers would pass profits taxes on in higher prices or else cease to manufacture, the revenues of the state depended predominantly on the success and prosperity of agriculture.[1] In this, Turgot was at one with the physiocrats, and also in his belief that the prosperity of agriculture would be ensured above all by freeing the market for food. Farmers were not allowed to move food within France, or to export it. Each region and city had markets which were locally controlled with the object of preventing famine, and establishing a level of prices which local administrations judged correct, but there were those who were privileged to benefit from the consequent régime of controls and restrictions.

In Rouen, for instance, the right to buy and store wheat, and the privilege of supplying bakers, had been conferred on a single company of merchants, and its monopoly privileges extended to the surrounding villages.[2] A similar situation prevailed in the market for meat in many cities. It was a central tenet of François Quesnay, the founder of the physiocratic school of économistes, that the market for food must be freed. This had also been the opinion of Jacques Vincent de Gournay, Intendant du Commerce from 1751 to 1758, who had created a school of young economists who sought to free markets and is the widely credited original author of advocacy of 'laissez faire et laissez passer'. There was indeed a group of officials, economic writers and even government censors,[3] who regarded the freeing of food markets as a necessary and desirable reform. The advantage they perceived, and which the physiocrats sought to demonstrate through calculations based on Quesnay's tableau, was that if farmers could sell their products in free markets, they would obtain higher prices for their food, especially if they were no longer obliged to sell to monopolistic companies. Farming would thereby become more profitable, and this would enable and encourage agricultural expansion. An expansion of food production would then enlarge agriculture's economic surplus, the ultimate source of taxation.[4] Higher tax revenues were desperately needed to solve the French government's financial problems where debts proliferated and revenues fell far short of expenditures.

Those who stood to lose from the freeing of agricultural markets included all those who benefited from the monopoly privileges which proliferated, while the reform of government finances would undermine those who ran the ramshackle system of taxes and borrowing which Louis XVI had inherited.

Turgot's appointment as Controller-General of Finances initially appeared a new dawn to those who favoured reform. D'Alembert, the editor (with Diderot) of the *Encylopédie* wrote: 'If good does not result, one must conclude that good cannot be done.'[5] His personal 'cabinet' included several non-physiocrats, but he appointed Du Pont as his Inspector-General of Commerce and room was also found for Quesnay de Saint-Germain, a grandson of the founder of physiocracy.[6] Turgot rapidly introduced measures which partially freed French food markets, but short-term difficulties rapidly emerged. The price of wheat was

50 per cent higher in 1775 than it had been in 1774.[7] By being able to sell wheat in provinces other than their own, farmers were able to receive higher prices, and those who bought bread had to pay more. In May 1775 a series of provincial bread riots reached Paris, and as a mob was smashing bakers' shops, the Marquis de Maurepas, Turgot's principal colleague in government, went to the opera and left the mob free to rampage. The Paris 'Parlement' met and passed a resolution which asked the King to:

> take the measures which his good sense and love for his subjects will inspire, to lower the prices of wheat and bread to a level appropriate to the needs of the people.

Turgot regarded it as vital to prevent the publication of this subversive decree which asked the King to revoke the laws of market economics. He dashed to Versailles in the middle of the night, had the King woken, had a musketeer sent to summon each member of the Royal Council, and obtained the King's agreement to prevent the circulation of Parlement's decree. Several ministers were replaced, and order was restored. Two members of the mob were hanged, many were imprisoned and a curate who had preached against the food riots received a pension and promotion (to a bénéfice).[8] But the fundamental difficulty that the policy of establishing a free market for food would initially raise food prices remained unsolved. Bachaumont speaks of a mob being ready to smash a bust of Quesnay 'on hearing that he was the cause of the current dearness of grain through false theories and the baneful influence he had had on government'.[9]

Turgot retained royal support throughout the crisis of 1775, but in February–March 1776 he proposed six reforming edicts which aroused still sharper opposition. These included the replacement of the corvée which obliged peasants to spend a number of days a year on local public works, financing this by local taxation to be paid by landowners. Other decrees proposed to free internal French food markets and to abolish local monopoly privileges such as those in Rouen. A large number of government posts associated with the administration of the markets Turgot was proposing to free would be abolished, and indirect taxes, such as those on salt, be replaced with a territorial tax which landowners and even the Church would have to pay, with a consequent loss of privileges for tax collectors.[10] Turgot knew that great opposition would be aroused by the speed of his reform programme, but he remarked when he became a minister at the age of 47, 'In my family we die at fifty' (Schelle, 1909, p. 211): he was actually 54 when he died in 1781.

Maurepas declined to support the six decrees, the Paris Parlement again voiced its opposition, and referred to 'The cry for an ill considered freedom' and 'a novel system introduced by books and articles, as inexact in their facts as their principles'. Yet Turgot still enjoyed the support of the King, and his six decrees were endorsed by the Council. Paris was illuminated that night, but Turgot's triumph was brief.

He was isolated in the Council. He attempted to appease his opponents by closing the physiocratic journals, but he failed to persuade the King to replace Maurepas or indeed to make any ministerial changes which would strengthen his position. There was indeed powerful and widespread opposition to his reforms which did not even enjoy the support of the unprivileged because the price of bread had risen. Many of those in receipt of government incomes saw that the reforms would destroy their jobs and their wealth, and the farmers who were beginning to benefit were mostly some distance from Paris. The King opened conversations with another Provincial Intendant, Clugny, who was appointed to succeed Turgot as Controller-General of Finances in May 1776.[11] Clugny proved a tinkerer who rearranged public debt without seeking to pursue policies which would produce sufficient revenues to place government finances on a sound footing. He was succeeded by others who failed equally to achieve the fundamental reforms which were needed.

Turgot actually wrote to Louis XVI immediately before the King replaced him, 'Never forget that it was weakness that placed the head of Charles I on the block' (Schelle, 1909, p. 238). The King had written to Turgot previously that, 'It is only you and I who love the people' (Schelle, 1909, p. 247). But he failed to sustain Turgot in office, and permitted Clugny to reverse the six decrees. His queen, Marie-Antoinette (who followed Louis to the guillotine during the Revolution) wrote to her mother, Marie-Thérèse, Empress of Austria, that she was not sorry that Turgot had fallen. The Empress responded that Turgot had tried to do too much too quickly (Schelle, 1909, pp. 251–2). That is always the problem that radical reformers face. Gustave Schelle has commented that if Turgot had moved more slowly, opposition to his reforms would have had more time to build up, and his position would have been undermined before much could be achieved (1909, p. 252). The optimum pace of reform when radical change is necessary is never clear.

The économistes fell with Turgot. Du Pont was ordered to leave Paris, and the editors of the physiocratic journals, which Turgot had closed in a vain attempt to appease his opponents, were exiled. But what had occurred became central to economic debate. The économistes had had an opportunity to give practical effect to their theories and they had failed.

The reasons for Turgot's fall have aroused continuing interest including a major work by Edgar Faure, a President of the National Assembly and member of several twentieth-century French governments. The reactions of Turgot's contemporaries to his reform programme and to the difficulties he encountered are also illuminating. The second part of this article will be especially concerned with the analysis of Étienne Bonnot, the abbé de Condillac, a strong supporter of Turgot's programme, who wrote at this time because of the exceptional interest in the economy which his reforms attracted. His account of their perverse initial results and the opposition they aroused also offer vivid insights which are as relevant to Russia's predicament in the 1990s as to France's in 1776.

Maurice Allais, a French Nobel Prizewinnner in economics, described *Le Commerce et le Gouvernement considérés relativement l'un à l'autre* (hereafter, *Commerce and Government*), the book Condillac published in March 1776, two months before Turgot's fall, as 'much superior to Adam Smith's' in that Condillac had developed 'a general theory of the generation of surpluses, of general economic equilibrium and of maximal efficiency' (Allais, 1992, p. 174). In 1871, Stanley Jevons acknowledged in *The Theory of Political Economy* that Condillac had produced the 'earliest distinct statement of the true connection between value and utility' (1871, p. xxviii), while Terence Huchison in his magisterial *Before Adam Smith* (1988), concluded that 'Condillac's work represented the crowning achievement in the long and distinguished line of Italian and French theorists of utility and subjective value', and that, 'it is Condillac, with his emphasis on ignorance, uncertainty and erroneous expectations, who has stronger claims than anyone else to be regarded as the founding father of subjectivist analysis in economic theory' (1988, p. 331).

The Abbé de Condillac's case for market economics

Condillac was a distinguished philosopher, and as such he won the youthful Turgot's respect. He was a philosophe who for a time dined weekly with Diderot and Rousseau.[12] He had been tutor to the Prince of Parma, for whom he produced a seventeen-volume account of what rulers needed to learn from the arts and sciences and the experience of other societies. This contains one passage of political economy which could have been penned by Adam Smith:

> Governing an economy requires a comprehensive genius who knows everything, who weighs everything,and who directs all the resources of government in perfect harmony. It would be difficult, or rather impossible to find such a genius. The best intentioned and most skilful statesmen have made mistakes through ignorance or through over hasty action, for it is so difficult to see all and bring all together without sometimes falling into error ... statesmen never do more harm than when they wish to interfere in everything. It is wisest to confine oneself to preventing abuses and otherwise to pursue a policy of laissez-faire. (Condillac, [1775] 1798, XX. p. 488)

In 1776, at the age of 62, almost the age (61) at which Quesnay first wrote on economics, Condillac published the first two Parts of *Le Commerce et le Gouvernement.*[13] The first, 'Elementary propositions on commerce, determined according to the assumptions and principles of Economic Science', provides a step-by-step statement of economic principles to establish the political economy which will most advance the wealth of nations. One of Condillac's notable philosophical works, his *Traité des Sensations* (1754), had opened with the assumption that human beings are statues, which he then relaxed in successive chapters to arrive at a clear account of complex human sensations. His economics followed a similar methodology. He opens Chapter 1 with a corn model (with corn the only commodity which is produced and consumed) and gradually relaxes the assumptions to provide a general account of a real economy. He believed that political economy could be presented simply and comprehensibly by creating a clear language for the presentation of economic analysis (which up to then was lacking), and by using this to move forward chapter by chapter to provide a comprehensive account of more complex economies. Hence his title of Part 1, with its emphasis on 'elementary propositions'. The approach is one very much to be expected of a philosopher of the first rank seeking to establish a sound basis for economic analysis, and Condillac completed his account of economic principles in 60 000 words.

The considerably shorter Part 2 is entitled, 'Commerce and government considered in relation to each other following some assumptions', has the same title as he gave to his book, with the significant addition of the words 'following some assumptions'. Condillac thus used the analysis he developed in Part 1 to elucidate the practical questions he was addressing. The expositional method he uses is generally a comparison between abstract countries in which some pursue disastrous policies while others adopt correct policies and perform far more successfully. But the pretence that it is hypothetical countries he is comparing is dropped in Chapter 15, subtitled, 'Obstacles to the circulation of grain when the government wishes to restore to trade the freedom it took from it', which is clearly concerned with the actual impact of Turgot's reforms. In Part 3, which was never written, Condillac proposed to consider what he had established in Parts 1 and 2 'according to the facts in order to rest as much on experience as on reasoning' (CG, p. 78) Richard Cantillon is said to have followed his largely theoretical *Essai sur la nature du commerce en général* (1755) with an empirical second volume which has not survived (Murphy, 1986, p. 251), and it has recently been suggested that Karl Marx's object in the third volume of *Das Kapital* (which he did not live to complete) was to provide an empirical account of the trade cycle in nineteenth-century Britain (Kennessey, 1991). Condillac might well have found it equally difficult to provide an account of 'the facts' to complete his work, but it is actually complete as it stands. The theoretical Part 1 and its development in Part 2 to illuminate practical questions and especially the failure of Turgot's reforms produces a wholly coherent book.

The most innovative aspect of the theoretical Part 1 is Condillac's account of the relationship between the utility derivable from commodities, the demand for them, and the impact this had on the motivation to produce. This was 100 years ahead of its time.[14] Farmers and manufacturers produce to generate 'value' for themselves which depends on the personal utilities they derive. The marginal utility they enjoy from each commodity they consume diminishes as the quantity consumed increases (CG, 84) As soon as there is a departure from the one-commodity corn model, with this analysis, farmers grow more corn only if they can exchange their surplus, which offers them no value because it has no marginal utility, for something else that they desire, and the same is true of the producers of all other commodities. Wherever production is surplus to a farmer's own needs, an absence of adequate opportunities to market this will remove any incentive to produce beyond the level which satisfies the farmer's personal desires. The absence of adequate markets therefore has highly adverse effects on the supply side of the economy:

> The surplus of the settlers [farmers] ... is wealth so long as they can find an outlet for it; because they procure for themselves something

> that has value for them, and they hand over something which has value for others.
>
> If they were unable to make exchanges, their surplus would stay with them, and it would have no value for them. Indeed, surplus grain, which I store in my barns without being able to exchange it, no more represents wealth to me than the grain which I have not yet pulled from the ground. So I will sow less next year. (CG, p. 101)

Markets for the produce of the land are provided by merchants:

> Now merchants are the channels of communication through which the surplus runs. From places where it has no value it passes into places where it gains value and wherever it settles it becomes wealth.
>
> The merchant therefore in a way makes something out of nothing. He does not till, but he brings about tillage. He induces the settler to draw an even greater surplus from the land ...
>
> A spring which disappears into rocks and sand is not wealth for me; but it becomes such, if I build an aqueduct to draw it to my meadows. This spring represents the surplus products for which we are indebted to to the settlers, and the aqueduct represents the merchants. (CG, p. 102)

Condillac's insistence that less food will be grown, if farmers cannot exchange what is surplus to their own needs for something else which has utility for them, is underlined by the Soviet Union's experience, where one-quarter of all food was grown in private plots which amounted to just 1 per cent of the land in cultivation.

Condillac goes on to explain that beyond the merchants who give value to surplus agricultural production are manufacturers who turn materials into ever-more desirable finished products, the availability of which encourages farmers to grow more food in order to obtain them:

> It is the farmer who provides all the primary material. But such primary material, as would be useless and without value in his hands, becomes useful and obtains value when the artisan has found the way to make it serve the needs of society.
>
> With each skill that begins, with each advance it makes, the farmer thus acquires new wealth, because he finds value in a product which previously had none.

> This product, given value by the artisan, gives a fresh spur to commerce for which it is a new stock in trade; and it becomes a new source of wealth for the farmer …
>
> Thus it is that all, farmers, merchants, artisans, come together to increase the mass of wealth. (CG, p. 104–5)

This statement was provocative to the physiocrat French économistes of 1776 who still held that agriculture was the sole source of wealth, and Condillac comments that 'industry gives value to a number of products, which otherwise would have none', so it is 'proved that in the final analysis industry is also a source of wealth'. He added that these clear propositions had been 'much obscured by some writers' (CG, p. 105).

The key role that the existence of adequate markets played in providing sufficient incentives for the supply side of the economy (which is one of the features of Condillac's work which greatly impressed Allais) is naturally central to the policy-oriented Part 2 of the book. Several chapters are concerned with the market for grain which figured so prominently in Turgot's reforms. Condillac's description of actual markets and his account of the rules on which policy was then based show how completely French practice had departed from conditions where farmers would obtain value for their produce, which was the central consideration for the functioning of a successful economy in the theoretical Part 1 of his book. Thus it was:

> forbidden to all persons to undertake trade in grain without having obtained permission for it from officials appointed for that purpose.
>
> It was forbidden to all others, farmers or landowners to interfere directly or indirectly in carrying out this trade.
>
> Any association between grain merchants was forbidden unless it had been authorized.
>
> It was forbidden to pay a deposit on corn or to buy corn unripe, standing, before the harvest.
>
> It was forbidden to sell corn other than in the markets.
>
> It was forbidden to make hoards of grain.
>
> It was forbidden to let it move from one province into another without having obtained permission. (CG, p. 262)

The disadvantages were compounded by corruption, for:

> You could not carry on the corn trade at all without having obtained their permission. But it was not enough to ask for it in

> order to get it; you also needed to have protection; and protection was hardly ever granted except to those who would pay for it, or who would give up a share in their profit. (CG, p. 264)

Because of the prevalent corruption, those who traded in wheat were viewed with social contempt:

> the people ... regarded the grain merchants as grasping men who took advantage of their needs. Once that opinion was rooted, a person could not engage in this trade if he cared for his reputation: it had to be left to those vile creatures who counted money for everything and honour for nothing. (CG, p. 268)

But the success of Turgot's reforms would depend upon the existence of a large number of merchants who would establish competitive prices:

> In dealing with the circulation of cereals we have seen that it can only be carried out by a host of merchants spread everywhere. These merchants are so many canals through which the grain circulates. Now these canals had been broken and it was time to mend them.
>
> Indeed, to succeeed in any type of trade, it is not enough to have the freedom to carry it on; one must ... have obtained contacts, and these contacts can only be the fruits of experience, which is often slow. One must also have capital, stores, carters, agents, correspondents: In a word one must have taken many precautions and many measures. (CG, p. 267)

Because the grain trade was a corrupt and despised profession, and because there had been no experience in trading, the infrastructure for the establishment of successful markets did not yet exist with the result that the first effects of freeing food markets would inevitably prove disappointing:

> So the freedom returned to the grain trade was a benefit that could not be enjoyed the moment it was granted. A word from the monarch had been enough to wipe out this freedom; a word did not restore it, and there was high price a few months later. (CG, p. 267)

Condillac was of course aware that 'the true price' (le vrai prix) which would follow the establishment of free markets might well be higher than the one which had prevailed previously:

> it must be seen that that high price is not dearness: it is the true price fixed by competition, a true price which has its high, its low and its middle limit. (CG, p. 204)

The people reacted extremely adversely to the rise in prices that followed the freeing of food markets: 'Look what freedom produces ... They thought that dearness was a result of freedom'. They did not appreciate that prices would only fall when there were 'enough merchants ... to set cereals at their true price'. But they said, 'we need bread every day' (CG, p. 267). They believed that:

> the one task of government was to procure them cheap bread ... So every time that it became dearer the people asked the government to have the price lowered.
>
> There were only two ways to satisfy them. The government had to buy grain itself to sell again at a loss, or it had to force merchants to deliver their corn at the price it had fixed.
>
> Of these two ways the first tended to ruin the state; the second was unjust and odious; and both accustomed the people to think that it was for the government to obtain cheap bread for them, whatever it cost either in money or in injustice. (CG, p. 268)

The people saw the problem of obtaining cheap bread as a conflict of 'The rights of humanity opposed to those of property' (to which Condillac the philosopher added, 'What gibberish!'), and everyone said 'the most absurd things to oppose the operations of the new minister ... It seemed that everyone was condemned to reason badly on this matter'. Turgot's opponents, many of whom had favoured the policy of freeing food markets until the immediate consequence of higher prices emerged, now included:

> poets, geometricians, philosophers, metaphysicians, in a word almost all literary men, and especially those whose trenchant tone hardly allows one to take their doubts for doubts, and who do not permit one to think differently from them. (CG, p. 269)

Opposition to Turgot also came from the vast bureaucracies which government had created, to administer regulated markets and to exploit monopolistic privileges in international trade:

> In the capital they need administrators, directors, clerks, employees: they need other administrators, other directors, other clerks, other employees wherever they form establishments. They also need, in addition to the counters and the warehouses, buildings as a monument to the vanity of the directors they employ. Forced to such outlays, how much will they not lose in embezzlement, in negligence, in incompetence? They pay for all the errors of those they employ to serve them; and all the more arise, as the administrators who succeed each other at the whim of faction, and who each see differently, never allow a sensible, sustained plan to be made. They form badly contrived enterprises: they carry them out as though randomly; and in an administration that seems to tie itself up in knots, they employ self-interested men to complicate it further. The direction of these companies is thus necessarily vicious. (CG, pp. 281–2)

Those with vested interests in the perpetuation of these bureaucracies added their voices to the opposition to Turgot's reforms. According to Condillac, 'the new minister showed courage', but, 'Such are the chief obstacles in the way of the re-establishment of freedom. Time will remove them if the government perseveres' (CG, p. 269). It became evident two months after the publication of *Commerce and Government* that Turgot was not to be allowed to persevere. After just twenty months, the opposition that Condillac describes led to his fall, and the reversal of his reforms by his successors. As Condillac remarked, 'when disorder has reached a certain point, a revolution, however good it may be, is never accomplished without causing violent reactions' (CG, pp. 266–7).

Condillac's book was published a few weeks before Adam Smith's *Wealth of Nations* and it presents an elegant statement of the same free market principles. But he published in the wrong country and the wrong manner.

The initial reaction in France to the brilliance and clarity of Condillac's presentation was highly favourable. Writing to Ferdinando Galiani in Naples in March 1776 immediately after its publication, Louise d'Épinay described it as, 'A classic work which makes the jargon of economics clearer than a mountain spring ... devotees of the subject applaud a masterpiece' (Galiani, 1992–6, V, p. 69). But the French reviewers were mainly physiocrats who regarded as heresy Condillac's statements that manufacturing and commerce added to the value of production. They condemned the book, and the flavour of their opposition can be inferred from a passage of remarkable dogmatism in the lengthy review by the abbé Baudeau in the *Nouvelles Ephémérides* which he was able to publish just before Turgot closed the journal as one of his last acts in government:

> True économistes can easily be characterised by one simple characteristic in a manner that the whole world can understand. They recognise one master, Dr Quesnay, one doctrine, (that of *Philosophie rurale* and *l'Analyse économique*), classical texts (*la Physiocratie*), and a single formula (*le Tableau économique*), and they use technical terms in the same way as the ancient scholars of China. (Baudeau, [1776] 1903, p. 433)

The physiocrat Le Trosne devoted almost twenty pages to *Le Commerce et le Gouvernement* in the book *De l'Intérêt Social* which he published in 1777, and he reproached Condillac for having found inadequate a doctrine which had been 'published, proved and demonstrated in several works in the last fifteen years' (Le Trosne, [1777] 1846, p. 886). Condillac was evidently not a true economist to the économistes. There has always been a powerful Colbertian element in official French economics, and nineteenth century writers in the mainstream French tradition found his economics over-theoretical and insisted that he had failed to recognise the complex realities which underpinned the case for detailed government intervention.

But as early as 1808 when dogmatic physiocracy was dead, Condillac was astonishingly accorded the highest possible praise by Du Pont, who had been one of the most dogmatic of physiocrats in the 1770s, He was the original editor of *Les Ephémérides*, and Turgot's Inspector-General of Commerce in 1774–6. In the account of the state of contemporary economics which he included in his nine-volume Turgot edition, he said that there were distinguished 'philosophes éclectiques' who had benefited from the work of both the physiocratic school and the school of Gournay without belonging to either, 'at the head of whom should be placed M. Turgot, l'abbé de Condillac and the celebrated Adam Smith' (Du Pont, 1808b, III, p. 316). So by 1808, Du Pont was placing Condillac alongside the great minister whose reforms both had so strongly supported, and Adam Smith, by then recognised as author of the supreme account of the benefits of competitive market economics.

At a fundamental level, a clue to the contemporary success of Smith's book and the failure of Condillac's to receive similar acclaim is to be found in Spencer Pack's interpretation (1991) of the relevance of Smith's *Lectures on Rhetoric and Belles Lettres* to the success of *The Wealth of Nations*. Smith advises that when an author is writing for those already receptive to what he has to say, a deductive method of presentation with a logical derivation of conclusions from axioms which readers are already prepared to acccept is appropriate. It is by far the easiest to follow and it is the most elegant. But where an author is writing for the unconverted, he should argue inductively, moving step by step from known facts to the conclusions he wishes to establish. Tariffs, restrictions on trade and detailed government interventions proliferated in both Britain and France in 1776, so Condillac and Smith were both addressing the largely unconverted, but Smith adopted the method of presentation which he had prescribed for such a situation:

> keep as far from the main point to be proved as possible, bringing on the audience by slow and imperceptible degrees to the thing to be proved, and by gaining their consent to some things whose tendency they cant discover, we force them at last either to deny what they had before agreed to, or to grant the Validity of the Conclusion ... if they are prejudiced against the Opinion to be advanced; we are not to shock them by rudely affirming what we are satisfied is disagreeable, but are to conceal our design and beginning at a distance, bring them slowly on to the main point and having gained the more remote ones we get the nearer ones of consequence. (Smith, 1983, pp. 146–7)

Pack has reminded us with this passage in mind that Smith only reached his critique of mercantilist policies after more than 500 pages replete with fascinating and convincing empirical detail.

Condillac, in contrast, used the deductive methodology of a distinguished philosopher and moved faultlessly and elegantly from proposition to proposition. But he failed to carry his French readers. His initial chapters lacked Smith's empiricism, and his French readers were unprepared to accept that a deductive argument, which moved from premises they did not recognise as relevant, had managed to arrive at conclusions which sensibly related to their country. His is nonetheless a forceful and highly pertinent book for a generation ready to accept a theory of value grounded in utility, and theorems which establish the superiority of free markets over any kind of microeconomic interventionism.

Moreover, by the time Condillac reaches his account of the difficulties that Turgot's reforms encounter he is empirical. These failed because of the build-up of opposition as a consequence of their immediate adverse impact on vested interests and upon food prices. That is strikingly similar to the impact of reform today in several East European economies and Russia in particular. What Condillac has to say of their predicament is as vivid now as the statements his fellow countrymen failed to appreciate thirteen years before the collapse of the Bourbons.

The failure of France's reforms in the eighteenth century and Russia's in the 1990s

There are apparent parallels. With the attempts at reform in both countries, markets were freed and prices rose sharply. In both countries, the large number of merchants and traders required to exploit freer markets was absent. In both countries, a bureaucracy with corrupt elements apparently threw much of the movement and trading of food and consumer goods into the hands of the semi criminal: the large number of middlemen and small trading companies that efficient wholesale and retail distribution requires had not emerged. In both cases, there were inefficient bureaucracies with vested interests in the prevention of any reforms that undermined their privileges and their raison-d'être.

Condillac was scathing about the adverse impact on the real economy of volatile monetary values, from which France suffered in the early eighteenth century as a consequence of John Law's failed financial experiments and which is equally damaging in Russia in the 1990s:

> once the monarch had changed the coins, one could no longer accept them with confidence, because one no longer knew what they were worth. One had either to be deceived or oneself to deceive. So the sovereign's deception placed deception in lieu of confidence in trade, and people could neither buy nor sell unless forced by need ... people did not know how to use a measure which, as it varied continually, was no longer a measure. (CG, p. 245)

The consequence was that:

> Cautious people who did not want to lay out their money at the risk of losing it locked it up ... They waited for the moment to use it again with less risk, and trade suffered from this ...

> ...mistrust was general and one saw no more silver in circulation. Merchants who had borrowed it did not have enough for every day essential expenditure. Then, forced to empty their warehouses and to sell at a 50 or 60 per cent loss, they saw how they had been deceived in their speculations. The majority became bankrupt. (CG, p. 246)

What is locked up in Russia in the 1990s, or sent out of the country, is not the silver which disappeared from circulation in eighteenth-century France, but the hard-currency dollars and D-marks which are as essential as gold and silver were in the eighteenth century for the purchase of the industrial materials and equipment without which production cannot proceed.

In eighteenth-century France and the Russia of the 1990s, there were unrepresentative Assemblies with pre-reform attitudes which believed that the state should exercise its power to control markets. In France, the reforming minister fell after less than two years. Condillac's explanation of the failure of the French reformers in the eighteenth century illuminates the intractable difficulties which have undermined the efforts of those who have sought to create an effective market economy in Russia in the 1990s.

Notes

1. The best modern accounts of Turgot's economics are by Groenewegen (1977, 1987) and Meek (1973).
2. See Du Pont (1808a), 1, p. 204.
3. See Murphy (1986), Chapter 15.
4. A detailed account of the impact of higher food prices on output and growth is set out by Quesnay in his '[Premier] problème économique' which is included in Daire (1846), pp. 107–24. See Eltis (1984), Chapter 2 for a modern restatement.
5. Turgot, *Oeuvres*, 4, p. 20.
6. Schelle (1909), p. 154.
7. Turgot, *Oeuvres*, 4, p. 45.
8. See Schelle (1909) Chapter 13, Turgot, *Oeuvres*, 4, pp. 44–55, and Faure (1961), Part 2, Chapters 3–4, for detailed accounts of the bread riots ('La guerre des farines') of 1775.
9. Hecht (1958), p. 276.
10. See Schelle (1909), Chapter 14, Turgot, *Oeuvres*, 5, pp. 1–12, and Faure (1961), Part 3, Chapters 4–5, for accounts of the February–March decrees.
11. See Schelle (1909), Chapter 16, Turgot, *Oeuvres*, 5, pp. 12–20 and Faure (1961), Part 3, Chapters 6–7, for accounts of Turgot's fall.
12. See S.M. Eltis (1997) and Lebeau 1903, Chapter 1 for biographical accounts of Condillac.

13. The book first appeared in March 1776 (Amsterdam, Et se trouve à Paris Chez Jombert & Cellot) and it has been reprinted many times in France. The first English language translation was published by Edward Elgar in 1997 (ed. by S.M. and W. Eltis) and the quotations from *Commerce and Government* in the present chapter are from that edition, with page references preceded by the letters CG.
14. In 1769 Turgot elegantly derived the relationship between the relative marginal utilities of commodities and their relative values in exchange in his uncompleted 'Valeurs et monnaies'. His rigorous analysis took the form of two persons trading two commodities. The influence of the opportunity cost of producing the commodities and the generalisation of the argument beyond two persons and two commodities is sketchily indicated. It is not known if Condillac saw Turgot's manuscript, and if he did, he certainly extended the argument, which is why he is widely credited with the principal French originality in the development of the relationship between utility and demand, and its implications for an efficient economy. Turgot's analysis of utility, value and demand is set out and discussed in detail in Faccarello (1992).

References

Allais, M. (1992) 'The General Theory of Surpluses as a Formalization of the Underlying Theoretical Thought of Adam Smith, his Predecessors and his Contemporaries', in *Adam Smith's Legacy*, ed. Michael Fry, London: Routledge.

Appleby, Joyce Oldham (1980) *Economic Thought and Ideology in Seventeenth Century England*, Princeton, NJ: Princeton University Press.

Arrow, K.J., H.B. Chenery, B. Minhas and R.M. Solow (1961) 'Capital–Labour Substitution and Economic Efficiency', *Review of Economics and Statistics*, 43, August.

Bacon, Robert (1980) 'The Effects of Public Employment and other Government Spending on the Rate of Wage Inflation', in *Public Finance and Public Employment*, Proceedings of the 16th Congress of the International Institute of Public Finance, Jerusalem, Detroit: Wayne State University Press.

Bacon, Robert and Walter Eltis (1975) 'The Declining Britain articles: 1 'Where We Went Wrong' 2 'The Chances We Missed', 3 'What We Would Do', The *Sunday Times*, 2, 9 and 16 November.

Bacon, Robert and Walter Eltis (1976) *Britain's Economic Problem, Too Few Producers*; 2nd edn 1978, London: Macmillan.

Bacon, Robert and Walter Eltis (1979) 'The Measurement of the Growth of the Non-Market Sector and its Influence': A Reply to Hadjimatheou and Skouras', *Economic Journal*, 89, June.

Bacon, Robert and Walter Eltis (1996) *Britain's Economic Problem Revisited*, 3rd edn of *Britain's Economic Problem: Too Few Producers*, London: Macmillan.

Balasubramanyam, V.N. (1993) 'Entrepreneurship and the Growth of the Firm: The Case of the British Food and Drink Industry', in J. Brown and M.B. Rose (eds), *Entrepreneurship, Networks and Modern Business*, Manchester University Press.

Bank Credit Analyst (1997) 'High tech's Positive Impact on the US Economy', May.

Bank Credit Analyst (1999) 'Where are we in the Long Wave?', February.

Bannock, G. and H. Albach (1991) 'Small Business Policy in Europe: Britain, Germany and the EC', London: Anglo–German Foundation.

Barro, R.J. (1974) 'Are Government Bonds Net Wealth?', *Journal of Political Economy*, 82 (November–December), pp. 1095–1118.

Barro, R.J. (1998) 'Reflections on Ricardian Equivalence', in J. Maloney (ed.), *Debt and Deficits: An Historical Perspective*, Aldershot: Edward Elgar.

Baudeau, l'abbé N. (1776) 'Observations économistes à M.l'abbé de Condillac par M. l'abbé Baudeau', *Nouvelles Ephémérides*, (April–May); reprinted in Lebeau (1903), pp. 423–45.

Bean, C.R. (1994) 'European Unemployment: A Survey', *Journal of Economic Literature*, 32, June.

Bean, C.R. and N. Crafts (1995) 'British Economic Growth since 1945: Relative Economic Decline ... and Renaissance?', *CEPR Discussion Paper*, 1092.

Blake, A.P. and N. Pain (1994) 'Investigating Structural Changes in UK Export Performance: The Role of Innovation and Direct Investment', *National Institute Discussion Paper*, 71.

Blaug M. (1995) 'Why is the quantity theory of money the oldest surviving theory in economics', in Blaug (ed.) *The Quantity Theory of Money from Locke to Keynes and Friedman'. Aldershot: Edward Elgar.*

Booth, A. (1983) 'The Keynesian Revolution in Economic Policy Making', *Economic History Review*, 36, February.

Bosher, J.F. (1965) 'French Administration and Public Finance in their European Setting', in *The New Cambridge Modern History*, 8, *The American and French Revolutions, 1763–93*, Cambridge: Cambridge University Press, pp. 565–91.

Brenton P.A. and P.J.N. Sinclair (1996) 'Explaining Recent British Export Performance', University of Birmingham for HM Treasury, unpublished.

Brewer, John (1989) *The Sinews of Power: War, Money and the English State, 1688–1783*, London: Routledge.

Budd, Alan (1996) 'Unemployment Policies since the War – The Theory and the Practice', in B. Corry (ed.), *Unemployment and the Economists*, Aldershot: Edward Elgar.

Callaghan, James (1987) *Time and Chance*, London: Collins.

Cantillon, R. (1755) *Essai sur la nature du commerce en général*, Paris.

Cantwell J.A. and C. Hodson (1990) 'Global R & D and UK Competitiveness', in M.C. Casson (ed.), *Global Research Strategy and International Competitiveness*, Oxford: Basil Blackwell.

Caves, R.E. (1980) 'Productivity Differences among Industries', in R.E. Caves and I.B. Krause (eds) *Britain's Economic Performance*, Washington DC: Brookings Institution.

Child, Josiah (1668) *Brief Observations Concerning Trade and Interest of Money*, London.

Clarke, Peter (1998) 'Keynes, Buchanan and the Balanced Budget Doctrine', in J. Maloney (ed.), *Debt and Deficits: an Historical Perspective*, Aldershot: Edward Elgar.

Competitiveness Policy Council (1993) *A Competitive Strategy for America*, Second Report to the President and Congress.

Condillac, l'abbé E. de (1754) *Traité des Sensations*, vol. 3 in *Oeuvres Complètes de Condillac*, 23 vols, Paris, 1798 (hereafter. *Oeuvres*).

Condillac, l'abbé E. de (1774–6) *Course d'Etudes pour l'Instruction de Prince de Parme* (vols 5–21 in *Oeuvres*).

Condillac, l'abbé E. de (1776) *Le Commerce et le Gouvernement Considérés relativement l'un à l'autre* (Paris). A 1795 edition (Paris) reprinted in 1980 by Slatkine Reprints (Paris – Geneva). A 1798 edition corrected by the author, printed as vol. 4 in *Oeuvres*. An 1847 edition edited by E. Daire in *Mélanges D'Économie Politique*, 1 (Paris). The first English-language edition translated, by Shelagh M. Eltis and edited by Shelagh M. and Walter Eltis as *Condillac: Commerce and Government*, Aldershot: Edward Elgar, 1997.

Congdon, Tim (1988) *The Debt Threat*, Oxford: Basil Blackwell.

Congdon, Tim (1996) 'The Coming Collapse of EMU: The Maastricht Treaty is Impractical to the Point of Impossibility', *Gerrard and National Monthly Economic Review*, August.

Congdon, Tim (1998) 'Did Britain have a Keynesian Revolution? Fiscal Policy since 1941', in J. Maloney (ed.), *Debt and Deficits: An Historical Perspective*, Aldershot: Edward Elgar.

Connolly, B. (1995) *The Rotten Heart of Europe*, London: Faber & Faber.

Coopers and Lybrand (1993) Final Report for Study in International Differences in the Cost of Capital for the European Commission London.

Corden, W.M. (1994) *Economic Policy, Exchange Rates and the International System*, Oxford: Oxford University Press.

Crafts, N. and G. Toniolo (1995) 'Post-war Growth: An Overview', *CEPR Discussion Paper*, 1095.

Cranston, Maurice (1957) *John Locke: A Biography*, Oxford: Oxford University Press.

Cummins, J.G. and R.G. Hubbard (1994) 'The Tax Sensitivity of Foreign Direct Investment: Evidence from Firm-Level Panel Data', *National Bureau of Economic Research Working Paper Series*, 4703.

Daire, E. (1846) *Collection des Principaux Économistes, Tome 2: Physiocrates*, Paris.

DeLong, J.B. and L.H. Summers (1991) 'Equipment Investment and Economic Growth', *Quarterly Journal of Economics*, 106, pp. 445–502.

Denison, E.F. (1967) *Why Growth Rates Differ*, Washington DC: Brookings.

Denny, K. and S. Nickell (1992) 'Unions and Investment in British Industry', *Economic Journal*, 102, pp. 874–87.

Dickson, P.G.M. (1967) *The Financial Revolution in England: A Study in the Development of Public Credit, 1688–1756*, London: Macmillan.

Domar, E.D. ([1944]1957) 'The "Burden of Debt" and the National Income', *American Economic Review*, 34, December, pp. 798–827. Reprinted in 1957 in *Essays in the Theory of Economic Growth*, New York: Oxford University Press, pp. 35–82.

Dornbusch, Rudi (1996) 'Euro Fantasies', *Foreign Affairs*, 75(5), September–October.

Dresdner Kleinwort Benson Research (1998) *The EMU Collection: What the EMU means for Europe*.

DTI (1998) *Our Competitive Future: Building the Knowledge Driven Economy*: analysis and background to the government's Competitiveness White Paper.

Dunning, J.H. and Walker, P. (1982) 'The Competitiveness and Allocative Efficiency of UK Manufacturing Industry and Foreign Direct Investment', mimeo.

Du Pont de Nemours, P. (1808a) 'Mémoires sur la Vie, l'Administration et les Ouvrages de M. Turgot, Ministre d'État', 1 of *Oeuvres de M. Turgot*, 9 vols, Paris.

Du Pont de Nemours, P. (1808b) 'Sur les Économistes', in *Oeuvres de M. Turgot*, III, pp. 309–20.

Eltis, Shelagh M. (1997) 'Étienne Bonnot, abbé de Condillac', 1714–80', Chapter 1 of Introduction to *Condillac: Commerce and Government*, Aldershot: Edward Elgar.

Eltis, Walter (1979) 'How Rapid Public Sector Growth can Undermine the Growth of the National Product', in Wilfred Beckerman (ed.), *Slow Growth in Britain: Causes and Consequences*, Oxford: University Press.

Eltis, Walter (1982) 'Do Government Manpower Cuts Correct Deficits when the Economy is in Deep Recession?', *Political Quarterly*, January–March.

Eltis, Walter (1984) *The Classical Theory of Economic Growth*, London: Macmillan.
Eltis, Walter (1985) 'Ricardo on Machinery and Technological Unemployment', in Giovanni Caravale (ed.), *The Legacy of Ricardo*, Oxford: Basil Blackwell, pp. 257–84.
Eltis, Walter (1996) 'How Low Productivity and Weak Innovativeness Undermined UK Industrial Growth', *Economic Journal*, 106, January, pp. 184–96.
Eltis, Walter, Douglas Fraser and Martin Ricketts (1992) 'The Lessons for Britain from the Superior Economic Performance of Germany and Japan', *National Westminster Bank Quarterly Review*, February.
European Commission (1993) *Growth, Competitiveness, Employment: The Challenges and Ways Forward into the 21st Century*, White Paper, Brussels – Luxembourg.
European Commission (1995) *The European Employment Strategy: Recent Progress and Prospects for the Future*, Brussels–Luxembourg.
European Commission (1997a) *The Competitiveness of the European Information and Communication Technologies (ICT) Industries*, Brussels, April, COM(97) 152.
European Commission (1997b) *Employment in Europe*, Brussels, October, COM(97) 479.
Faccarello, G. (1992) 'Turgot et l'économie politique sensualiste' in *Nouvelle histoire de la pensée économique*, Paris: Editions la Découverte, 1, pp. 254–88.
Faure, E. (1961) *La Disgrâce de Turgot, 12 Mai 1776*, Paris: Gallimard.
FitzGerald, Niall (1997) *Tomorrow's Europe*, Lecture, London School of Economics, 12 June.
Fukao, M. (1993) 'International Integration of Financial Markets and the Cost of Capital', *OECD Economics Department Working Paper*, 128.
Galiani, Ferdinando (1992–6) *Correspondance with Louise d'Épinay*, (ed.) Georges Dulac, 5 vols, Paris: Desjonquères.
Gedmin, Jeffrey (ed.) (1997) *A Single European Currency*, Washington, DC: American Enterprise Institute.
Gemmell, Norman (1993) 'Wagner's Law and Musgrave's Hypothesis', in Norman Gemmell (ed.), *The Growth of the Public Sector: Theories and International Evidence*, Aldershot: Edward Elgar.
Gershon, Feder and Richard Just (1984) 'Debt Crisis in an Increasingly Pessimistic International Market: The Case of Egyptian Credit 1862–76', *Economic Journal*, 84, June, pp. 340–56.
Giersch, Herbert (1986) 'Economics as a Public Good', *Banco Nationale del Lavoro Review*, 158, September, pp. 251–73.
Giersch, Herbert (1991) 'Eurosclerosis', in *The World Economy in Perspective*, Aldershot: Edward Elgar.
Gregg, P., S. Machin and D. Metcalf (1993) 'Signals and Cycles? Productivity Growth and Changes in Union Status in British Companies, 1984–89', *Economic Journal*, 103, pp. 894–907.
Groenewegen, P. (1977) *The Economics of A.R.J. Turgot*, The Hague: Martin Nijhoff.
Groenewegen, P. (1987) 'Turgot, Anne Robert Jacques, Baron de L'Aulne', *The New Palgrave Dictionary of Economics*, London: Macmillan.
Haley, K.H.D. (1968) *The First Earl of Shaftesbury*, Oxford: Oxford University Press.

Hannah, Leslie (1994) *Education, Employment and Business Leadership* (London: Foundation for Manufacturing and Industry, 1994).
Harrod, R.F. (1939) 'An Essay in Dynamic Theory', *Economic Journal*, 49, March, pp. 14–33.
Healey, Denis (1975) 'The Government Alone Cannot Put Britain Back on its Feet', *The Sunday Times*, 14 December.
Hecht, J. (1958) 'La vie de François Quesnay' in *François Quesnay et la Physiocratie*, 2 vols, Paris: Institut National d'Études Démographiques.
HMSO (1994) *Competitiveness: Helping Business to Win*, Cm 2563.
HMSO (1995) *Competitiveness: Forging Ahead*, Cm 2867.
HMSO (1996) *Competitiveness: Creating the Enterprise Centre of Europe*, Cm 3300.
HM Treasury (1997) *UK Membership of a Single Currency: An Assessment of the Five Economic Tests*, October. Preface by the Rt Hon Gordon Brown MP, Chancellor of the Exchequer.
Hoeller, Peter, Marie-Odile Louppe and Patrice Vergiete (1996) 'Fiscal Relations Within the European Union', *Economics Department Working Paper*, 163, OECD: Paris.
Horsefield, J. Keith (1960) *British Monetary Experiments 1650–1710*, London: Bell.
Hume, David ([1752]1985) *Political Discourses*, Edinburgh. Reprinted in 1985 in Eugene Miller (ed.), *David Hume: Essays Moral, Political and Literary*, Indianapolis: Liberty Fund.
Hutchison, T. (1988) *Before Adam Smith: The Emergence of Political Economy 1662–1776*, Oxford: Basil Blackwell.
IBM/LBS (1994) *Made in Europe: A Four Nations Best Practice Study*, November.
IMF (1997a) 'EMU and the World Economy', in *World Economic Outlook*, Washington DC, October.
IMF (1997b) 'International Economic Outlook: Enhancing Labor Market Flexibility in Europe', *World Economic Outlook*, Washington, DC, October.
Jevons, S. (1871) *Theory of Political Economy*, London.
Jones, D.W. (1988) *War and Economy in the Age of William III and Marlborough*, Oxford: Basil Blackwell.
Kelly, Patrick Hyde (1991) 'General Introduction' and Tables, in Locke (1991).
Kennessey, Z. (1991) 'Why Das Kapital Remained Unfinished', in William J. Barber (ed.), *Perspectives on the History of Economic Thought*, 5, Aldershot: Edward Elgar.
Keynes, John Maynard (1925) *The Economic Consequences of Mr. Churchill*, London: Macmillan. Reprinted in 1972 in *The Collected Writings of John Maynard Keynes*, Basingstoke: Macmillan, IX, pp. 207–30
Keynes, John Maynard (1937) 'Borrowing for Defence: Is it Inflation? A Plea for Organised Policy', *The Times*, 11 March. Reprinted in 1982 in *The Collected Writings*, XXI, pp. 404–9.
Keys, W, S Harris and C. Fernandez (1996) *Third International Mathematics and Science Study*, Part 1, London: NFER.
Knoester, Anthonie and Nico van der Windt (1987) 'Real Wages and Taxation in Ten OECD Countries', *Oxford Bulletin of Economics and Statistics*, 49, 1.
KPMG (1995) 'Study on Outward Investment', Study prepared for Department of Trade and Industry.
Krugman, P. (1994) 'Competitiveness: A Dangerous Obsession', *Foreign Affairs*, March–April.

Lascelles, David (1996) *The Crash of 2003. An EMU Fairy Tale*, Centre for the Study of Financial Institutions (CSFI), December.

Lebeau, A. (1903) *Condillac: Économiste*, Paris.

Le Trosne, G. ([1777]1846) *De l'Intérêt Social*, Paris. Reprinted in Daire (1846), pp. 885–1027.

Lindbeck, Assar (1979) 'Imported and Structural Inflation and Aggregate Demand: The Scandinavian Model Reconstructed', in Assar Lindbeck (ed.), *Inflation and Employment in Open Economies*, Amsterdam: North-Holland.

Locke, John (1689a) *Two Treatises of Government*, London.

Locke, John (1689b) *Essay Concerning Human Understanding*, London.

Locke, John (1692) *Some Considerations of the Consequences of the Lowering of Interest and Raising the Value of Money*, London. Reprinted in Locke (1991), pp. 206–342.

Locke, John (1695) *Further Considerations Concerning Raising the Value of Money*, London. Reprinted in Locke (1991), pp. 401–81.

Locke, John (1976–89) *The Correspondence of John Locke*, ed. E.S. de Beer, 8 vols, Oxford: Clarendon Press.

Locke, John (1991) *Locke on Money*, ed. Patrick Hyde Kelly, 2 vols, The Clarendon Edition of the Works of John Locke, Oxford: Clarendon Press.

Longford, Elizabeth (1972), *Wellington: Pillar of State*, Weidenfeld & Nicolson.

Lowndes, William (1695) *A Report Containing an Essay for the Amendment of the Silver Coins*, London.

Madden, Geoffrey (1981) *Geoffrey Madden's Notebooks*, ed. J.A. Gere and John Sparrow, with an Introduction by Harold Macmillan, Oxford: Oxford University Press.

Maddison, A. (1991) *Dynamic Forces in Capitalist Development*, Oxford: Oxford University Press.

Maloney, John (1998) 'Gladstone and Sound Victorian Finance', in J. Maloney (ed.), *Debt and Deficits: An Historical Perspective*, Aldershot: Edward Elgar.

Malthus, Thomas R. ([1806] 1989) *An Essay on the Principle of Population*, 3rd edn. Reprinted in 1989, ed. Patricia James, 2 vols, Cambridge: Cambridge University Press.

Marx, Karl ([1867]1974) *Das Kapital*, Hamburg. In 1974 English-language edition with posthumous 2nd and 3rd vols, Lawrence & Wishart for Moscow: Progress Publishers, 3 vols. The first English-language edition of vol. 1 was published in London in 1887, and the Lawrence & Wishart edition reproduces the original translation by Samuel Moore and Edward Aveling.

Mason, G. and B. van Ark (1993) 'Productivity, Machinery and Skills in Engineering: An Anglo–Dutch Comparison', *National Institute Discussion Paper*, 36.

McCauley, R. and S. Zimmer (1989) 'Explaining International Differences in the Cost of Capital: The United States and the United Kingdom versus Japan and Germany', *Federal Reserve Bank of New York Research Paper*, 8913.

McKinsey (1992) *Service Sector Productivity*, New York: McKinsey Global Institute.

Meek, R. (1973) *Turgot on Progress, Sociology and Economics*, Cambridge: Cambridge University Press.

Mitchell, B.R. (1988) *British Historical Statistics*, Cambridge: Cambridge University Press.

Mun, Thomas (1664) *England's Treasure by Foreign Trade. Or, the Ballance of our Forraign Trade is the Rule of our Treasure*, London.

Murphy, Antoin (1986) *Cantillon: Entrepreneur and Economist*, Oxford: Oxford University Press.

O'Brien, Patrick (1988) 'The Political Economy of British Taxation', *Economic History Review*, 41, 1, pp. 1–32.

OECD (1980–96) *The Tax Benefit Position of Production Workers*, Paris: OECD.

OECD (1990) *OECD Employment Outlook*, Paris: OECD.

OECD (1995) *Annual Economic Survey of the UK*, Paris: OECD.

OECD (1998) *The Tax/Benefit Position of Employees, 1995–1996*, Paris: OECD.

OECD/Statistics Canada (1995) *Literacy, Economy and Society*, Paris: OECD.

Office of National Statistics (ONS) (1997) *Adult Literacy in Britain*, London: ONS.

O'Mahony, M. (1995) 'International Differences in Unit Labour Costs: A Disaggregated Study', study prepared for the Department of Trade and Industry.

Owen, Sir Geoffrey (1994) *National Environment and International Competitiveness: A Comparison of the British Pharmaceutical and Electronics Industries*, London: Foundation for Manufacturing and Industry.

PA Cambridge Economic Consultants (1995) 'Assessment of the Wider Effects of Foreign Direct Investment on Manufacturing in the UK', study prepared for the Department of Trade and Industry.

Pack, S. (1991) *Capitalism as a Moral System: Adam Smith's Critique of the Free Market Economy*, Aldershot: Edward Elgar.

Pain, N. (1993) 'An Econometric Analysis of Foreign Direct Investment in the United Kingdom', *Scottish Journal of Political Economy*, 40, pp. 1–23.

Palgrave's Dictionary of Political Economy, ed. R.H. Inglis Palgrave (1894–1900), 3 vols, London: Macmillan. *The New Palgrave Dictionary of Economics*, eds John Eatwell, Murray Milgate and Peter Newman (1987), 4 vols, London: Macmillan.

Pennant-Rea Committee (1997) *The Ostrich and the EMU: Policy Choices Facing the UK*, London: CEPR, May.

Phelps Brown, Henry and Sheila V. Hopkins (1981) *A Perspective of Wages and Prices*, London: Methuen.

Porter, M.E. (1990) *The Competitive Advantage of Nations*, New York: Free Press.

Prais, S.J. (1981) *Productivity and Industrial Structure*, Cambridge: Cambridge University Press.

Pratten, C.F. (1976) *Labour Productivity Differentials Within International Companies*, Cambridge: Cambridge University Press.

Prodi, Romano (1998) 'European Industry and Finance Face World Competition', *Banca Nazionale del Lavoro*, 51, June, pp. 101–17.

Quesnay, F. (1767) *Physiocratie, ou Constitution Naturelle du Gouvernement le Plus Advantageux au Genre Humain*, ed. Du Pont, Paris. Reprinted in Daire (1846), pp. 41–304.

Quesnay, F. and Victor Riqueti, Marquis de Mirabeau (1763) *Philosophie Rurale*, Amsterdam.

Ricardo, David (1817) *Principles of Political Economy and Taxation*, London, 2nd edn 1819, 3rd edn 1821. Reprinted in 1951–73, ed. P. Sraffa, as vol. I of *The Works and Correspondence of David Ricardo*, 11 vols, Cambridge: Cambridge University Press. (hereafter, *Works and Correspondence*).

Ricardo, David (1819) 'Evidence on the resumption of cash payments', in *Works and Correspondence*, V, pp. 350–457.

Roach, Stephen S. *et al.* (1996) *The Economics of Competitive Advantage*, London: Morgan Stanley, November.

Romer, P.M. (1993) 'Idea Gaps and Object Gaps in Economic Development', *Journal of Monetary Economics*, 32, pp. 543–73.

Romer, P.M. (1994) 'The Origins of Endogenous Growth', *Journal of Economic Perspectives*, 8, 1, pp. 3–22.

Sargent, T.J. and N. Wallace (1981) 'Some Unpleasant Monetarist Arithmetic', *Federal Reserve Bank of Minneapolis Quarterly Review*, Fall.

Sato, R. (1970) 'The Estimation of Biased Technical Progress and the Production Function', *International Economic Review*, 11, June.

Schelle, G. (1909) *Turgot*, Paris.

Skidelsky, Robert (1992) *John Maynard Keynes: The Economist as Saviour*, London: Macmillan.

Small Business Research Centre (1993) 'Growth, Innovation and Competitive Advantage in Small and Medium Size Firms', University of Cambridge.

Smith, Adam. ([1776]1976) *An Inquiry into the Nature and Causes of the Wealth of Nations* 2 vols, London. Reprinted in 1976, eds R.H. Campbell, A.S. Skinner and W.B. Todd, in *The Glasgow Edition of the Works and Correspondence of Adam Smith*, Oxford: Clarendon Press.

Smith A. (1983) *Lectures on Rhetoric and Belles Lettres*, ed. J.C. Bryce, Oxford: Clarendon Press.

Söderström, Hans and Staffan Viotti (1979) 'Imported and Structural Inflation and Aggregate Demand: The Scandinavian Model Reconstructed', in Assar Lindbeck (ed.), *Inflation and Employment in Open Economies*, Amsterdam: North-Holland, pp. 71–98.

Soros, George (1996) 'Can Europe Work?' *Foreign Affairs*, 75, 5, September–October.

Steuart, James ([1767]1998) *An Inquiry into the Principles of Political Oeconomy*, 2 vols, London. Republished in 1998, ed. Andrew S. Skinner, 4 vols, London: Pickering & Chatto.

Turgot, A.R.J. (1766–9) *Réflexions sur la Formation et la Distribution de Richesses* (*Oeuvres*, 2, pp. 533–601).

Turgot, A.R.J. (1769) 'Valeurs et monnaies' (*Oeuvres*, 3, pp. 79–98).

Turgot, A.R.J. (1913–23) *Oeuvres de Turgot et Documents le Concernant*, ed. G. Schelle, 5 vols, Paris (hereafter, *Oeuvres*).

van Ark, B. (1993) *International Comparisons of Output and Productivity*, University of Gröningen.

Vaughn, Karen Iversen (1980) *John Locke: Economist and Social Scientist*, London: Athlone Press.

Vickers, Douglas (1959) *Studies in the Theory of Money 1690–1776*, New York: Chilton.

Vickers, J. and G. Yarrow (1988) *Privatisation: An Economic Analysis*, Cambridge Mass.: MIT Press.

Wadhwani, S.B. (1985) 'Inflation, Bankruptcy, Default Premia and the Stockmarket', *Discussion Paper*, 194, Centre for Labour Economics, London School of Economics.

Wagner, Adolph (1876) *Grundlegung der Politischen Ökonomie*, Leipzig.

Winch, Donald (1998) 'The Political Economy of Public Finance in the "Long" Eighteenth Century', in J. Maloney (ed.), *Debt and Deficits: An Historical Perspective*, Aldershot: Edward Elgar.

Young, G. (1994) 'The Influence of Foreign Factor Prices and International Taxation on Fixed Investment in the UK', *National Institute Discussion Paper*, 66.

Index

Note: figures and tables are indicated by *italics*, unless there is related text on the same page.